ETHICS EDUCATION I

Ethics Education in the Military

Edited by

PAUL ROBINSON
University of Ottawa, Canada

NIGEL DE LEE
University of Hull, UK

DON CARRICK
Institute of Applied Ethics, University of Hull, UK

ASHGATE

Published by
Ashgate Publishing Limited   Ashgate Publishing Company
Gower House   Suite 420
Croft Road   101 Cherry Street
Aldershot   Burlington, VT 05401-4405
Hampshire GU11 3HR   USA
England

Ashgate website: http://www.ashgate.com

British Library Cataloguing in Publication Data
Ethics education in the military
  1. Military ethics 2. War - Moral and ethical aspects
  I. Robinson, Paul, 1966- II. De Lee, Nigel III. Carrick,
  Don
  174.9'355'00683

Library of Congress Cataloging-in-Publication Data
Ethics education in the military / edited by Paul Robinson, Nigel de Lee and Don Carrick.
        p. cm.
    Includes bibliographical references and index.
ISBN: 978-0-7546-7114-5 (hardback)
ISBN: 978-0-7546-7115-2 (pbk)
  1. Military ethics. 2. Ethics. 3. War--Moral and ethical aspects. I. Robinson,
Paul. II. Lee, Nigel de. III. Carrick, Don.
  U22.E831 2008
  174'.935500683--dc22
                                                            2007037046

ISBN: 978-0-7546-7114-5 (Hbk)
ISBN: 978-0-7546-7115-2 (Pbk)

Printed and bound in Great Britain by TJ International Ltd, Padstow, Cornwall.

Contents

PART II: RESPONSES

List of Figure and Tables

Figure

Tables

Notes on Contributors

Tor Arne Berntsen is chaplain and instructor in military ethics at the Royal Norwegian Air Force Academy in Trondheim. He is currently working on a PhD on reintegration of child soldiers in northern Uganda at the Stavanger School of Mission and Theology. He is also managing editor for the *Journal of Military Ethics*.

Don Carrick is a Lecturer in Philosophy and Researcher/Research Assistant in the Institute of Applied Ethics at the University of Hull. He was for many years a lawyer in private practice, and is currently working on a doctoral thesis in military ethics.

Martin L. Cook is Professor of Philosophy and Deputy Department Head at the United States Air Force Academy. Prior to that, he was Professor of Ethics in the Department of Command, Leadership and Management (DCLM) of the United States Army War College (USAWC) in Carlisle, PA in 1998, and was awarded the Elihu Root Chair in Military Studies in 2001.

Jamie Cullens served for 19 years as an infantry soldier and commanded from platoon through to regiment. He saw operational service in Kashmir with the UN and in Panama with US forces. He then worked in a management position in the mining industry in Northern Australia before being appointed as the first director of the Centre for Defence Leadership Studies in 2002, supporting command, leadership, management and military ethics programme development at the Australian Defence College and across the Australian Defence Force.

Stephen Deakin has taught for many years at the Royal Military Academy Sandhurst and has a particular interest in military ethics, leadership, management, and civil-military relations.

Nigel de Lee has lectured in War Studies and associated subjects at Sandhurst and the Joint Services Command and Staff College in the UK and also at military academies in the Netherlands, the USA and Norway. He has published several papers on military ethics. He is now a lecturer in the Department of Politics and International Studies at the University of Hull where he teaches modules in Security and War Studies and International Relations.

Yvon Desjardins joined the Canadian Forces in 1974 and served as an Air Traffic Controller until 1986. He then joined the Public Affairs Branch. For 20 years, he has held numerous key Public Affairs positions in Canada and abroad. In February 2006, he was appointed Director of the Defence Ethics Program at National Defence Headquarters in Ottawa.

Henri Hude is the Head of the Centre for Military Ethics at Saint-Cyr Military Academy, France. His latest published work is *L'Ethique des Décideurs* (*The Ethics of Decision Makers*) (2004).

Asa Kasher is a Senior Research Associate of the Israel Defence Force (IDF) College of National Defense. He has also taught Military Ethics in other IDF colleges. He is the vice-Chair of the Jerusalem Centre for Ethics and also an Emeritus Professor of Philosophy at Tel Aviv University, where he held until recently the Chair of Professional Ethics and Philosophy of Practice. He won the Prize of Israel for general philosophy 2000.

Patrick Mileham, a graduate of Cambridge and Lancaster universities, experienced active service with the British Army in South Arabia and Northern Ireland. Between 1992 and 2006 he held a number of university posts. With many publications, notably on military ethics and professionalism, he is now a defence analyst working for the Ministry of Defence and other institutions, with interests in security sector reform in nations such as Ukraine and Colombia.

Alexander Moseley is the author of *An Introduction to Political Philosophy* (2007) and *A Philosophy of War* (2002), and co-editor of *Human Rights and Military Intervention* (2002). After lecturing at the University of Evansville he founded a private educational company which he now runs with his wife. He has authored two philosophical-adventure novels under the nom-de-plume William Venator.

Peter Olsthoorn holds a PhD degree from Leiden University in political theory. He is Assistant Professor of Sociology at the Netherlands Defence Academy, where he teaches on ethics. He is the author of a number of articles on subjects such as military honour, the suspension of the draft in the Netherlands, and the relationship between humiliation and terrorism.

Fumio Ota is Director of the Centre for Security and Crisis Management Education at the National Defence Academy of Japan. He was a serving officer in the Japanese Navy before assignment to the Maritime Staff Officer. Following a diplomatic assignment as Defence and Naval Attaché at the Japanese Embassy in Washington DC, he became President of the Joint Staff College of the Japanese Defence Forces and then Director of Defence Intelligence Headquarters, prior to taking up his present post.

Paul Robinson is Associate Professor in Public and International Affairs at the University of Ottawa. He is the author and editor of numerous works on military history, military ethics and defence policy, including *Just War in Comparative Perspective* (Ashgate, 2003) and *Military Honour and the Conduct of War: from Ancient Greece to Iraq* (Routledge, 2006). He has served as an officer in both the British and Canadian armies.

Raag Rolfsen is head of the Department of Education in the Chaplaincy of the Norwegian Armed Forces. He is presently working on a doctoral thesis on 'The Significance of the Political in the Philosophical Formation of Emmanuel Levinas'. He is also leading The Commission on International Affairs in the Church of Norway Council on Ecumenical and International Relations. Until 1999 he worked as a minister in a local congregation in the Church of Norway.

Stefan Werdelis is a Protestant Minister, and is now Military Dean and Lecturer in Ethics in the Centre for Leadership and Civic Education of the Armed Forces of Germany in Koblenz. He served for six months in the Balkans with KFOR in 2004.

Jeffrey Wilson is a lieutenant colonel in the United States Army. He is currently an Assistant Professor of Philosophy at the United States Military Academy, West Point. He is especially interested in cosmopolitanism, the philosophy of education, and issues of alienation in modern society.

Jessica Wolfendale is an Australian Research Council Postdoctoral Research Fellow at the Centre for Applied Philosophy and Public Ethics at the University of Melbourne. She has published on military ethics, moral philosophy, and the ethics of torture. She is the author of *Torture and the Military Profession* (Palgrave Macmillan, 2007).

Foreword

Major General (Retd) Patrick Cordingley DSO DSc

In February 1991 the United Kingdom's 7th Armoured Brigade, the Desert Rats, was in Saudi Arabia, as part of the US 7th Corps, waiting to attack into Iraq. For one week we bombarded the Iraqi positions immediately to our front. As a result our initial advance was almost unopposed. For two days we manoeuvred, attacked and overcame weakly held enemy positions. It was then that I met with my commanders to work how we could continue without killing so many Iraqi soldiers. We had trained and were equipped to fight the Warsaw Pact. Then we could only hope to survive by using maximum force. How could we suddenly change our approach to minimize the loss of enemy life without endangering our own troops? We tried, and we took casualties as a result. We tried to be ethical.

In the second Gulf War I was surprised that the Coalition Forces used as much force as they did in the first encounter. Was it necessary? Was it ethical? Afterwards there were insufficient troops on the ground to bring security to a country that had lost its own army and police. The chain of command became stretched to near breaking point. Soldiers, unsupervised by default, performed tasks that they were not prepared for. Their behaviour from time to time was unacceptable, even criminal. But how do you control such behaviour while peacekeeping in a lawless country? Every army has its share of soldiers who may, under stress, mistreat captives. Even those in authority can abuse their positions. Human nature seems to dictate that the stressed will tend towards abuse. How do we regulate this on battlefields and in detention cells?

It has to be through the teaching of ethics. The chapters in this volume constitute an important step in exchanging ideas and practices in arguably one of the most critical areas of modern soldiering. I recommend them strongly to all those responsible for training the soldiers of the future.

Patrick Cordingley, commissioned into the 5th Royal Inniskilling Dragoon Guards, commanded the 7th Armoured Brigade during the first Gulf War. A short time later he was promoted to command the UK's 2nd Division. He retired in September 2000 and is now chairman of MMI Research and the Defence and Security Forum. He is also a military commentator working mainly for the BBC.

Chapter 1

Introduction:
Ethics Education in the Military

Paul Robinson

Aims and Content

Within liberal democratic countries, demands that the ethics of public office be formally codified are becoming ever louder. 'Ethics committees' and the like are a growth industry. This is especially true in the militaries of the Western world, where the work of the armed forces is held up to unprecedented public scrutiny. Furthermore, many military missions are now justified in humanitarian terms, using the language of 'humanitarian intervention' and the 'responsibility to protect'. The British armed forces, for instance, claim that their mission is to be 'a force for good'. Clearly, if such claims are to be more than self-serving rhetoric, military personnel must uphold the highest ethical standards. This in turn means that military institutions must pay increasing attention to the ethical education of their members.

Until recently, ethics education policies in military forces were developed on an *ad hoc* basis, rather than drawn from any systematically considered ethical theory or embedded within any pragmatic, workable education programme. This has begun to change, and many countries are establishing new military ethics programmes directly based on the work of academic philosophers and social scientists. The philosophical principles behind these programmes are, however, often very different from one nation to another, producing significant variation in the methods used to tackle the common problem.

One of the reasons for this variation is a degree of semantic confusion concerning the meaning of key terms, most especially 'ethics'. As will become clear in this volume, for some ethics is synonymous with 'morality'. The aim of ethics education, therefore, is seen as being what many refer to as 'character development', in other words the creation of morally upright persons through the instillation of certain key qualities or dispositions of character (commonly known as 'virtues'). Others, however, disagree, and consider ethics to be somewhat distinct from general morality. Instead, ethics are more properly seen as being related to a given profession and its requirements. The focus of ethics education therefore shifts from character development to creating an understanding of the purpose and methods of the profession and the values which underpin it. Complicating matters still further, some institutions shy away from the word 'ethics' and prefer to speak of 'ethos', the intangible tone or spirit which guides a community and the behaviour of its members. The consequence of this semantic confusion is the occasional elision and overlap of terms such as 'ethics', 'morality', 'ethos', and 'character'. While regrettable, the fact that there is no firm agreement on definitions means that this is unavoidable. Rather than try to impose a narrow definition of ethics, the editors have therefore chosen to allow contributors to indicate how it is understood in the institutions they are describing, and to allow the resulting tensions to become clear.

In addition, the book looks at ethics education broadly, covering both institutional and operational ethics, in both peacetime and wartime, rather than limiting the scope of enquiry to particular activities (be they conventional war, counter-insurgency, peacekeeping, or anything else). A narrower study of ethics education for 'operations other than war' is, however, planned for the future.

The essays contained in this volume constitute the first academic survey of the work being carried out in the area of ethics education in the military. The book brings together philosophers, military officers (including chaplains), and social scientists from around the globe to analyze the ethics education schemes currently in place within the armed forces of a large sample of countries, and to conduct a critical comparison and evaluation of those programmes. The authors examine the philosophical principles upon which existing programmes are based, discuss the reasons why those principles have been selected and how they translate into practice, and determine, as far as is possible, their suitability and effectiveness.

In putting this volume together, the editors and contributors had a variety of related aims and objectives:

- to identify and examine a representative selection of current methodologies of ethics education programmes; to exchange ideas and best practices from within the realm of military education; and to inform practitioners of what others are doing, and thereby facilitate the further development of suitable military ethics education;
- to identify the explicit or tacit theoretical underpinnings of individual ethics education programmes (such as utilitarian, deontological, contractarian, or virtue theories); to determine why the programmes exist and why they are constructed in the way they are; and to carry out a critical evaluative comparison of the advantages and constraints of adopting one or other of these theories as the basis for constructing such programmes;
- to investigate the effect of cultural and national differences on the content and rationale of individual programmes;
- to apply the results of these investigations to a consideration of the relationship between the dictates of 'ordinary morality' and 'role morality' given the practicalities of military operations (should we be seeking to create soldiers who are morally 'good' or merely to imbue soldiers with the ethics required for them to carry out their tasks?);
- to consider the appropriate roles of military personnel, chaplains, philosophers, and others within the structure of a military ethics education programme; and

- to investigate the advisability and feasibility of developing common principles and methods for ethics education programmes across all the countries studied in this volume.

The book consists of two parts: the first part contains a dozen essays outlining and analyzing the military ethics education programmes of ten democratic states, namely the United Kingdom, United States, Canada, Australia, Norway, Germany, France, Netherlands, Israel and Japan; the second part contains critical responses to these essays by moral philosophers.

Describing the practices of the British armed forces, Stephen Deakin and Patrick Mileham note in Chapters 2 and 4 a continuing resistance to the intellectualization of ethics. The British approach is thoroughly pragmatic; as Deakin comments in Chapter 2, 'abstract ethical theory is kept to a minimum; practical hands on experience of dealing with the issues is emphasized'. This does not mean that the British military produces men and women whose ethical standards are noticeably inferior to those of other armed forces; on the whole its methods appear to work. However, there is, as Mileham says, 'an intellectual doubt about how to articulate and codify what actually is intuitively well understood' (see Chapter 4).

By contrast, the academic study of ethics is well established in US military academies, as described by Jeffrey Wilson and Martin Cook in their studies of the US Military Academy at West Point and the US Air Force Academy (Chapters 3 and 5 respectively). Both view Aristotle as the 'intellectual father of the enterprise'. They disagree to some extent about the effectiveness of their respective institutions' efforts to build moral character in their charges. Wilson comments favourably that 'history is replete with fine examples of how well West Point has done in living up to its mission of producing leaders of character', whereas Cook more negatively notes 'confusion about the meaning of central terms of this discourse (such as 'integrity' and 'professionalism') ... the balkanized approach to the teaching/training of cadets in this area', and 'a fundamentally incoherent and confused welter of programmes justified, if at all, by the belief that if ethics is important, throwing lots of resources at the subject from any number of angles and approaches must somehow be doing good'.

Such alleged incoherence contrasts with the more centralized approach adopted by the Canadian Department of National Defence in its Defence Ethics Programme, described by Yvon Desjardins in Chapter 6. This strikes a 'balance between judgment based on values and absolute compliance', with the level and depth of ethics instruction varying according to rank and responsibility. Whereas ethics education in most countries (and consequently in most of the chapters in this book) is overwhelmingly focused on officers, the Canadian Defence Ethics Programme features activities specifically directed at non-commissioned members. It also aims to incorporate ethical problems into field training.

In this way the Canadian Defence Ethics Programme shares something with the approach adopted by the Australian Defence Force (ADF). In Chapter 7, Jamie Cullens makes special note of the ADF's use of the case study method, and particularly of the fact that it is 'willing to debate contentious contemporary issues' and to involve those actually involved in the incidents in question. 'The nature of Australian culture', Cullens claims, 'allows the ADF to examine sensitive and contentious issues in ways that other militaries are reluctant to consider'. In this regard, he concludes, 'the ADF is well ahead of our coalition partners'.

In most countries, responsibility for ethics education lies primarily with military officers, sometimes with the assistance of academic philosophers. The two countries examined in Chapters 8 and 9 (Norway and Germany) constitute an exception, in that military chaplains take the leading role. As shown by Tor Arne Berntsen and Raag Rolfsen, this is especially true in Norway. The German concept of *Innere Führung* described by Stefan Werdelis also provides an interesting contrast to the ideas put forward in some other chapters. Historical experience has given the Germans a justified suspicion of lofty ideals of military exceptionalism, and one of the aims of *Innere Führung*, as described by Werdelis, is to prevent such 'praetorianism' from gaining a foothold. Rather than seeing the soldier as a repository of virtue, the German perspective is to view him as a 'citizen under arms', and the purpose of ethics training as to instil a 'democracy-oriented model of professional ethics'.

As far as the French Army is concerned, Henri Hude argues in Chapter 10 that 'Standards and values which have come to count for little or nothing in civil society have continued to be cultivated, and have to go on being cultivated, in the sphere of the armed forces'. Formal ethics education is a recent phenomenon at the Coëtquidan Military Academy, but according to Hude has now been placed at the very centre of officer training, as one of three core areas (ethics, politics and tactics). Hude concludes with a plea for international cooperation 'to reach an understanding of, and harmony on, ethical issues'.

Most of the programmes described in this volume more or less follow the principles of virtue ethics. Chapters 11 and 12, by Peter Olsthoorn and Asa Kasher, describing their experiences in the Netherlands and Israel respectively, present some scepticism about the appropriateness of this model. While noting that virtue ethics underlie ethics education at the Netherlands Defence Academy, Olsthoorn believes that current expectations may be too ambitious. Referring to the work of Lawrence Kohlberg (Kohlberg 1981), he comments that we may need to accept that we will not always be able to produce men and women capable of autonomous ethical thinking. We should therefore set our sights somewhat lower. Professor Kasher takes yet another approach; for him, character development should not be the primary aim of ethics education in the military at all. Rather, military ethics is, he says, 'a conception of the proper behaviour of a person as a member of a military force'. Ethics education should focus not on changing character but on providing service men and women with an understanding of their professional identity, and of what it means to be a military professional in general and more specifically a military professional in a liberal democracy.

In the final chapter in Part I, Fumio Ota provides an Eastern perspective on the issues covered in this book, contrasting the ethics of Bushido, of the *Imperial Precepts to the Soldiers and Sailors*, issued by the Japanese Emperor in 1887, and of the *Ethos of Self Defence Personnel*, issued by the Japanese government in 1961 and still the official ethos of the Japanese Defence Forces. The *Imperial*

Precepts, he concludes, were superior both to the code of Bushido and the *Ethos of Self Defence Personnel*, because the *Imperial Precepts* include the precepts of Valour and Simplicity, and also because they have more 'emotional charge'. This introduces an important point – that ethics education needs to appeal to the emotions as well as the intellect.

Part II of this book contains responses to all of the above chapters by Jessica Wolfendale, Alexander Moseley, and Don Carrick. Wolfendale questions whether military commanders have given sufficient thought to the purpose of ethics education. It is obvious that to some it has a purely functional purpose, reflecting the belief that a soldier who is in some sense morally good will also be a more efficient soldier; however, it is also obvious that to others, the moral improvement of soldiers is seen as an aim in itself. Confusion about the purpose of ethics education leads in turn to confusion about the methods chosen to achieve that purpose, perhaps explaining some of the incoherence described by Martin Cook and others. Meanwhile, Moseley argues, like many others in this volume, that the purpose of ethics education should be to create service men and women who can think for themselves about ethical issues. Taken to its logical conclusion that means accepting that on occasion soldiers may wish to disobey orders or even withdraw entirely from combat. Finally, Carrick draws a comparison between ethics education in the military and in the medical and legal professions. Appealing to the notion of 'professional role morality', he finds that the traditional methodology and moral grounding of ethics education in the military are inadequate to meet the practical and moral demands made of soldiers taking part in 'new wars' and operations other than war. Favouring the approach to ethics education described by Asa Kasher, he suggests that the way forward might be to redefine the professional role of modern soldiers (and consequently to reconsider the values, norms and principles which underlie the role morality), and ethically re-educate them into being soldier-policemen.

Values and Virtues

Taken together, these essays raise as many questions as they answer, if not more. Why have ethics education in the military? What should be included in a military ethics programme? How should it be conducted? And by whom should it be taught and organized? As noted in many of the chapters which follow, the predominant principle which most military ethics education programmes have adopted is that of virtue ethics. This aims to ensure virtuous behaviour among those who serve in the military by means of 'character development'; in other words to produce people who will act virtuously because they *are* virtuous. Unfortunately, there exists a certain methodological and terminological confusion in this regard because 'virtues' are often mixed up with 'values' (virtues representing desirable characteristics of individuals, such as courage; and values representing the ideals that the community cherishes, such as freedom). All the same, the lists of prime military virtues and values produced by the various armed forces discussed in this volume provide a useful basis for examining whether there exists some common set of virtues or values which could be used to build a universal concept of military ethics.

In light of the widely held belief, echoed by Fumio Ota, that 'servicemen's virtues do not change over time and geography', it is worth comparing the lists of virtues and values produced by the armed forces studied in this book, as shown in Table 1.1.

A number of points arise from this table. First, there is great variation among the virtues and values, and also great variation in the length of the lists, although there are sufficient similarities among them to suggest that it might be possible to find some common ground. Most notably, 'loyalty' or 'comradeship' appear on eight of the 12 lists, and some variation of 'courage' also appears on eight. The dominance of these themes, along with others such as 'self-sacrifice' (four mentions in one form or another) and 'discipline' (five mentions) suggests that the authors of the lists still view the military virtues in a manner which would have been understandable to soldiers of more ancient times. However, the focus is undeniably inward looking: the virtues listed are overwhelmingly those required to make a soldier effective in a purely functional sense. They seem to ignore the fact that the purpose of military ethics is not solely to produce soldiers who will be efficient, but also to limit the use of force and to protect others from the power that soldiers wield. As a result, there is a striking gap in the virtues and values listed. Very few indeed relate to restraint, respect for non-combatants, and so forth (although the Canadian Department of National Defence does elsewhere list 'respect the dignity of all persons' as a separate 'core principle'). An argument could be made that these are included within the scope of 'respect' (which in some form appears six times), but the fact that this is sometimes given as 'mutual respect' suggests that the framers of the lists have in mind more the need for military persons to respect one another than the need to respect the rights of outsiders. The code of the Israel Defence Forces appears to be unique in including respect for human life, a value which surely merits inclusion if military ethics is to fulfil its role of limiting the activities of armed forces.

In addition, the lists of values and virtues reflect in many cases a clearly-held belief that what matters most is soldiers' role as soldiers. Virtue ethics is context-dependent; different roles require different virtues. As Alasdair MacIntyre says, 'The concept of what anyone filling such-and-such a role ought to do is prior to the concept of a virtue; the latter concept has application only via the former' (MacIntyre 1997, 121). If a military person's primary role in life is his or her military one, the list of virtues he or she must aspire to will be different than if he or she is, as Stefan Werdelis claims, a 'citizen in uniform'; in the latter case, it is the virtues of a citizen which must have priority. Perhaps these lists need further refinement in the light of a more thorough analysis of what the role and identity of military personnel, and the purpose of military ethics education, ought to be.

Table 1.1   Military values and virtues

Israel	Australia	Canada	US Army
Mission perseverance	Professionalism	Honesty	Loyalty
Responsibility	Loyalty	Loyalty	Duty
Credibility	Innovation	Integrity	Respect
Personal example	Courage	Courage	Selfless service
Respect for human life	Integrity	Fairness	Honour
Purity of arms	Teamwork	Responsibility	Integrity
Professionalism			Personal courage
Discipline			
Comradeship			
Sense of mission			

Japan	Norway	Germany	France
Awareness of mission	Respect	Loyalty	Mission
Individual development	Responsibility	Duty	Discipline
Fulfilment of responsibility	Courage	Discipline	Initiative
		Valour	Courage
Strict observation of discipline		Moral values	Self-controlled force
		Democracy	Fraternity
Strengthening of solidarity			

Royal Navy	Royal Marines	British Army	Royal Air Force
Mutual respect	Humility	Integrity	Integrity
Loyalty	Unity	Respect	Mutual respect
Courage in adversity	Courage	Loyalty	Service before self
Discipline	Fortitude	Courage	Excellence
Teamwork	Unselfishness	Discipline	
High professional standards	Professional standards	Selfless commitment	
Leadership	Determination		
Determination	Adaptability		
'Can do' attitude	Commando humour		
Sense of humour	Cheerfulness		

Methods of Ethics Education

How armed forces seek to carry out ethics education inevitably reflects their perceptions of its purpose. Utilitarian ethics are almost universally rejected as unsuitable in a military context. As previously stated, the predominant model is that of virtue ethics. (Although not everybody agrees with that approach; Asa Kasher, for instance, argues that it is not appropriate for the military in a democratic state to seek to change people's characters, that it should merely seek to change behaviour (see Chapter 12).) In line with the preference for virtue ethics, most military training seeks to instil habits through a system of punishment and reward, combined with repetition and practice, which should in theory eventually lead those being trained to internalize the virtues in question.

The primary criticism of this approach in the pages which follow is that military educators tend to be poor at instilling what Aristotle called *phronesis* ('practical wisdom'), described by Martin Cook as 'the ability to reflect on *why* the habits being formed and the pains and pleasures the institution uses to regulate behaviour do indeed serve important functional requisites of military behaviour' (see Chapter 5). Again and again in the pages that follow, readers will find authors urging that the military teach its members to think independently, while lamenting that they are not very good at this. Patrick Mileham, for instance, comments that 'The difficulty a high proportion of [British] officers have had with military ethics is that they would prefer ethical judgment to be prescribed and rendered as orders, drills, procedures and instructions, not a matter for their personal interpretation of observed events against hard to understand, abstract principles' (see Chapter 4). Similarly Jamie Cullens notes in Chapter 7 that in ethics workshops in the Australian Defence Forces, 'Many of the students still struggle with the fact that so many of the issues are not black and white, and there are always a handful who miss the point of the discussion'.

Many officers in English-speaking militaries speak frequently about 'integrity' and 'moral courage'. This implies having the courage to do what one believes is right in the face of pressure from others to do something different. 'The heart of all ethics', writes James H. Toner in an article on military professionalism, 'consists in the ability morally to transcend the group' (Toner 2002, 318) (a point of view contradicted in Chapter 11 of this book by Peter Olsthoorn). John Mark Mattox also argues that, 'Army officers are not, and indeed cannot be, automatons. They are moral agents who must recognize their responsibility (1) never to issue an immoral order, and (2) to refuse an order – or even a suggestion – to undertake military operations inconsistent with the ideals they are sworn to defend' (Mattox 2002, 303). This in turns implies having a capacity and a will to truly think deeply about issues, and to have sufficient understanding of the concepts involved to do so in a meaningful way. Otherwise, choosing one's own preference in the face of others, who possibly know better, could be interpreted as mere vanity. Yet it is not always clear that the military really does want its members to think deeply and independently. Consequently, as Alexander Moseley points out in Chapter 15, its rhetoric about integrity runs the risk of being 'mere cant'. 'If military authorities are going to be serious about teaching ethics to soldiers', Moseley argues, 'they must accept that it implies encouraging unlimited criticality'. But when service personnel practise such criticality, the tendency is to descend on them like the proverbial ton of bricks. Officers such as Flight Lieutenant Malcolm Kendall-Smith and Lieutenant Ehren Watada, who have refused to obey orders to serve in a war they consider immoral and illegal (the Iraq conflict), have shown the virtue of integrity which the military claims to value so highly – they have thought about the issues, and reached an autonomous decision on what is right and refused to compromise their values – but the military's response is to punish them. This may in fact be necessary for the maintenance of discipline and order, and there is no room here for a detailed analysis of the ethics of selective conscientious objection, but if that is so, integrity and moral courage are not quite the absolutes that they are made out to be. It would appear that the military needs to think more deeply about exactly what it actually wants and expects in terms of ethics. It is not clear that military commanders have really thought through the ramifications of what they preach.

Putting that to one side, how in practice do military institutions carry out ethics education? A number of methods are identified in the chapters which follow, namely:

- A pragmatic method in which there is no formal ethics education, but in which the 'ethos' of the institution is instilled into trainees by a process of osmosis (the British armed forces rely on this method, and their preference for the word 'ethos' rather than 'ethics' is notable in this regard). With this method, ethics are 'caught' not taught; the sheer force of the institution, via its traditions and the examples of commissioned and non-commissioned officers, shapes soldiers in the desired directions through unseen, but nonetheless powerful, processes. Supporters of this approach would agree with the sentiment expressed by Patrick Mileham, and common in the British armed forces, namely 'why intellectualize and make problematical what experience has taught and sustained over a long period?' (see Chapter 4).
- Formal classes in moral philosophy. These are carried out in some officer training academies, such as those in the United States, but not in all. It is generally felt that such classes would not be appropriate for all ranks, but could have some benefit for officers, in terms of enhancing their abilities to think critically and with understanding about ethical issues. Supporters of this approach would probably answer Mileham's question above by stating that moral problems *are* problematic, and cannot be adequately understood without some degree of intellectualizing.
- Case studies. These are probably the most favoured pedagogical method because they give abstract theories practical relevance and show the importance of the issues under discussion. Particularly useful are sessions in which students present case studies from their own experience. Apart from these, there is some disagreement as to which are the best studies – the usual preference is for negative cases, which demonstrate ethical failure of some sort, but some commentators feel that positive cases of exemplary behaviour might be more suitable. Jamie Cullens identifies two types of case studies: dilemmas,

and integrity cases. The former involve situations in which 'a member of the military is faced with a number of options, often all of them bad, and the difficulty arises out of the fact that it is not obvious which of these options is the ethically correct one to follow', whereas the latter are cases in which 'they know which is the ethically correct option to choose, but where there is considerable pressure on them to choose the ethically wrong option' (see Chapter 7). It is the former which are most often used in military training, but J. Joseph Miller has warned elsewhere that in fact 'very few moral problems truly constitute dilemmas', and there is a danger that use of poorly constructed cases can 'seduce practitioners into … the quasi-reflective life … that relies upon moral judgments that are inadequately grounded in theoretical commitments' (Miller 2004, 210). The military tendency to demand clear cut solutions to such problems enhances this problem.

- Motivational speakers. These are of numerous types, but there is a widespread feeling that speakers with military experience, talking about military cases, are more likely to hold the interest of their audiences than other speakers, such as sportsmen or businessmen, however extraordinary the latter's personal achievements.
- Role models, battlefield tours, and museum visits. These are designed to provide positive examples which soldiers can aim to emulate.
- Integration of ethics into other aspects of military training. With this method, ethics need not be taught as a separate subject, since it appears within the other aspects of training. This, for instance, is the approach adopted by the German *Zentrum für Innere Führung*. According to Stefan Werdelis, it is the 'very limits set to the ethical education effort which, in my view, would make it reasonable to deal with ethical education and instruction in conjunction with education in other fields, such as law, history, and politics' (see Chapter Nine). Ethical problems can also be introduced into field training, an approach adopted by the Canadian Forces.

Responsibility for Ethics Education

The final question to answer is who should be responsible for ethics education in the military. There are many candidates, with military officers (commissioned and non-commissioned), chaplains, academics, and lawyers being the obvious examples. As Stephen Deakin notes, at the Royal Military Academy Sandhurst, officer cadets imbibe the ethos of the army from their platoon colour sergeants, and also to some degree from their platoon captains. Chaplains have a lesser role, and academics almost none. By contrast, where formal ethics classes exist, as for instance at US military academies, philosophers have a much larger part to play, and in some circumstances, such as in Norway, the chaplains take the leading role.

There are arguments for and against all of these participants. As I have noted elsewhere (Robinson 2007), national differences may be significant. The involvement of chaplains in ethics education in Norway may be less controversial than it would be in, say, Canada, due to the relative religious homogeneity of the former compared with the latter.

The involvement of academic philosophers also varies considerably from country to country. In an article in *Journal of Military Ethics*, J. Joseph Miller, himself a philosopher, has argued that their role in military ethics education should be enhanced. The assumption that because an officer has high moral qualities he is suitable for teaching ethics is not, in Miller's opinion, sustainable:

> While all soldiers have a role to play in moral education, namely that of serving as role models, it is trained philosophers who have the skills necessary to facilitate the theoretical and dialectical components of a soldier's education. Military institutions should draw upon some of that collective expertise by making sure that their moral education programs include sustained work with philosophers. (Miller 2004, 212–13)

This is an argument which has some force, but may be resisted by some. One compromise is to provide those military officers who are to carry out ethics education with some training in moral philosophy. Henri Hude, for instance, comments that the French military academy is planning to 'train the trainers', enrolling in a French university the captains who train the cadets at Coëtquidan so that they can obtain a masters degree in 'ethics, strategy and management of human resources' (see Chapter 10). Miller, however, casts some doubt on the usefulness of sending military officers to graduate school and then using them as teachers, saying that they 'lack the time to absorb a real feel for the open, free-wheeling inquiry of the academic life' (Miller 2004, 213). The validity of this observation might be questioned by some, but it appears clear that the question of who 'owns' ethics education in the military (to use Martin Cook's phrase) is one that requires further investigation.

Conclusion

It is unlikely that the importance of ethics education in the military will diminish in coming years. On the contrary, it is likely to become an ever more vital aspect of military life. Notwithstanding scandals such as the prison abuses at Abu Ghraib in Iraq, the service men and women of the armed forces of democratic states appear in general to behave in a manner consistent with the principles of the societies that they serve. For every scandal, one can easily find numerous instances of exemplary behaviour. Nevertheless, it is always possible to do better. Exemplary behaviour may be more common than the opposite, but even the slightest abuse of military power can have a catastrophic strategic effect. It is our hope that the chapters of this book can provide a basis for further discussion and improvement.

Acknowledgments

I wish to thank the Arts and Humanities Research Council and the Institute of Applied Ethics at the University of Hull for their support. Thanks are also due to C.R., to Flick Lawes of the Institute of Applied Ethics, and to all the contributors to this volume.

Bibliography

Crisp, R. and Slote, M. (eds) (1997), *Virtue Ethics* (Oxford: Oxford University Press).

Kohlberg, L. (1981), *Essays on Moral Development* vol. I: *The Philosophy of Moral Development: Moral Stages and the Idea of Justice* (New York: Harper and Row).

Matthews, L.J. (ed.) (2002), *The Future of the Army Profession* (Boston: McGraw-Hill).

Mattox, J.M. (2002), 'The Ties that Bind: the Army Officer's Moral Obligations', in L.J. Matthews (ed.), pp. 293–312.

MacIntyre, A. (1997), 'The Nature of the Virtues', in R. Crisp and M. Slote (eds), pp. 118–40.

Miller, J.J. (2004), 'Squaring the Circle: Teaching Philosophical Ethics in the Military', *Journal of Military Ethics* 3:3, 199–215.

Robinson, P. (2007), 'Ethics Training and Development in the Military', *Parameters* 37:2, 23–36.

Toner, J.H. (2002), 'A Message to Garcia: Leading Soldiers in Moral Mayhem', in L.J. Matthews (ed.), pp. 313–36.

PART I
CASE STUDIES

Chapter 2

Education in an Ethos at the Royal Military Academy Sandhurst

Stephen Deakin

The British Army and Sandhurst

The Royal Military Academy Sandhurst (RMAS) is widely regarded as one of the world's leading military academies. The Academy reopened after the Second World War in 1947 as the sole Army initial officer training establishment and it set itself the primary aim of, 'The development of the cadet's character, his powers of leadership, and a high standard of individual and collective discipline' (Shepperd 1980, 159). The current mission statement of the Academy is, 'Through military training and education, to develop the qualities of leadership, character and intellect demanded of an Army Officer on first appointment' (The Royal Military Academy Sandhurst website). These statements make a number of ethical points. Character and leadership are required of a student officer and these of course have strong ethical dimensions. The Academy's aim is to develop students' ethical and moral strength so that they can cope with the incredibly demanding circumstances of leading soldiers in battle.

The main part of the student body consists of 700 to 800 officer cadets (around 10 per cent of them women and 10 per cent from overseas) taking the year-long commissioning course for the regular army. This course is intensely demanding, physically and mentally. Students' days are long and filled with activity and they are often physically and mentally tired. As the graduates of this course go on to lead the regular army, it provides the main focus of this chapter (ethics education elsewhere in the British armed forces is covered by Patrick Mileham in Chapter 4). However, it should be noted that in addition to the regular commissioning course, Sandhurst runs four week-long courses for doctors, dentists, nurses, vets, lawyers and padres, two week-long courses for reserve officers of the Territorial Army, and four week-long courses for late-entry officers being commissioned from the ranks. Together these courses mean that every army officer who now gains a commission is educated and trained at Sandhurst. It is the spiritual home of the British Army officer corps and the Army's and Sandhurst's ethics are inseparable.

Sandhurst has both a military staff that teaches the myriad military skills and qualities required of an officer, and a civilian academic staff that teaches military history, defence policy, international affairs, leadership and management. Military and academic parts of the course integrate with each other where possible. For example, civilian academic staff teach peacekeeping in the classroom and it is then practised in the field on exercise under military instruction with the support of the academic staff.

However, the academic study of ethics plays very little part in student life at the Academy. Students spend hardly any time studying the great ethical thinkers or such issues as utilitarianism, determinism, moral relativism and the like. Instead, they study practical applied ethics. This teaching is part of much of what goes on at Sandhurst. Opportunities on military exercise in the field test and develop student's moral qualities; in the classroom they are presented with numerous ethical dilemmas. These range from what they will do if a soldier under their command gives them stolen military kit, to the finer points of the application of the Geneva Convention. Staff make great efforts to help students become practical ethical thinkers. Sandhurst is a very ethical institution that aspires to instilling high moral standards in all its students.

A small number of British students on the regular commissioning course gain entry from the ranks or straight from school, but 85 per cent of them have already attended university. Sandhurst students today are typically aged around 23 or 24 years old on entry and many have taken a year off between school and university. Unlike other military academies, Sandhurst is not a degree-awarding institution and it has never been one. One advantage of this policy is that students enter the Army with a wider perspective and with more experience of life than if they had joined at 18 straight from school to study for a degree in a military environment. They are probably less malleable because of this prior experience, but they are also more thoughtful and more able to think independently; these are qualities that the modern army requires.

Sandhurst students seem to have many of the ethical insights of their generation in civilian life. This means that they usually, unthinkingly, endorse some sort of moral and cultural relativism with a dash of utilitarianism thrown in for good measure. Yet they also accept the moral absolutism involved in belief in contemporary human rights – which they usually accept without question.

The important point to recognize here is that both Sandhurst and the Army it serves are British institutions with long histories. Traditionally, the British, and their military, have been pragmatic and impatient of abstract reasoning and philosophy in public affairs (a fascinating example here concerns when British soldiers have thought it right to disobey their orders. See de Lee 2002). Instead, they have favoured shared, tacit, understandings of the right way to do things. That Sandhurst has never been a degree awarding institution is perhaps testimony to this ideal of pragmatism. The view taken has been that the trainee Army officer only requires a practical education and training. Because of this, until quite recently, talk of 'ethics' or 'military ethics' has not sprung naturally to the lips of the British military.

At Sandhurst, for long periods, students came from the right sort of family and attended the right sort of public school before, in many cases, going directly to Sandhurst. As the Sandhurst chaplain remarked in one of his sermons to students before the First World War in the Academy Chapel, 'We ask you to give us examples worthy of the best traditions of the Schools you have left' (Archibald 1912, 15). Together, family and public school were expected to have prepared a new arrival with the right ethical standards and so further explicit ethical tuition was not required at Sandhurst. Such expectations are no longer held.

Ethical Influences on Sandhurst and the British Army

The most obvious source of ethics of Sandhurst and of the British Army is the Christian religion and the Bible. To put it another way, each institution would be very different if its source of ethics had been other religions such as Buddhism, Islam or Hinduism. Since the creation of the modern British Army in the sixteenth century, the British military has been required by law to adopt the Christian religion. From that time, the British military has been organized, spiritually and ethically, to behave much like a diocese of the state church, the Church of England (Deakin 2005, 97–105). The *public and organizational* ethical language of the British military has been Christianity. Soldiers have routinely participated in Christian rituals such as worship services, military funerals, marriages, blessing of regimental colours and the like. Christian ethics and Christian understandings shaped military law and military organizational procedures. The military have had official Christian chaplains, their own church buildings and, in the case of the Royal Navy, their own chapter of prayers in the Church of England's Book of Common Prayer. Chaplains routinely accompanied their soldiers into battle. Nine chaplains were at Waterloo in 1815 (Smyth 1968, 47). Sixty-six chaplains were with the British Expeditionary Force in 1914 (Brumwell 1943, 16). There were 15 chaplains at Arnhem with the 1st Parachute Division (Johnstone and Haggerty 1996, 241).

Christian teaching and education received great emphasis among the military. This Christian commitment was enshrined in military law. For example, Article 1 of the *Articles of War* in 1641 made it a duty for the military to 'diligently frequent Divine Service and sermon' (Walton 1894, 809). This requirement was for many years Article 1 until in 1847 it was moved to another part of the military code (Clodde 1874, 76). *The Articles of War 1662–3* gave the duty of every chaplain: 'The Chaplains to the Troops of Guards and others in Regiments shall every day read the Common Prayers of the Church of England to the Soldiers respectively under their charge, and to preach to them as often with convenience shall be thought fit' (Walton 1894, 809). By the 1970s this had become, in Queen's Regulations, which applied across all three Services; 'Chaplains are commissioned by Her Majesty the Queen to provide for the spiritual well being of Service personnel and their families. They are to be given every assistance to fulfil their ministry' (*Queen's Regulations* 1975). Queen's Regulations in 1971 stated;

> Commanding Officers have the primary responsibility for encouraging religious observance by those under command, but it is important that all who exercise authority should set a good example in order to lead others to an intelligent acceptance of Christian principles in the life of the Armed Forces' (*Queen's Regulations* 1971). Queen's Regulations 1975, as had earlier versions, gave special attention to places of education such as Sandhurst, 'Commanding officers are to ensure that the curricula of training

and educational establishments provide for appropriate religious instruction to young personnel (*Queen's Regulations* 1975).

This is not to suggest that members of the Army always behaved in a manner consistent with Christian ethics – clearly, they did not. Indeed, for long periods from the sixteenth century, a common understanding amongst the civilian population was that soldiers and sailors were members of a particularly godless community. More recently, academic studies have argued the case that Christianity was a control mechanism used to inculcate obedience amongst military personnel (see e.g. Spiers 1980 and Skelley 1977), or that Christianity was used as part of a policy in the nineteenth century to integrate the Army and civilian society (see Hendrikson 1998). The obvious starting point here is that Britons considered themselves a Christian nation and that they held Christian beliefs. Naturally, therefore, military law and the procedures used to organize the military provided a Christian framework for the military. At times of Christian revival, this framework was clothed with further Christian developments. This was particularly the case with the Christian revivals in the mid-nineteenth century that were part of a movement that saw the military further Christianized and the good soldier, by the end of the century, was now a fully Christian soldier (see Anderson 1971). The Victorians rebuilt the Army as a respectable permanent state institution and Christianity played an important role in this activity.

Christianity has not been the only ethical influence at work among the officer corps in the British Army and at Sandhurst. Throughout its history, many student officers came to Sandhurst from public schools that taught and embodied the ideal of the Christian English gentleman (see Mason 1982). A unique institution, Sandhurst modelled itself similarly (Shepperd 1980, 76). From the beginnings of Sandhurst in 1812, students were known as 'GCs' or Gentlemen Cadets (a title which eventually fell into disuse, possibly when the College was renamed as an Academy in 1947). This elusive ideal of the Christian, English, gentleman was a hybrid of Christianity, Plato's guardians, Aristotle's character development, and more. Much of it drew from Christian ethics, and with them the need for character development, plus an optional spiritual faith, thereby making for an easier, yet satisfying, religion for the English.

Indeed, this emphasis on moral character is an important element in the Western military tradition (Watson 1999, 55–72). British public schools emphasized 'character' above academic learning and this developed through enduring hardship and team games in addition to the School chapel – all strong features of Sandhurst throughout its history. This, sub-Christian, view of character has shaped Sandhurst a good deal. For example, its influence appears in the Academy Standing Orders of 1900 (reprinted in Mockley-Ferryman 1900). These placed considerable emphasis on students being Christian gentlemen – although, true to the British way of shared, tacit understandings, this is implicit rather than explicit in the Orders; students were to be dismissed for 'serious misconduct, or for moral or physical unfitness' (Mockley-Ferryman 1900, 293). At the time everyone obviously knew what immoral behaviour was, since it is not elaborated in the Orders. It was misbehaviour according to Christian ethics and the ideal of the Christian gentleman. Members of the military staff were instructed, 'to make themselves acquainted with the character' of their cadets; they were to, 'endeavour to the utmost … to promote that honourable and gentleman-like tone which ought to prevail among them' (Mockley-Ferryman 1900, 296). Anxious to protect the morals of its students, the Academy Orders insisted that, 'Only Gentlemen will be permitted to visit cadets in their rooms at any time' (ibid., 302). Major General J.F.C. Fuller, a well-known military historian and strategist in his time, who was at Sandhurst in 1897 and 1898, wrote, 'When I was at Sandhurst we were not taught how to behave like gentlemen, because it never occurred to anyone that we could behave otherwise' (quoted in *The Queen's Commission*, 14). A British Army general's 1978 study of fighting spirit summarizes part of this elusive ethical stream very well: 'since history undoubtedly proves that a sound religious faith is a strong component of high morale – a war winning factor – it is clearly the duty of every officer, whatever his private beliefs, to be seen as a Christian, even if he can only be what I call "an Army Christian"' (*The Queen's Commission*, 14).

This emphasis on individual good character is evident in the Academy's mission statement today. The ideal is that of the gentleman, with unspoken and unconscious Christian ethics, who has a sure, but unarticulated, grasp of decent behaviour and right and wrong – but who, we assume, does not take his Christian faith too seriously. These beliefs are very powerful and effective ones, for from them Sandhurst and the Army and have created a British military ethical community that has successfully held together and fought through battle after battle and war after war. This ethic was challenged by the changes that started in the 1960s when a secular revolution began in Britain and elsewhere that rejected Christianity and the ideals of the Christian gentleman. The new ethics were individualistic, materialistic, egalitarian, morally relativistic and secular. This was a great challenge to how the Army and Sandhurst viewed life.

The Post-Christian Army

The changes in ethics brought about by the 1960s revolution gradually made themselves felt in the Army. By the 1980s, senior officers were expressing concern about the ethical beliefs and standards of the Army. They worried about what they saw as the changed, and less satisfactory, ethics of young officers. Whilst in the past regular officers were encouraged to view their time in the Army through the Christian metaphor of vocational service, a spiritual calling, now youngsters acted as if it was simply a job. No longer could they be relied upon to support publicly the Army's official Christian ethics of the past. The new ethics were making it harder to for the Army to form a moral community based on self-sacrifice, trust and social cohesion.

The Army responded to this concern with policy documents that codified its ethical beliefs and standards. In 1993 it produced an internal unpublished paper *The Discipline and Standards Paper*. This document was clear that its thinking was a response to the new secular movement.

> Within society the formative influences in promoting positive attitudes towards authority have been in steady decline: religion, education and the family no longer always provide the framework of behaviour, social structure and responsibility they have in the past. More liberal attitudes prevail, leading many parts of society to reflect or reduce in importance those values which the Armed Forces seek to maintain and regard so highly: sense of duty, loyalty, self-discipline, self sacrifice, respect and concern for other. (*The Discipline and Standards Paper* 1993)

This paper emphasized virtuous character as a requirement of being a successful member of the Army. In many respects, the ethics of this paper were a modernized version of sixteenth century military law, with its Christian understanding of good behaviour – although the paper did not mention Christianity. This sort of thinking however was increasingly out of step with secular civilian society's views and it came under pressure. The Army responded with an unpublished internal paper, *The Right to be Different* (some discussion of which can be found in Mileham 1998, 170), which made the case that the Army's unique task – to kill or to be killed on the battlefield – required it to have a special ethical basis drawn from traditional morality. In the ethical climate of the 1990s, this argument did not prove to be sustainable. The Army then produced another ethical statement of its core beliefs, *The Values and Standards of the British Army*. The ethics of this paper straddled the demands for good (unspoken Christian) gentlemanly character with a post-Christian emphasis on values and utilitarianism. Like its predecessors, it also saw its purpose as being to clarify the Army's ethics in a post-Christian age. It argued:

> The Army recruits from a society in which there is less deference to authority and a greater awareness of individual rights. It is also a less cohesive society, one in which traditional, shared values are less effectively transmitted, and concepts such as honour and loyalty are less well understood. (*The Values and Standards of the British Army* 2000, para 2)

An important feature of the Army's response in these ethical documents is that it seized on the term 'ethos' rather than on 'ethics' as the basis of its moral thinking. The 1993 *Discipline and Standards Paper,* was subtitled *The Military Ethos (The Maintenance of Standards)*, whilst *Values and Standards 2000* identifies the Army's ethos as 'That spirit which inspires soldiers to fight. It derives from, and depends upon, the high degrees of commitment, self-sacrifice and mutual trust which together are so essential to the maintenance of morale' (*The Values and Standards of the British Army* 2000, para. 9). Ethos and ethics relate closely to each other, but they are not the same. Ethics concerns the moral principles that should guide us. Ethos describes the characteristic spirit of a community; it is concerned with the way in which a community actually lives.

This appeal to ethos is both clever and revealing. The study of ethics often involves abstract and applied thought about complex problems informed by the world's great thinkers. The appeal to ethos neatly sidesteps this. It promotes and reinforces an ideal British Army way of life and in doing so it seems to avoid much ethical discussion. It is not prescriptive in a legalistic sense and this appeal to the spirit of its community fits the pragmatic British military culture with its shared implicit understandings. Ethos appears at first glance to be neutral, yet it carries within it all the characteristics of the British Army. It is a strong socializing device. It communicates that this is the way that the British Army military community does things. It says to all soldiers: accept the principles of our military community. Its use expresses the British military distaste of abstract philosophy and reasoning and instead it celebrates how a community lives.

Although the word ethos has only come into popular use in British military circles in the last twenty years or so, it is clear that the term captures the practice of hundreds of years. Soldiers have always been educated in the British military ethos. Sandhurst has played an important part in this. Sandhurst has taught its students right and wrong not by study of academic, philosophical, ethics, but by a process of absorbing practical and applied ethics. The educational model used has been a time-honoured, 'hear, see, do' one, where one military generation passes its ethics on to the next.

Ethical Education at the RMAS Today

Sandhurst is an imposing institution, whose grounds and buildings communicate power, order, discipline and purpose. Past students knew the initials RMA as standing for 'Right Mental Attitude'. Although this has now passed into disuse, the sentiment is still very much part of the education at Sandhurst. Students are encouraged to be enthusiastic, positive and to push themselves to the limit of their abilities.

Sandhurst makes a determined effort to change the thinking and the behaviour of its students, and so it is inevitably involved in moral education. It would be impossible to complete the course unless one learnt military etiquette. To succeed, students need to change their thinking about themselves, about others and about the military community that they are joining. It may be possible to bluff about this changed thinking, yet Sandhurst puts students in such demanding, tiring and stressful circumstances, and then evaluates how they behave, that this seems unlikely.

The first five weeks of the year-long course are an intense period of military instruction and training, which aim to instil basic soldier skills into students. They learn to dress properly, to march and to polish boots, and so on. Students must show that they can salute and march correctly before they complete this experience at the beginning of the course. After this, students learn the myriad subjects that an officer needs to know about. Teaching takes place both in the classroom and in the field on exercises away from the Academy. Many of these exercises build and test physical and mental resilience as well as character.

Although there is much teaching and learning of military practice here, there is also an expectation of osmosis concerning the ethics and ethos of the Army. Rather than learn ethical principles in an academic fashion, the emphasis is on absorbing the time-honoured ethos of the British Army and its officer corps. Of note here is the important role of the Colour Sergeant in each platoon. He is a specially selected senior Non-Commissioned Officer who is trusted to lead the platoon in day-to-day matters and who acts as a powerful conduit to channel the flow of the Army's ethos to students. Students receive the British Army's wisdom of the ages, its history, common sense and pragmatism. The long history of the Academy helps in this; the corridors of the older buildings are ones where the great men of the past have walked; Churchill, Montgomery and the like. This is a model of ethical education where the wisdom of the older generation passes to the younger one. The ideal of ethos is very appropriate here since this is an education in the characteristic spirit of the British Army community and particularly in that of its officer corps. Some of this spirit is clear and unambiguous: some of it is intuitive and intangible: some is caught and some is taught.

A noticeable feature of this ethos is that of good manners and politeness. Students, of course, salute senior officers. They are also expected to do other things such as to say 'Good morning, Sir' when passing a civilian or to hold doors open for others. With this goes teaching about how to behave at formal dinners, in the Officers Mess and in others' homes. A thank you letter for hospitality received must follow, promptly, an invitation to someone's home for a meal. Students dress smartly both in uniform and in their civilian clothes. They must dress at all times in a way that would not attract the critical attention of a Regimental Sergeant Major. Punctuality and good organization are expected. All of this is part of the ethos of being a British officer. Some of it is justified in terms of effectiveness: an efficient officer is better than one who is not. Some of it prepares officers to live with others in stressful conditions on operations. Good manners and thoughtfulness oils relationships and makes it easier to get the job done. Some of it, good manners and politeness, integrity and personal honour are part of being a Christian English gentleman.

The developments in the Army's ethical thinking outlined above have had their impact at Sandhurst. Christianity has been the official religion at Sandhurst throughout its history. For much of this period, students have attended compulsory Christian worship. The list of kit that students had to bring to Sandhurst in 1849, for example, included a Bible and a Church of England prayer book. At this time, the student day began with a compulsory 15-minute Christian service in the Academy Chapel. Sandhurst's motto since the end of the Second World War, 'Serve to Lead', reflects the words and example of Christ in the Bible (Matthew 20: 28). In 1813 the first Academy Chapel for Christian worship was built, and the second in 1879, and this latter one was greatly enlarged in the 1920s and 1930s. For much of its history Sandhurst has had full time military Christian chaplains who taught this religion to students and staff, carried out pastoral duties and were responsible for the spiritual wellbeing of staff. The Academy has its own Christian cemetery within its grounds where are buried some former staff and students. The influence of biblical Protestantism on the origins of the modern Army in the sixteenth century carried through to the twentieth century at Sandhurst. A Catholic Chapel did not exist within the Academy grounds until after the end of the Second World War. Prior to this, Catholic students marched into the nearby town of Camberley to attend church. The protestant, Church of England,

Academy Chapel is a huge and impressive building that occupies a central site within the grounds. It is the parish church of both students and staff.

This Christian ethic continues but it is hard to evaluate its role and importance today. Since the 1960s, in common with other countries in the West, Britain has seen the rise of secular humanism, which has replaced large parts of the former Christian ethics. The impact of this movement on the Army and on Sandhurst is difficult to discern accurately. There is still much that is Christian, and much of the Christian English Gentleman about Sandhurst and the British Army ethos. Yet in British civilian society support for Christian ethics and the ethics of the Christian gentleman is probably much weaker than in the past.

Currently, the Academy employs three full time, uniformed, Christian military chaplains whose primary purpose is the spiritual welfare of students and staff. They lead worship, provide pastoral support and teach some ethics to students. In contrast to many American military academies, few staff or students at Sandhurst today are overt Christians and religious belief is largely a private matter. However, in the absence of a chaplain, Queens Regulations require officers to lead Christian services for their soldiers, when necessary. Sandhurst chaplains provided tuition for students in how to do this.

Whereas once the Academy relied on an innate sense of decency and an agreement about ordinary civilized behaviour in its students, derived from the ideal of the Christian English gentleman, this can no longer be assumed. Since its publication in 2000, the Army booklet, *Values and Standards* has become the ethical bible of the Academy. Students are told to keep the booklet to hand and to refer to it often to remind them of what is expected of them. It is necessary then to consider the ethical content of *Values and Standards*. The booklet is a mixture of ethical appeals and the result is not always a happy one, not least for the academic ethicist, who will find inconsistencies in its argument (see e.g. Deakin 2006, 39–46). Much of the booklet's appeal is to traditional Christian gentleman virtue ethics – although it labels these as values; these are selfless commitment; courage; discipline; integrity; loyalty and respect for others. The justification for adopting these virtues is not developed in the booklet, but it is clear that it is a utilitarian one. Soldiers will be better soldiers if they adopt these virtues is the implicit argument.

The core principle of the booklet is what it calls the Service Test. It is worth citing in full:

> When considering possible cases of misconduct, and in determining whether the army has a duty to intervene in the personal lives of soldiers, commanders at every level must consider each case against the following Service Test: *Have the actions or behaviour of an individual adversely impacted or are they likely to impact on the efficiency or operational effectiveness of the Army?* This Service Test lies at the heart of the Armed Forces Code of Social Conduct, and is equally applicable to all forms of conduct. (*The Values and Standards of the British Army*, para. 20, my emphasis)

Whilst this formulation may work well at the everyday level; 'don't do that, it will harm the Army' – and this is the sense in which it is taught at Sandhurst – at a deeper ethical level, there are numerous problems with it. It is very similar to John Stuart Mill's harm principle in *On Liberty* and it has many of the problems that his critics found with that. In *On Liberty*, Mill attempted to identify the boundaries where the community can rightfully interfere in individual's lives. He argued that it may only do so when they are causing harm to others. 'The only purpose, for which power can be rightfully exercised over any member of a civilized community against his will, is to prevent harm to others' (Mill 1998, para. 68).

The Service Test tries to solve the ethical problems associated with role morality, the ethics of the soldier doing his or her job, and the morality required of a civilian. It argues that the Army will not intervene in the lives of its personnel unless they harm the Army. This is an application of the common liberal principle that people have both a private and a public life and that one should not interfere in the private sphere. There are numerous ethical problems with this formulation, especially when applied to a cohesive Army community that fights and perhaps dies together. Indeed, elsewhere in *Values and Standards* appeal is made to a holistic morality that encompasses the total individual. For example, *Values and Standards* argues, under the heading of moral courage, the need 'to insist on maintaining the highest standards of decency and behaviour at all times and under all circumstances. In the end this will earn respect and trust' (*Values and Standards*, para. 12). Later it asserts, 'every soldier must strive to achieve and maintain the highest professional and personal standards' (ibid., para. 19). The conclusion must be, despite the Service Test, that the Army *is* interested in the personal life of its members.

The Service Test is utilitarian and the utilitarianism ethic often does not work in a military community. It is not the ethic of a virtuous person desiring to do good in every circumstance, which is what the Army and Sandhurst want. Rather, it is the ethic of a highly educated rational calculator who is constantly considering whether an action is harmful to the Army or not, and, inevitably, what he can get away with. This principle's emphasis on costs and benefits is individualistic and draws attention from a shared moral understanding and it acts to undermine the community cohesion that the Army sees as so vital to fighting power. Remarkably, this Service Test formula prohibits many acts of bravery by soldiers since these, being often particularly risky, are most likely to harm the operational effectiveness of the Army.

Recently, the Academy has developed a concept of 'Officership' as an umbrella term for its important ethical concepts. This now informs much education and training at the Academy. A booklet has been produced for each officer cadet, *The Queen's Commission – A Junior Officer's Guide*. Its first sentence is revealing, 'This is a guide about Officership, a term that has gained in currency in an age of changing social and moral standards' (*The Queens Commission*: introduction). This supports the argument earlier in this chapter that the Academy is fighting to preserve the essential qualities of an officer in a time when civilian society does not fully support them. Whilst in the past there was often an intuitive shared understanding of what a good officer was, the issuing of this booklet symbolizes the belief that these intuitions now require codifying in written form or they will be lost. The booklet defines Officership as 'Officership ... is about what an officer must be and the essential standards that he must uphold ... these qualities of leadership, character and moral integrity... without them the trust that is essential ...will be eroded' (ibid). Officership is intended to encapsulate what it is to be an officer. As the foreword to the booklet suggests, 'Officers must be the embodiment of leadership, character and indispensable moral values ... dedicated to the essential qualities of moral courage, commitment and self sacrifice' (ibid.). Officership incorporates the traditional military virtues recognized throughout much of British history as essential to the successful leading of soldiers. The term is also a modern expression of the ideal of the English Christian gentleman and would have been as acceptable in the Academy Standing Orders of 1900 as it is now.

Another important recent ethical initiative at the RMAS is the decision to increase the prominence given to studying the law of armed conflict. The emphasis here is not on political decisions about going to war but on the actual conduct of war fighting. Since some students will be leading soldiers in conflict quite soon after leaving the Academy, this is a subject that attracts much student interest. The Academy teaches the law of armed conflict as part of Officership. Civilian academic staff provide classroom-based education into such issues as how prisoners of war should be treated; the need to avoid civilian casualties where possible; and fighting according to the Geneva Conventions. These sessions include numerous practical case studies where students can place themselves in the sort of situation that they may face once they leave the Academy.

These classes are stimulating ones since, inevitably, they quickly engage students in ethical debate. What about 'illegal combatants'? Does adhering to the law of war give an opponent an advantage? What about suicide bombers? Am I always responsible for the conduct of my soldiers in this area? Students can choose to write a long dissertation about a topic in this area if they wish. This classroom-based education is followed by a two week exercise in the field where students face a complex emergency situation and have to deal with refugees, prisoners of war, terrorists, insurgents, suicide bombers, and rioters. Members of the Academy military staff, with the support of civilian academic staff, lead this exercise. As well as exercising as soldiers, students find themselves role-playing hostages, negotiators, rioters, and NGO staff. Students have to show here a developing knowledge and understanding of the law of armed conflict. Post-exercise discussions are held with students by the academic staff, who draw out the ethical and legal dilemmas that students encountered. Students report that the law of armed conflict package is one of the highlights of the whole course. The treatment of this subject exemplifies the Academy approach to the teaching of ethics. Abstract ethical theory is kept to a minimum; practical hands on experience of dealing with the issues is emphasized.

How Successful is Ethical Education at Sandhurst?

The British Army has a good ethical record. British soldiers have largely avoided the ethical problems that other armies have experienced in the last 50 years or so.

Indeed not since 1812 at Badajos in Spain have large numbers of British soldiers shown serious indiscipline. Of course, in almost any conflict, ethical problems and failures will occur. In the case of the British Army criticism is sometimes made about incidents in Kenya, Aden, the Falklands, Northern Ireland and Iraq, to name a few. However, the British Army has avoided the sort of ethical problems that the Americans got into in Vietnam, or the Dutch in the Balkans or the Canadians in Somalia or the French in Algeria. British troops have maintained their military ethics in some very difficult situations indeed in the past decades. The Army has been remarkably successful in the five conflicts, together with Northern Ireland, that it has been involved in since the Blair government came to power in 1997. Given this, although it cannot be quantified, the success of the ethical contribution of Sandhurst's education and training must be acknowledged.

Sandhurst today faces numerous ethical dilemmas. It recognizes as it always has done that good soldiering requires a strong ethical sense and the creation of a moral community in the British Army. The numerous recent complex emergency operations that the Army has undertaken have only highlighted the value of this. Sandhurst does its best to inculcate an ethos of traditional moral virtue and moral character in its students. Yet, in many ways, character is out of fashion in British public policy making; instead, the state often wishes to be morally neutral. One commentator has described much contemporary British morality as an invented 'quasi-morality', where older virtues such as courage, fairness, love, prudence and honesty have been replaced by equality, anti-discrimination, environmentalism, self-esteem and a caring attitude (Anderson 2005, 9). Hence, there is pressure on people to avoid smoking, to recycle their rubbish, to reduce their energy use, to avoid drinking alcohol and not to be overweight. Yet, there is a lack of commitment to public policies that support traditional moral virtues. For example, the British tax system does not currently discriminate in favour of marriage.

The Army's Service Test is best seen as the Army's attempt to acknowledge and come to terms with this ethically neutral civilian society that it serves. Utilitarian formulations such as the Service Test focus attention on the outputs that people create rather than on their characters. This avoids the need to discriminate over people's character and morality, something that the new morality sees as immoral since it has no fixed view of the good. Yet, focusing on the consequences of actions and not on their morality weakens the moral community and communicates that morality does not matter. Consequences are very important, of course, but primary emphasis on them will lead soldiers to become rational calculators who consider only consequences rather than the morality of the wider Army community.

The need to write formal codes of ethics as in the *Values and Standards* booklet is a sign of the passing of an age when people knew what a British officer stood for. He was a gentleman; a Christian English gentleman, who, whilst he might not take his religion too seriously, could be relied upon to do the right thing and to know what ordinary decent correct behaviour was without even thinking about it very much. It is revealing in this context to look at the official thinking that led to the creation of a military Academy at Sandhurst in 1812. It included the following reasoning; 'The uncircumscribed extent of land, which admits to the buildings being so placed as to avoid neighbourhood injurious to the morals of cadets, and which allows space also for military movements, and the construction of military works without interruption' (Mockley-Ferryman 1900, 15). Sandhurst was founded, therefore, on a concern for the morals of its students. As ever, these morals were not detailed, for everyone knew what a British Army Gentleman Cadet should behave like: He should be a Christian English gentleman – even if he was Scottish, Irish or Welsh!

Sandhurst has responded well to his passing by identifying its core ethics and by emphasizing them in its education and training. What of the students themselves? A year at Sandhurst appears to have a hugely formative ethical effect on students; yet is one that they are often unaware of and that they often deny. At the end of the course students usually remain the moral relativists and utilitarians that many of them were when they entered Sandhurst. However, they also see that their unique profession must have virtuous ethical absolutes, which they accept as part of their employment. Of course, Sandhurst is only the beginning of their career and when students leave to join their regiments, another very powerful ethos begins to affect them.

Meanwhile, senior officers continue to fight for the older, gentlemanly, Christian virtues. In December 2006, General Jackson, recently retired as Britain's top soldier, the Chief of the General Staff, gave an important speech about defence matters. In part of it he expressed his concern about the ethos of the British Army:

> I also worry, not only where the Ministry of Defence is concerned, but more generally at large, that there is a failure, even an unwillingness, to understand the fundamental nature of the ethos of soldiering. It is difficult to overestimate the importance of ethos: the can-do, the us-us approach, rather than me-me, we can hack it. At the heart of this are perhaps some old-fashioned words – duty, honour, selflessness, discipline. These may not rest easily with some of today's values, but if they are not there you will not have an Army, certainly not an Army which can do what it has to do. (Jackson 2006)

General Jackson's successor, General Sir Richard Dannatt, gave an interview in 2006 in which he also supported these ethics. He said;

> In the Army we place a lot of store by the values we espouse. What I would hate is for the Army to be maintaining a set of values that were not reflected in our society at large – courage, loyalty, integrity, respect for others; these are critical things. ... I think it is important as an Army entrusted with using lethal force that we do maintain high values and that there is a moral dimension to that and a spiritual dimension. ... Our society has always been embedded in Christian values; once you have pulled the anchor up there is a danger that our society moves with the prevailing wind. ... There is an element of the moral compass spinning. I am responsible for the Army, to make sure that its moral compass is well aligned and that we live by what we believe in. It is said we live in a post-Christian society. I think that is a great shame. The Judaic-

Christian tradition has underpinned British society. It underpins the British Army. (Dannatt 2006)

Acknowledgments

I am grateful for the helpful comments of a number of people including Nigel de Lee and Alan Ward. As ever, responsibility for the arguments herein rests with the author alone.

Bibliography

Anderson, D. (2005), *Decadence* (London: Social Affairs Unit).

Anderson, O. (1971), 'The Growth of Christian Militarism in the Mid-Victorian Army', *English Historical Review* 86:338, 46–72.

Archibald, M.G. (1912), *Sundays at the Royal Military College* (London: Macmillan).

Brumwell, M. (1943), *The Army Chaplain* (London: Charles Black).

Clodde, C. (1874), *The Administration of Justice Under Military and Martial Law* (London: Murray).

Dannatt, Gen. Sir R. (2006), interview with Sarah Sands, *The Daily Mail*, 12 October.

Deakin, S. (2005) 'British Military Ethos and Christianity', *British Army Review* 138, 97–105.

Deakin S, (2006), 'Ethics and the British Army's Values and Standards', *British Army Review* 140, 39–46.

de Lee, N. (2002), 'British Approaches to Military Obedience: Pragmatism, Operational Necessity and Moral Dilemmas', *British Army Review* 135, 97–105.

Hendrikson, K.E. (1998), *Making Saints* (London: Associated University Press).

Jackson, Sir M. (2006), *The Richard Dimbleby Lecture*, <http://www.telegraph.co.uk/news/main.http://www.telegraph.co.uk/news/min>.

Johnstone, T. and Hagerty, J. (1996), *The Cross on the Sword* (London: Cassell).

Mason, P. (1982), *The English Gentleman* (London: Andre Deutsch).

Mileham, P. (1998), 'Military Values and the Right to be Different', *Defense Analysis* 4:2, 169–90.

Mill, J.S. (1998), *On Liberty and Other Essays*, John Gray (ed.) (Oxford: Oxford University Press).

Mockley-Ferryman, A.F. (1900), *Annals of Sandhurst* (London: Heinemann).

The Queen's Commission – A Junior Officer's Guide, 14, privately printed at Sandhurst.

Queen's Regulations 1971 (London: HMSO, J1427).

Queen's Regulations 1975 (London: HMSO 5.269).

Richardson, F.M. (1978), *Fighting Spirit: Psychological Factors in War* (London: Leo Cooper).

The Royal Military Academy Sandhurst website, <hrrp://www.sandhurst.mod.uk/courses/commissioning.htm>.

Shepperd, A. (1980), *Sandhurst* (London: Hamlyn).

Skelley, A.R. (1977), *The Victorian Army at Home* (London: Croome Helm).

Smyth, J. (1968), *In This Sign Conquer* (London: Mowbray 1968).

Spiers, E. (1977), *The Army and Society 1859–1914* (London: Longman).

The Values and Standards of the British Army (2000) (London: HMSO).

Walton, C. (1894), *History of the British Standing Army* (London: Harrison).

Watson, B.C.S. (1999), 'The Western Ethical Tradition and the Morality of the Warrior', *Armed Forces and Society* 26:1, 55–72.

Chapter 3

An Ethics Curriculum for an Evolving Army

Jeffrey Wilson

In his July 2003 Arrival Message, former United States Army Chief of Staff General Peter J. Schoomaker made explicit his view of the ethical foundations of the American profession of arms, emphasizing that the United States Army is, always has been, and 'will remain a values based organization, where the core identity of Soldier is centred around a self-conception of the "Warrior of character" whose "non-negotiable" commitment to the values embodied in the Constitution of the United States "will not change," no matter what the exigencies of operational deployments or the character of our enemies' (*Warrior Ethos Briefing* 2003, 1). When Schoomaker characterized the American soldier as the professional who, in some ways more than any other epitomizes the spiritual underpinnings of American national identity, he was conveying much more than motivational hyperbole: he was evidencing his own awareness of, and commitment to, a plausible – but by no means universally accepted – ideal centre of gravity in the relationship between soldiers and the states they serve. The eloquent and provocative British General Sir John Winthrop Hackett succinctly expressed this ideal in his 1970 Harmon Memorial Lecture at the United States Air Force Academy. Laying aside the obvious fact that, since military organizations are created by the state to protect the state, the effectiveness of a military organization will be judged largely on instrumental grounds (i.e., on how well they contribute to deterring war and, when deterrence fails, how well they conduct themselves in war), Hackett offered the noble idea that 'the highest service of the military to the state may well lie in the moral sphere, [as a] well from which to draw [moral] refreshment for a body politic in need of it' (Hackett 1970, 19).

If we agree with Hackett – and Schoomaker's remarks seem to imply that American military professionals ought to do just that – then we judge soldiers as good or bad soldiers by, in effect, looking into their souls, rather than by looking merely at how well they perform their instrumental functions. Given that soldiers come from varying socio-economic strata within the political communities they serve, the moral character of the brand new soldier is indeterminate. The military establishment assumes the burden of defining good moral character, developing methods for teaching soldiers how to develop good moral character, somehow assessing the quality of the soldiers' moral character at a given time (the end of basic training, for example), and giving character some sort of measurable (even quantifiable) weight in the overall professional evaluation of soldiers as they progress through their careers. Pluralist political communities, of which the United States is perhaps the most radical example, have a greater training and educational challenge than political communities more authoritarian in governance or more racially and ethnically homogeneous in population. Authoritarian communities value the simple norm of obedience above all: one is good to the extent to which one does what the duly constituted authority directs. In racially and ethnically homogenous societies, where communal values are shared to a larger extent throughout various parts of the community than they perhaps are – or can be – in more diverse communities, it will likely be easier for the military to mould large numbers of people into a cohesive team with a shared vision of right and wrong, both inside and outside the scope of their professional duties.

Given the American population's socio-cultural diversity, United States Army leaders debated for many years whether or not a formal code of ethics for all soldiers (or separate codes for officers and enlisted soldiers) ought to be a part of the process of creating good soldiers (see for instance Hartle 1992 and Matthews 1994a and 1994b). The rhetorical question framing this decades-long debate, earnestly begun in the 1960s, was one of whether or not the hallowed West Point mantra of 'Duty, Honor, Country' was enough of an ethical lighthouse for the American military in the foggy ethical climate of the mid-twentieth century. The many arguments against a formal code of ethics centred around the idea that the more instrumental and traditional martial virtues such as loyalty, courage, and a conception of selfless service were self-evidently the basis for a soldier's character, regardless of rank. Further, those antagonistic to an Army code of ethics often took a compartmentalized view of character, arguing rather simplistically (yet forcefully) that a fighter who fights and a leader who is able to lead under fire demonstrate all the character necessary to rise through the ranks and be worthy of respect within the profession of arms (see the essays in Matthews and Brown 1989). One of the most outspoken proponents of this compartmentalized view was Second World War hero (later Superintendent of the US Military Academy (USMA) and US Army Chief of Staff) Maxwell Taylor, who saw no moral problems in serving with a combat ready officer who is 'loyal to his superiors and his profession but disloyal to his wife', or keeps physically fit but has 'General Grant's weakness for strong drink' (Taylor 1989, 131). For Taylor, a good soldier, even a good officer, *could be a bad man*. For Hackett, this statement is a non-sequitur. Seeming to address Taylor directly, Hackett opined in his Harmon Lecture that a person 'can be selfish, cowardly, disloyal, false, fleeting, perjured, and morally corrupt in a wide variety of other ways and still be outstandingly good in pursuits in which other imperatives bear than those upon the fighting man ... what the bad man cannot be is a good sailor, or soldier, or airman' (Hackett 1970, 18).

It would take a book-length study to describe the often torturous process of self-examination that led the US Army from an institutional view of which Taylor's remarks are but an authoritative recapitulation to the more enlightened view reflected in Schoomaker's remarks. The broad correlation of events and ideas leading to this shift is fairly well known. The intense escalation of the American war in Vietnam between 1965 and 1970 necessitated a rapid increase in the size of the Army, with a corresponding decrease in attention paid to ethics education and training. The drug use, racial tensions, and ethical relativism characterizing American society in the 1960s darkened the ethical fabric of the American Army. Although an isolated incident, the 1968 My Lai massacre, in which a company-sized unit of American soldiers slaughtered hundreds of innocent Vietnamese civilians, was the event that signalled to Army leadership and the American public just how degenerative the ethical decay had become. The tragedy of My Lai was doubled by the facts that so few American soldiers were held legally accountable for their actions, and that only one officer (Lieutenant William Calley) ever served time in jail. The commander of the division of which Calley's unit was a part became Superintendent of the US Military Academy, but later resigned because he felt, correctly, that his association with the massacred tainted the Academy (Ellis and Moore 1974). According Richard Gabriel and Paul Savage, self-centredness and careerism had become rampant in the Army officer corps of the 1960s and 1970s (Gabriel and Savage 1978).

Although the ethical climate in the US Army went from bad to worse in 1975 with the advent of the all-volunteer force, by 1980 the senior officers and non-commissioned officers who had borne the brunt of the Vietnam War started to turn the situation around from the bottom up. The period between Ronald Reagan's election as President in 1981 and the end of the first Gulf War in 1991 is generally acknowledged to be one of the great intellectual renaissances in American military history, of which the Army's ethical renaissance was a part (Romjue 1984 and 1993). This period culminated with the formal codification of the seven Army Values as the official Army Ethic in the late 1990s, encompassing the ethical ideals set forth in the oaths of enlistment and officer commissioning, the Code of Conduct, and the West Point Honor Code.

Beginning in the 1990s, then, the Army formalized the relationship between adherence to a clearly defined set of professional virtues that become one's personal *values* – a set of professional characteristics necessary for instrumental success on the battlefield – and the *actions* the soldier takes to interact with other people and the environment. In order to be 'persuasive in peace, invulnerable in war', the twenty-first-century soldier is immersed in the Army Ethic in Army service schools for enlisted soldiers from basic training to the Sergeant Major Academy. Officer education programmes in ethics at the pre-commissioning level and in junior officer schools are somewhat more theoretical, yet still overwhelmingly pragmatic, in appreciation of the unique position the young lieutenant occupies in the organizational hierarchy, where the youngest and least experienced officers are charged with the most demanding leadership challenges. The United States Military Academy at West Point, established in 1802, today carries on in its 204th year of service as the flagship of ethics education and training for officers, and the well from which all other US Army ethics training and education programmes spring.

West Point's mission is to 'educate, train and inspire the Corps of Cadets so that each graduate is a commissioned leader of character committed to the values of Duty, Honor, Country and prepared for a career of professional excellence and service to the Nation' (*Cadet Leader Development System* (*CLDS*) 2005, 7). The Academy mission statement implicitly reveals the Army's commitment to a communitarian conception of virtue and the primacy of principle over consequence in ethical decision making. If General Sir John Winthrop Hackett is right in assessing the primary virtue of a state's military establishment in the context of its function as a repository of virtue, then West Point's emphasis on building men and women of character who will infiltrate all walks of American life as ethical beacons around which like-minded people will coalesce during and after their Army service is perhaps more valuable to the long term viability of the United States as a political community than the mere fact that it graduates about 1,000 new second lieutenants annually to populate the ranks of Army units.

West Point's communitarian ethic has philosophical roots that are evident in Plato's *Republic*, itself a foundational text of the eighteenth-century political liberalism upon which the United States' system of government is grounded. That not everyone is born with the temperament, both intellectual and moral, to be a good soldier is a fact acknowledged in Book II of *The Republic*. The basic dichotomy of the profession of arms, that the guardians of the state (soldiers) must be by temperament 'gentle towards their own people, but rough towards their enemies' (Plato 1984, 172), creates the initial impression among *The Republic's* interlocutors that 'a good guardian cannot possibly be', for a person whose nature it is to be 'both gentle and full of high temper' – by implication a person able to be educated and trained to apply only the right amount of force toward the right objective for only the right amount of time – is seemingly impossible to find in the actual world (ibid., 172). As the dialogue progresses, Socrates reminds the others of what he thinks they are missing: that observation of creatures other than humans reveals the existence of 'natures such as we thought there were not, which have all these opposite things' (ibid., 172). Socrates uses the example of 'well-bred dogs', who possess a 'character' which allows them 'to be as gentle as can be to those they are used to, those they know, but are opposite to strangers' to show that 'we don't go against nature in seeking such a guardian' (ibid., 172).

This is not to say that such people are any more plentiful in the community than are well-bred dogs, who, according to Socrates, possess in their own way a 'real love of wisdom' which enables such dogs to display 'something refined' in their ability to discern between friend and foe (ibid., 173). Concluding first that the well-bred dog is by nature a 'lover of learning if he distinguishes his own and others' by understanding and ignorance', then further arguing that, because 'love of learning and love of wisdom are the same thing', the well-bred dog is, therefore, a lover of wisdom, Socrates notes with pleasure that 'we can confidently set down the same as true of a man also; if he is to be gentle to his own people, whom he knows, he must be a lover of learning and a true lover of wisdom' (ibid., 173).

Reaching the satisfying conclusion that the guardian must be a 'lover of wisdom' in addition to being 'quick and strong' is only the first step in manning the state's ramparts for Plato. Ascertaining the 'basis of his character' leads Socrates in *The Republic* directly to the question of 'how ... our guardians [shall] be trained and educated' (ibid., 173). In the end, to educate guardians for the state, Socrates recommends 'gymnastic for the body and music for the soul', which I think can translate into the modern era as a well-balanced blend of physical and liberal arts education (ibid., 174).

It should not be surprising, then, that the United States, whose founders conceived of their nascent experiment in democracy as the heir to the idealism of ancient Greece, has adopted the basic Platonic framework from *The Republic* as a foundation for military education and training at its Military Academy. All United States service academies, of which West Point is the eldest and perhaps most grounded in classical concepts of the relationship between soldier and state, educate and train young men and women in a four year programme that would look, it seems, very familiar in both form and substance to what Socrates in *The Republic* appears to have envisioned for his ideal state.

The conceptual link between character and professionalism that Plato seems to establish in *The Republic* comes to light in the USMA operational definition of character as 'those moral abilities that constitute the nature of a leader and shape his or her decisions and actions' (*CLDS*, 9). Further, USMA instructs cadets that the 'leader of character seeks to discover the truth, decide what is right, and demonstrate the courage and commitment to act accordingly' (ibid.). If character, as USMA defines it, also 'includes not only moral and ethical excellence, but also finesse, resoluteness, self discipline, and sound judgment' (ibid.), then this set of excellences certainly increases the strength of the intuitive connection between Plato's conception of the guardian and the modern West Point graduate. As a commissioned officer, the cadet will in theory be a person who will set 'the professional example by personifying' character that displays 'an awareness of and commitment to something bigger than [one's] self' (ibid.). Above all else, the West Point graduate should be a person others can trust. If there is anything that separates the American professional military ethic from that of other nations, it is perhaps the emphasis on the character trait of trust as the link that binds seniors with subordinates, peers with peers, and commitment to principle with commitment to personal behavioural values. Contrary to the traditions of European armies, where, historically, trust can be argued to grow more out of associations with social class and family than from character, West Point has since its inception in 1802 assumed that trust was a character trait that can be inculcated primarily through example.

If the essence of leadership based upon trust is the ability to influence 'people while operating to accomplish the mission and [improve] the organization' (*CLDS*, 8), then the leader must exemplify in personal behaviour on and off duty those character traits deemed essential to earning the respect of others in the organization. Respect for fellow professionals *in* the organization is a central prerequisite for embracing one's status as a member *of* the organization as an integral part of one's identity. Due in large measure to the American repugnance toward the idea of leadership through fear or position, American soldiers simply cannot be effectively led – except, perhaps, in the most desperate of circumstances – through measures based upon these foundations. The commitment to the ideal of egalitarianism in the American socio-cultural fabric all but ensures this, as much now as in the past. American officers (and non-commissioned officers, for that matter) have to work hard to establish a personal credibility with soldiers that will transcend what I see as socio-culturally ingrained cynicism and scepticism about authority (Brogan 1944; de Tocqueville 2003, ch. 25; Samet 2004). Therefore, USMA takes great pains to instil essentially Aristotelian virtues into the cadets in order to build a character worthy of trust.

The virtues come to light in the cadet Honor Code, which exhorts cadets never to 'lie, cheat, steal, or tolerate those who do' (*CLDS*, 9). The dual intent of the code – to internalize the necessity to take upon one's self the responsibility for enforcing ethical standards among fellow members of the profession to an equal degree that one takes such responsibility for one's own ethical behaviour in order to maintain ethical equilibrium in the organization – forces commitment to the virtue of integrity to a degree that some even today find almost unreasonable. On the one hand, the code demands internalization of the character traits of honesty, loyalty, and trustworthiness. On the other hand, it demands selfless adherence to the deontological notion of the absolute primacy of principle in any conceivable situation involving a breach of character in another person. The code hits hardest, of course, when the person in question (whose actions cannot under the code be tolerated) is a person with whom one enjoys a close *personal* relationship that complements and perhaps transcends the professional one. The code not only demands that cadets hold themselves to a high standard of personal integrity, where integrity is understood as a moral makeup that is consistent across the spectrum of one's personal and professional activities and relationships; it also demands such a level of integrity from all members of the organization. Not all of the American service academies have embraced the so-called toleration clause, and debate continues about the extent to which one can judge how the toleration clause affects the overall ethical composure of the graduate.

Central to this discussion, though, is the importance of the toleration clause to USMA's conception of itself as the well-spring of the Army ethic, binding all soldiers, regardless of rank, into the professional culture of trust. All soldiers are indoctrinated in the Warrior Ethos, which the US Army defines as 'the foundation for the American Soldier's total commitment to victory through exemplification of the Army Values of loyalty, duty, respect, selfless service, honor, integrity, and personal courage' (*Warrior Ethos Briefing* 2003, 15). This ethos is supposed to instil a character foundation that will enable the soldier to put the mission first, refuse to accept defeat, never quit, and never leave behind a fellow American [with] absolute faith in themselves and their team (ibid.). The theory behind the honour code is that it will enable – in fact, motivate – cadets to learn how to 'elevate [themselves] above self interest, [thereby allowing] the Corps of Cadets, the Army, and ultimately the Constitution of the United States [to] emerge as higher and nobler loyalties [than any other]' (*CLDS*, 9).

If, as Aristotle contends, a virtue is a mean between two extremes, then USMA is decisively Aristotelian in its four-year developmental process of ethics training and education, emphasizing balance and equanimity within and between the '"four interrelated roles" that comprise the identity of the Army officer: warrior, servant of the Nation, member of a profession, and leader of character' (*CLDS*, 12). The so-called 'West Point Experience' focuses on 'development of the whole person', implying that the identity embraced by the overarching term 'officership' is personal as well as professional (*CLDS*, 13).

Like Plato, Aristotle links the individual human *telos* with that of the community. As essentially social beings, persons are, in his view, to cultivate virtues that enhance the community *of* community, beginning with a self-awareness of one's inextricable embedding within a complex array of social relationship from birth to death that both shape the present self and set many of the parameters for defining future selves. Ignoring Aristotle's naturalistic account of the potential for virtue in any given individual, his immersion of individual identity in a collective of collectives is a fitting grounding for a professional ethic which seeks, as Aristotle does, to unite the virtues into a holistic conception of personhood that guides individual action in both public and private space.

USMA's holistic evaluation process of potential cadets (known as 'candidates' during the application process) reflects a distinctly Aristotelian conception of the linkage between intellectual and moral virtue. The candidate questionnaire is deceptively simple, asking for raw standardized test scores and a list of the candidate's high school extra-curricular and scholastic activities, to include positions held and honours earned. From this, USMA personnel glean a picture of the candidate's relationship with the communities of which he or she enjoys membership. Individual excellences, particularly those the display of which presupposes an effective and reciprocal sharing of risk and reward, such as leadership positions on competitive athletic and academic teams, are especially valued. Serving as a religious youth group leader, earning the rank of Eagle in the Boy Scouts of America, or forgoing such challenges to hold full time jobs outside of school as a primary wage earner in the family, couple with the candidate's paragraph-length responses to a few carefully worded values-based questions to indicate the candidate's potential to apprehend the sorts of obligations a commitment to military service presupposes, whether the person serves beyond the minimum number of years required or not.

There are obviously many fine officers – including general officers – who would perhaps not have made fine USMA cadets, so one can arguably cast suspicion on the correlation between empirical measurements of academic, physical, and moral well-roundedness in high school and the potential for effectively fulfilling the obligations of service as an armed forces officer within the community of military professionals. For those less well rounded (among them, this author), there are alternative routes to a commission: civilian college-based officer training programmes (known in the United States as the Reserve Officer Training Corps programmes, or ROTC), and the Officer's Candidate School for college graduates without ROTC training and enlisted soldiers who desire to become officers (although soldiers can also apply to USMA out of the ranks, as well). USMA, though, does not claim that non-USMA officers are of lesser moral calibre than the members of the Long Gray Line. The intuition is more that the USMA graduate will be the officer best equipped to lead, by example and otherwise, the character development process in his or her Army units, due to the theoretical and practical underpinnings the four-year immersion in a process of character development has provided.

USMA uses its three pillars of education and training (Academic, Physical, and Military) to mutually reinforce the internalization of the four roles of officership in the person of the cadet. Capitalizing on Aristotelian notions of community responsibility for inculcation of values in the individual, the West Point community beyond the Academy itself reinforces the three developmental pillars through one-on-one faculty mentorship, provision of opportunities for cadets to work as mentors in youth programmes such as scouting and ski instruction, and a variety of clubs and activities that integrate the cadet's on- and off-duty experiences under like-minded role models.

Religion, too, is an important part of many cadets' lives. The West Point community offers a robust foundation for cadet spiritual development, with regular Protestant, Catholic, Jewish, and Lutheran services in the four on-post chapels. There are Army chaplains embedded in the United States Corps of Cadets chain of command itself, as there are in any other major US Army unit organizational structure, available for individual counsel and able to offer advisory insight to the chain of command concerning cadet well-being. The inter-faith Cadet Religious Activities Centre facilitates religious services for cadets affiliated with religions other than those represented in the four on-post chapels. While there is a strong evangelical presence at West Point, the Academy has been successful in keeping religion in the private sphere and avoided the problems associated with the overt proselytizing noted by Martin Cook at the US Air Force Academy (see Chapter 5).

Within the academic curriculum, an Introduction to Philosophy course grounds the cadet in basic logic, major ethical theories in Western philosophy, and the Just War Tradition during their second year at the Academy. Formal instruction in the Honor Code is complemented by broader discussions of the Professional Military Ethic in regular seminars throughout the four-year curriculum that use case study methodology to exemplify application of the Army ethic to practical problems of the sort cadets will encounter as officers. In addition, the Department of Military Instruction reinforces character development during Cadet Field Training in the summer through trust-based team building experiences and role playing exercises based on actual situations. Thus, all 'programs [are synchronized by USMA leadership, through the Simon Center for the Professional Military Ethic] in a sequential, progressive, and integrated manner' (*CLDS*, 19).

The current wars in Iraq and Afghanistan have brought issues of military ethics training and education to the forefront of American public discourse. Each real or perceived ethical mis-step is analyzed in detail by pundits who often display little or no appreciation for the lengths the United States Army goes to in order to field an ethically aware force of soldiers who consciously desire to conduct operations in accordance with the bedrock values of respect for human rights and appreciation of the dignity of persons *qua* persons. Dramatic incidents such as the American abuse of prisoners at Abu Ghraib prison in Iraq highlight both the *pragmatic* challenges the Army has in assessing the effectiveness of ethics training and education *before* deployment and the reinforcement training and education across the spectrum of active and reserve units *actually deployed*, as well as the more philosophical challenges posed by the fact that so many leaders failed across the length and breadth of the organizational hierarchy at Abu Ghraib to stop, report, condemn, and prosecute the offenders until prompted from the outside. To say that there is more work to be done is not to say that nothing has been done at all. Whereas it may *seem* a bit far fetched to argue that every soldier take a college level introduction to ethics and international relations during basic training, there certainly is a place for more theoretical foundation-laying at the lowest level of the military hierarchy, before soldiers become immersed in the normative proscriptions of the law of land warfare (which are often presented to soldiers in 'PowerPoint' briefings delivered without passion by lawyers or chaplains and reinforced only by the handing out of Rules of Engagement cards) and (in many, perhaps most cases at the time of writing) almost immediate deployment after initial training. Further, the ever-widening scope of what counts as soldierly duty may indeed make Army ethics training and education more academic in the theoretical sense, if we expect individual soldiers to serve as peacekeepers, peacemakers, and *de facto* police officers, as well as warriors. Like the Army itself (and the individual persons who make up that Army), ethics training and education is forever a work in progress.

Although senior enlisted and officer education curricula have greatly evolved in the past 30 years, nowhere is the sense of evolution perhaps more evident in Army ethics training and education than in the ongoing revision of foundational ethics education and training for Army officers in Army pre-commissioning programmes, grounded in that of the United States Military Academy. USMA reaches out to the field via the internet with its platoonleader.mil and companycommander.mil sites, encouraging the informal exchange of ideas among leaders already deployed and between those deployed now and others in the Army, who either have returned, are preparing for deployment, or are in some position (such as USMA faculty) to resource the discussion with doctrinal reference. In the core philosophy course, illustration of the ties between the normative law of land warfare and the theoretical constructs of the just war tradition in philosophy has been greatly enhanced by more guest lecturers with recent combat experience (including some from other armies) and direct participation from the USMA Department of Law. Recent wartime incidents, especially those involving USMA graduates, are used carefully and largely informally in a variety of classes to further enhance the links between the world of plastic black shoes and that of dusty brown boots.

One might point out that West Point and other service academy graduates commit war crimes and other offences at rates similar to less well 'bred' soldiers. USMA must account for the cases where its graduates have neither lived up to the Honor Code and the Professional Military Ethic themselves, nor enforced the toleration clause in relation to others. Over the past two years, I have noted with satisfaction the use of misconduct cases involving USMA graduates in ethics education classes, analyzing their ethical failures in light of the Professional Military Ethic and the Cadet Leader Development System. Obviously, the more instances there are of ethically aberrant behaviour among West Point Cadets, West Point-educated officers in the Army, or West Point and Army alumni in the fabric of American society, the louder the argument for closing its gates once and for all.

In response, one might suggest that, although the ethical fabric of particular West Point graduates has varied, there is little purchase in attempting to assess the fecundity of an institution so old, one that has so consistently produced leaders of character for the Army and the Nation for so long, by dwelling on those who did not live up to the institutional ideal. General Hackett's observation that, to 'see how bad men can be in any profession [or, by implication, how good men can indeed do bad things] is to learn little about it [or, perhaps, them] worth knowing', might encourage the student of military professionalism to study the lives of those USMA graduates 'who display its essential characteristics in exceptional degree' in order to 'measure the worth' of a particular 'way of life' or, by implication, any institution within the parameters of that way of life (Hackett 1990, 41). History is replete with fine examples of how well West Point has done in living up to its mission of producing leaders of character for the Army and the Nation. In fact, a favourite USMA History Department slogan notes with only slight hyperbole that 'much of the history we teach was made by the people we taught'. It is not the intent of this overview of ethics training and education in the US Army to defend the continued relevancy of the fortress on the Hudson that has become synonymous with the core values of the American republic as much as it represents the core values of the American Army. However, in closing, I think it pertinent to remind students of military professionalism that, in times of fiscal restraint, where maximization of utility in resource management often defaults to consolidation of functions, institutions such as the United States Military Academy possess intrinsic value as brick-and-mortar symbols of the ideals which we say we are willing to preserve with the blood of our sons and daughters, giving substance to the form of those ideals in the minds and hearts of their graduates.

Bibliography

Brogan, D.W. (1944), *The American Character* (New York: Knopf).

Cadet Leader Development System for Cadets (2005) (West Point, NY: United States Military Academy).

de Tocqueville, A. (2003), *Democracy in America* (London: Penguin).

Ellis, J. and Moore, R. (1974), *School for Soldiers: West Point and the Profession of Arms* (New York: Oxford University Press).

Gabriel, R. and Savage, P. (1978), *Crisis in Command: Mismanagement in the Army* (New York: Hill and Wang).

Hackett, J.W. (1970), *The Military in the Service of the State: Harmon Memorial Lectures in Military History Number 13* (Colorado Springs: US Air Force Academy).

Hackett, J.W. (1990), *The Profession of Arms* (Washington, DC: US Government Printing Office).

Hartle, A.E. (1992), 'Do Good People Make Better Warriors?', *Army* 42:8, 20–23.

MacIntyre, A. (1984), *After Virtue* (2nd edition) (Notre Dame, IN: University of Notre Dame Press).

Matthews, L.J. (1994a), 'Is the Military Profession Legitimate?', *Army* 44:1, 14–23.

Matthews, L.J. (1994b), 'The Need for and Officer's Code of Professional Ethics', *Army* 44:3, 20–5.

Matthews, L.J. and Brown, D.E. (1989), *The Parameters of Military Ethics* (Washington, DC: Pergamon-Brassey's).

Parfit, D. (1984), *Reasons and Persons* (Oxford, UK: Oxford University Press).

Plato (1984), 'The Republic', in *Great Dialogues of Plato* (New York: Mentor).

Romjue, J.L. (1984), *From Active Defense to Airland Battle: The Development of Army Doctrine, 1973–1982* (Fort Monroe: US Army Training and Doctrine Command).

Romjue, J.L. (1993), *The Army of Excellence: The Development of the 1980s Army* (Fort Monroe: US Army Training and Doctrine Command).

Samet, E. (2004), *Willing Obedience: Citizens, Soldiers, and the Progress of Consent in America, 1776–1898* (Stanford: Stanford University Press).

Warrior Ethos Briefing (2003) (Washington, DC: US Government Printing Office).

Chapter 4

Teaching Military Ethics in the British Armed Forces

Patrick Mileham

Cannon to the right of them, Cannon to the left of them,
Cannon in front of them, Volley'd and thundered.
Alfred Lord Tennyson, *The Charge of the Light Brigade*.

Intellectual Courage

The current fighting in Afghanistan and operations in Iraq are deadly serious, physical tests of Britain's armed forces. Nothing following in this chapter should belittle that fact. However, in another, cerebral, context, a 'Balaclava moment' has been reached in their comprehension of 'military ethics' and the 'moral component of military effectiveness and fighting power' (The three 'components', first identified in a Ministry of Defence publication *British Military Doctrine* (MoD 1989), are 'physical', 'intellectual' (formerly 'conceptual') and 'moral'). While research is being hurriedly conducted to establish first principles of 'military ethics' (Stage One in the Haldane-Spearman Consortium Project 2006), guns to the right are firing volleys demanding 'keep it simple; our [combat] soldiers have a reading age of eleven years', and guns to the left guns thunder 'where is the intellectual rigour?' Guns in front pound away at the mature and traditional pragmatism of institutional practice – consisting of the steady logical, military thinking and appropriate counter-intuitive insights of British commanders, the genius for practical solutions of non-commissioned officers, and the solid commonsense of the troops (see, for instance, de Lee 2004).

So what have they been doing for the last 40 years? This chapter will show that there has been much more learning about the wider bounds of military morality than there has been teaching of military ethics in the armed forces. Commenting in October 2006 on the British approach in Northern Ireland, the Dutch Secretary of State for Defence praised the military and political response to the security problems in that Province:

> With incredible patience and without budging an inch ... the response was as controlled as possible ... [showing] the democratic face of a state that subjects itself to human rights and to standards of propriety ... In the long term the ... situation in Northern

Ireland is looking relatively favourable, a victory thanks to moral superiority. (Van de Knaap 2006)

The part played by the Army was also recognized by John Keegan: 'The most important element in the Ulster experience is what it has *not* done to the British Army. It has not politicised it, nor has it brutalised it' (Keegan 1994). If the Army's professional and moral standing has remained largely intact for nearly four decades, why then intellectualize and make problematical what experience has taught and sustained over so a long period?

It is generally agreed that many military persons prefer to experience concrete activities and maybe even periodically 'advance into the valley of death' rather than read about abstract ideas and indulge in philosophical argument, contemplate ethical principles and worry about moral behaviours, which are intangible and abstruse. Indeed of the three 'components', the moral component in Britain has not received the attention it should and the study of military ethics – the study of the quality of military behaviour – is not nearly as advanced as, say, in Canada, Australia, the Netherlands or the United States, although that is not to state that the behaviour of the British armed forces is not as exemplary as any.

Two recent factors have caused military men and women to doubt the standing of their armed forces as 'moral organizations'. First, there is disquiet and a growing intensity of debate about the lawfulness and the morality of the use of force in general, prompted of course by the 2003 invasion of Iraq and the questions that it raised internationally. Gone are the days when the *jus ad bellum* tradition meant that politicians alone took responsibility for justifying the use of force and soldiers, with relatively clear consciences, attended to the technical details, including lethal means and maybe wide scale destruction. Second, there is the recent handful of court martial proceedings following highly publicized allegations of unlawful acts by British soldiers against prisoners, or at close proximity to potential adversaries in peace support operations, although the number of cases of actual, provable, immoral or unlawful behaviour by British servicemen and women are tiny in proportion to the numbers deployed on operations since the end of the Cold War.

What other underlying reasons are there for this moment of tension and doubt so obviously afflicting the military chain of command, the rank and file, and members of the concerned civil population? Answers lie not in a lack of physical or moral courage as such, but in intellectual doubt about how to articulate and codify what actually is intuitively well understood. The subject, however, must be acknowledged to exist at more than one level and certainly raised above what has sometimes disparagingly been called 'folk-morality' (for a robust defence of this notion, see Montmarquet 2003).

Thus the momentary loss for words is probably due to a last ditch stand by the anti-intellectual culture in the British armed forces, before those guns fall silent. 'Who dares wins' is a well-known regimental motto. With a desire for heavyweight military thinking by an increasing proportion of military officers both commissioned and non-commissioned, '*Sapere aude*' (Horace, 'dare to be wise') seems an appropriate aspiration. As Charles Moskos foretold it must, the day of the dual-purpose, 'soldier-scholar' (Moskos 1990, 15) is arriving in Britain.

Moral Dynamics

It cannot be disputed that the British armed forces are amongst the most mature and experienced professional military institutions in the world. They have taken part in more 'international armed conflicts since 1946 than any other nation' (21, compared with France 19, the USA 16, and Russia 9) (United Nations and University of British Columbia 2005, 16). They possess a collective wisdom and memory of considerable breadth and depth. They have learnt about the rightful use of force over long exposure and have felt the moral forces that interact with physical and intellectual forces. 'Moral dynamics' is the phrase this author believes they have been intuitively searching for.

What are the inherent dynamics of coercion by military force, whether in hard conflicts or peace enforcement? The answer lies in what Clausewitz meant when he wrote that force is based on persuasion: 'Moral elements are among the most important in war. They constitute the spirit that permeates war as a whole, and at an early stage they establish a close affinity with the will that moves and leads the whole mass of force. (Practically merging with it). Since the will is itself a moral quantity' (Clausewitz 1984, 184).

This deliberate word 'quantity' accords with Napoleon's frequently quoted view that the ratio of the persuasive moral effect of force should be as three to one with the physical. British military officers frequently quote the French Emperor. It is not, however, just simply weighing the numbers and morale (underlying mood), of one side against the other. The end purpose of operations is achieved when the will-power of the one side overcomes the will of the other, by deterring, discouraging, demoralizing, defeating and disarming the latter, in Clausewitz's words again, 'killing the enemy's courage rather than his men' (ibid., 259). Military effectiveness and fighting power is all about persuasion. To make sense of the notion of 'moral quantity' and moral dynamics, the dictionary meaning of moral also includes this deliberate enabling human factor of indirect and psychological persuasiveness of force, with the direct purpose of altering the will-power and intentions of others. 'Moral suasion', 'moral support', 'moral victory', the 'moral effect of artillery fire' are all included in dictionaries. In operations between intense combat and passive peace support, it has been recognized that 'in the eyes of the warrior, counter-insurgency calls for some decidedly un-warriorlike qualities, such as emotional intelligence, empathy, subtlety, sophistication, nuance and political adroitness' (Kiszely 2006, 20). *A fortiori*, these are acute moral sensitivities.

Enemies, of course, do not give up the fight lightly. They may have to be persuaded to, sometimes by robust, lethal methods, or else more subtle means over a long period. Optimistically, Sun Tzu (fourth century BC) suggested the supreme act of war is to 'subdue the enemy without fighting' (Sun Tzu 1963, vii). The moral consistency of means used and proper end-state desired, is at the heart of 'moral dynamics' and 'military ethics'. Much of this was learned slowly and sometimes painfully by the British Army in Malaya (from 1948), Aden, Borneo, Cyprus (1960s) and Northern Ireland (from 1968). Physical force alone makes no sense. In the end, there can be no purely military solutions; they are always intellectual, political and moral.

Moral Courage and Mission Command

In British military literature, both formal and historical, there is much encouragement of military men, and now women, to be motivated not only by physical bravery, but inspired by moral courage, which is a personal virtue. How far their actions are inspired by conscious choice, intuition, instruction, habit or rote training, when physical courage alone is not enough or inappropriate, is hard to judge.

Successful military actions do not happen by accident. British military leaders well understand the concepts of, and knowingly apply, 'force enablers and force multipliers' (Wallace 2004, 158). It must be obvious that 'moral dynamics' of military power are therefore inextricably interactive with the 'physical' and 'intellectual dynamics' of military power. Synergy can be generated by physical, intellectual and moral forces within military people and units working together. Synergies, however, do not happen by chance in military operations; they require mental and physical effort. In implementing the best military plans, many Clausewitzian 'frictions' (physical, intellectual and moral) have to be overcome, as well as the actions of adversaries. Synergy can often work in reverse, and ill-conceived interactions of dynamic forces may end in political, military, physical and moral disaster.

The British armed forces teach the concept and practice of 'Mission Command', whose purpose is to delegate to junior commanders, including non-commissioned officers, not just decision-making, but judgment about when and how to act. It is defined as the 'fundamental responsibility to act, or in certain circumstances to decide *not* to act, within the framework of the commander's intent' (MoD (Army) 2005, 11). As moral agents, commanders must be , as Alasdair MacIntyre says, '... justifiably and uncontroversially held responsible [firstly] for that in their actions which is intentional ... [secondly] for incidental aspects of those actions of which they should have been aware ... and [thirdly] for at least some of the reasonably predictable effects of those actions' (MacIntyre 1999, 312). Junior as well as senior commanders take on the status of moral agents whenever they issue orders. Having done so, they carry the moral consequences at 'second-' and 'third-order' responsibility in the cause-effect chain within the theory of 'agency' and 'action' (for more on this, see recent work on the philosophy and theory of action in e.g. Moya 1990 and Davies 1979). The complex relationship between intention, action and consequences, and the associated effects on the accountability of everyone in the chain of command and beyond, are matters of considerable practical as well as theoretical importance, particularly at a time when the 'I was only obeying orders' defence is no longer legally or morally tenable, but they are not specifically addressed in British military programmes. If military ethics is to be better taught and better understood, serious consideration should be given to incorporating a brief study of the notions of moral agency and responsibility into the education syllabus.

Recent doctrinal concepts and practices introduced into the armed forces for the conduct of war and operations, follow on from an understanding, deliberate or intuitive, of the importance of the 'end-state' of the mission namely, in the words of a mid-nineteenth-century Secretary of State for War, the achievement of 'a safer peace' (Fifth Duke of Newcastle 1925 in Bird 1925, 7). Through absorption of the works of such military thinkers as Colonel G.F.R. Henderson, Major General J.F.C. Fuller and Sir Basil Liddell Hart, the current day concept of the Effects Based Approach (see MoD 2007) to operations has emerged. A particular means of attaining the desired end-state, and lessening the reliance on brute military force, is the 'Manoeuvrist Approach to Operations' (see ibid. and MoD (Army) 2005). Essentially, it means the act of 'moral persuasion' by outmanoeuvring, outgunning and outwitting an enemy, defeating his will-power and cohesion – in other words demoralizing him and causing disintegration to his will to fight as well as his physical integrity. Such concepts have to be used carefully in practice, since peace has to be won after war has ended. 'All warfare', noted Sun Tzu, 'is based on deception, peacemaking is not' (Sun Tzu 1963, 66). 'Hearts and minds' policies of peacekeeping are about truth and confidence building.

One can infer that Britain's armed forces have gained their reputation for honest dealing through skill in differentiating when and when not to use robust or subtle military methods – proportional to the politico-moral effects desired and sustained by adherence to the law of armed conflict. But little mention or emphasis has been accorded to the Kantian, utilitarian and virtue ethics approaches. It seems that the armed forces have been so busy with operations and developing their skills and thinking in the physical and intellectual dynamics, that they have not had the luxury of time to articulate, in moral and philosophical terms, what they have done and the successes they have achieved. That having been said, they have been 'learning organizations' for generations, and long before government ministers and management professors coined the phrase. Armed forces personnel of all levels spend proportionately more of their time, individually and collectively, on training and education than any other comparable organization, in learning how best to conduct their professional roles and tasks.

In sum, one can confidently conclude from their actions over many years and the external and independent judgments stated above, that the British armed forces very well understand the moral dynamics of what they have achieved in the past and what they are doing in Afghanistan and Iraq in 2007. If formal teaching in moral dynamics and military ethics appears to be scanty, an enormous amount of informal, indirect education and training has enabled soldiers, sailors and airmen to learn, and has sustained their moral behaviour and reputation over many operations since 1946. Much of the moral dynamics and principles adhere to correct physical and technical (in its professional sense) military actions, with commendable consistency of careful planning by commanders at the strategic level. At the tactical level, much of the moral development is part of the ethos – that metaphysical word should be used sparingly – of the internal cohesion generated by such circumstances and relationships in the 'regimental system', the 'officers' messes' and 'sergeants' messes', and other means of organically adding to and retaining corporate memory and wisdom. Each generation is inducted and sustained by such means. One can call this subliminal learning and differentiate it from training. It happens. It works. It cannot be ignored, or decried because it is wanting in pedagogical refinement. That is on its way.

Documentary Developments

'Military ethics' began to be formally codified in Britain only as recently as 1989. Three years later, at the time of the post-Cold War drawdown of the armed forces, a mood of inevitable and quite serious internal tension was recognized, particularly in the Army. In 1993 the Adjutant General issued a general instruction with a triple title, namely *The Discipline and Standards Paper. The Military Ethos. (The Maintenance of Standards)* (MoD (Army) 1993). The fact that the third title was in parentheses indicated hesitation, if not unwitting equivocation. The use of the word 'ethos' acknowledged, again probably unwittingly, the deeper, even inexpressible metaphysical qualities of military service. What followed was a mixture of spiritual, even metaethical statements mixed up with what looked like direct orders about personal moral behaviour, backed by legal requirements of military law. In the opinion of this author, the lack of differentiation between four discernible moral categories has ever since inhibited the development of clear thinking of the whole subject of military ethics in Britain.

Those categories are:

- the moral dynamics of live interpersonal behaviours, cultures, relationships and actions by military personnel in base or shipboard amongst themselves and with the civil population;
- the need for military persons to accept the spirit of such matters as anti-discrimination norms and legislation, equal opportunities, health and safety and employment laws, as well as breaches of criminal laws on such matters as drug and alcohol misuse;
- best practice in personnel management, corporate governance and corporate social responsibility by the Ministry of Defence and the chain of command;
- the moral dynamics of live, interpersonal behaviours with or against actual or potential adversaries (or enemies) and indigenous populations on operational deployments.

While much is now covered by national and international legislation and regulation, it is advisable to consider what has passed as the study and application of the 'moral component of military effectiveness' under two very distinct headings: 'Institutional Ethics' (which also apply to most public institutional and commercial organizations) and 'Operational Ethics'. The former consist of the more static principles and relationships, such as the first three categories above. One can conceive of the principles as domestic and routine, or even the basis of what is often known as an organization's 'psychological contract' or 'covenant'. The latter, covered by the fourth category, consist of dynamic precepts and experiences and should be clearly understood as what happens, or should happen, during operations. While differentiating the two for purposes of study, education and training, if Institutional Ethical standards are high, then standards of Operational Ethics are also likely to be high. Moral consistency between them should be achieved by exemplary leadership and firm command.

Many of the policies and practices of the armed forces concerned with Institutional Ethics were investigated in the 1995 *Bett Review* (Bett 1995) and policy changes were made accordingly. The following year the Army Board considered and issued a Paper entitled *The Extent to which the Army has a Right to be Different*. That process was essentially a rearguard exercise attempting to 'ring fence' certain matters of self-regulation outside the political process, in order to preserve military command and control over institutional matters apparently already conflicting with society's norms and government legislation and regulation. A number were to do with questions of sexual relationships and exemption from some legal restraints. This was ultimately futile; it became obvious that the Army and other two services did not have an absolute right to establish and maintain their own rules, policies and practices free from public scrutiny – unless they could bring to bear the strongest irrefutable evidence of operational necessity.

In 2000 three documents were published and promulgated. The doctrinal statement was in *Soldiering. The Military Covenant* (MoD (Army) 2000) alongside two versions of *The Values and Standards of the British Army* (MoD 2000, 63813 and 63812), one for commanders and one for all ranks including private soldiers. General statements about human resource management, authority, duty, discipline, professional and personal relationships, and alcohol and drug misuse, were included. Little direct mention of actions and relationships within the category of Operational Ethics was made: even to date those considerations of moral (rather than just legal) behaviours in regard of adversaries, would-be adversaries and local populations remain implicit. Four particular statements and explanations were significantly included in these Army documents.

The 'Military Covenant' is a new concept, acknowledging that a 'formal contract of employment' is inappropriate and impractical for the profession of arms in Britain. A covenant in a general sense is akin to a 'psychological contract': some aspects can be expressed in words but others must remain implicit or open-ended. There is an ongoing debate about how far the assumed military covenant is genuinely two-way, reflecting its biblical provenance, or weighted towards one party (the state) in accord with the legal status of a covenant in English civil law. There is current thought that it should be three–way, between individuals in the armed forces, the government and the population.

The second notion introduced in *Soldiering* was that of 'unlimited liability'. This was articulated by General Sir John Hackett in describing why armed forces are different from other occupations in advanced liberal democracies: 'The essential basis of military life is the ordered application of force under an unlimited liability. It is the unlimited liability which sets the man who embraces this life somewhat apart. He will be (or should be) always a citizen' (Hackett 1983, 208). It is the last sentence which admits why the armed forces do not have an absolute 'right to be different'. How far this forms part of a military covenant within the moral component of military effectiveness and fighting power, has yet to be determined.

Two further statements are important in these Army documents, both setting out the basis of Institutional Ethics and acknowledging, up to a point, Operational Ethics in military service. First the Army's 'ethos' is described as: 'that spirit which inspires soldiers to fight. It derives from, and depends upon the high degree of commitment, self-sacrifice and mutual trust which together are essential to the maintenance of morale' (MoD 2000, 2–3). The second statement is known as the 'Service Test' and it poses a question about the consequences of routine behaviour outside fighting duties, both on and off duty: 'Have the actions or behaviours of an individual adversely impacted or are they likely to impact on the efficiency or operational effectiveness of the Army?' (MoD 2000 63813, 13)

Ethics is a branch of moral philosophy and philosophy, by definition, is not factual: its precepts and practices are established by argument, not direct and tangible evidence, as in criminal law and the natural sciences. While principles can be taught, developing the ability to form moral judgments can only be achieved up to a point. That requires acute imagination and intelligence. The difficulty a high proportion of officers have had with military ethics is that they would prefer ethical judgment to be prescribed and rendered as orders, drills, procedures and instructions, not a matter for their personal interpretation of observed events against hard to understand, abstract principles. The interpretation of the moral quality of circumstances, relationships and events is not part of mainstream education in Britain, and the British *Defence Doctrines* of 1996 and 2001 did not elaborate on the moral component of military effectiveness. It is likely that formal doctrine on the subject will soon be attempted. It will be very difficult to devise and write, because in moral philosophy there are no absolutes of fact or authority.

More recently, each service has been encouraged to produce its own separate list of values and standards. The Royal Navy and Royal Marines have written and published their own versions, namely *Royal Navy Ethos. The Spirit to Fight and Win* (MoD (Navy) Royal Navy Ethos 2004) and *Royal Marines Ethos* (MoD (Navy) Royal Marines Ethos 2004). The Royal Navy's ethos statement includes a 'fight and win' clause, but that of the Royal Marines idiosyncratically defines ethos as 'what a group does and how it does it'. The Royal Air Force drew on an earlier working paper with the title *RAF Culture – A Model to Strengthen Commitment* for their authoritative document *Ethos, Core Values and Standards of the Royal Air Force* (MoD (RAF) 2004). That also has an ethos statement, which writes about 'air power' in the abstract, rather than fighting or combat, and is mainly about internal, domestic moral behaviour, i.e. Institutional Ethics. It mentions the word 'covenant', but does not add detailed obligations for either party. Exemplary personal behaviour is expected, even exalted, in all these documents, while the metaphysical and spiritual term 'ethos' is used to denote institutions that have high degrees of confidence, self-belief, and commitment to their work. The term 'moral ethos' put forward by Robin Snell is useful (Snell 1993, passim). It is almost certainly what the armed forces mean whenever they use the expression.

The point to be made about all these documents is that they are not formally designated as 'doctrine', based on research conducted within academic standards. None of them appear to draw on any external sources of general moral philosophy, although Chapter 7 ('The Moral Component') of the Army's most recent publication MoD (Army) *Land Operations* 2005, cites a number of military thinkers whose collective wisdom on 'moral dynamics' cannot be faulted. The in-house publication of 1999 for Royal Navy officer cadets, however, was written to academic standards and was properly referenced with the help of the present author. It has been circulated with some success within the Royal Navy (see Britannia Royal Naval College 1999).

While the above commentary seems overly critical, each single service has put much thought into their list of values, virtues, standards, qualities and elements of ethos, and this work is continuing. The themes are shown as follows, the order adjusted for purposes of comparison. One detects that different meanings and inferences are intended, even if the same word is used by different Services.

Education and Training

So what is taught in Britain's armed forces about 'military ethical principles' and moral philosophy in general? This penultimate section is chiefly descriptive.

Since 2001, the new Defence Academy has brought together the Royal College of Defence Studies, the Joint Services Command and Staff College (JSCSC, itself a recent amalgamation of the former three single service staff colleges), and the Defence College of Management and Technology (DCMT, part of Cranfield University, and formerly the Royal Military College of Science). One detects a transition phase in syllabus development, striving to understand the analysis of ethical principles as distinct from the law of armed conflict and rules of engagement. Certainly the Higher Command and Advanced Staff courses tackle the paradoxes and internal contradictions of security and defence matters seriously. In a lecture to the Advance Course entitled 'Ethics and the Military' on 2 November 2006, Dr David Rodin advised working towards achieving a 'reflective equilibrium'. His advice was to reconcile the elements of force and restraint necessary on operations, as well as finding answers to questions posed by factors within the fields of both *jus ad bellum* and *jus in bello* – such as urgency, proportionality, human rights, avoidance of collateral damage, death and injury, minimum force and when to hesitate before opening fire – in order to achieve the immediate effects desired and the mission as a whole. A number of students at JSCSC and at DCMT now research aspects of moral philosophy applicable to defence. A high proportion of students at these two institutions gain masters degrees. A corpus of research and knowledge is building up within the Defence Academy, an institution which proclaims itself as providing 'Intellectual Excellence in Defence'.

Table 4.1   Values and standards, British armed forces

Royal Navy	Royal Marines	Army	Royal Air Force
		Integrity	Integrity – courage, honesty, responsibility, justice
Mutual respect	Humility	Respect for others	Respect, mutual
Loyalty	Unity	Loyalty	
Courage in adversity	Courage [personal] Fortitude	Courage	
Discipline		Discipline	
Teamwork	Unselfishness [personal]	Selfless commitment	Service before self – loyalty commitment, teamwork self-discipline and control pride
High professional standards	Professional standards		Excellence – personal excellence excellence in the use of resources
Leadership			
Determination	Determination [personal]		
'Can do' attitude	Adaptability		
Sense of humour	Commando humour Cheerfulness [personal]		
		* Additional themes are: voluntary professionalism; and regimental spirit	

Note: The Army has an acronym for its list, 'SOLID C', and the Royal Air Force uses the
        acronym 'RISE'.

Britain has four initial education/training establishments for officer cadets.
Mention has been made already of the *Britannia Guide to Military Ethics*. It is a
formal if brief publication from which 'informed judgments' can subsequently
be made, by means of 'open forum' educational interventions for candidates
for commissions in the Royal Navy. At the Royal Military Academy Sandhurst,
particular emphasis has been placed in the past three years on education and
training in 'officership', a concept new to the British Army (see Chapter 2 of this

book, RMAS 2004, and Mileham 2003 for more detail), but long established in the better English dictionaries, and adopted already by the US Military Academy West Point and the Royal Military College of Canada. It can be defined as the 'concept, character, practice and quality' of being a commissioned officer, and incorporates many intangible factors that do not fall comfortably within the categories of command, leadership and management. Military ethics is one of these groups of intangible factors and underlying its teaching is the ideal of a person holding a commission (as a public office) who 'personifies' those principles within the 'virtue ethics' approach to moral understanding and behaviour. More development is expected of this concept and its teaching. At the Royal Air Force College Cranwell officer cadets are introduced to the core values and standards of the Royal Air Force, and at the Commando Training Centre, Royal Marines, Lympstone, similar induction training on the elements of the Royal Marines 'ethos' is conducted. Again more work is required in developing and refining the teaching and learning at these establishments.

Critical comment has been made above about the lack of clear differentiation between Institutional Ethics and Operational Ethics. This is most clearly shown in the syllabus of the Army's Military Annual Training Test No. 6 (MATT 6), which is introduced during initial training for all soldiers and repeated within units as part of annual continuation training for adherence to Army Values and Standards. The MATT 6 policy statement, with a curious caveat, asserts that: 'The standards underpin the ethos of the British Army and that ethos supports the moral component of fighting power. Although the standards are about maintaining combat effectiveness, rather than attempting to seize the moral high ground per se, without moral validity the standards are useless and bankrupt' (see MoD (Army) (2007), and MoD Army Training and Recruiting Agency 2000 and 2006).

Why the hesitation about the moral high ground? The statement affirms the 'Balaclava moment' of uncertainty, referred to at the start of this chapter, and yet indicates the wish to abide by the Aristotelian 'mean' in avoiding excess. In detail, the six 'Values and Standards' (SOLID C, see above) as well as law of armed conflict (LOAC), security, substance misuse, and Equality and Diversity are brought together, unfortunately without sufficient differentiation of category, for which different moral philosophical arguments should apply. Nevertheless Institutional Ethics is supported by an admirable booklet of 2004 entitled *Soldier Management* (MoD (Army) 2004). It is worth stating that the British Army's interpretation of moral philosophy, including the Service Test, has been challenged by Stephen Deakin as being too strongly based on the ethics of utilitarianism (Deakin 2006, 42). Moral imagination, identity and humanity are not notions that an individual should be encouraged to turn on and off like a tap. Moral courage and personal integrity should be striven for 24 hours every day, each week in the year, which is why they are virtues.

Unease about existing Values and Standards training being derived from heuristics rather than academically based research, has led to the 'first principles' work mentioned in this chapter's opening paragraph. It is fortunate that the law of armed conflict (explained in MoD (Army) 2002) and rules of engagement (specific to the campaign) actually prescribe and take account of most of the possible moral breaches during operations, and are part of pre-operational training for all units preparing for deployment. LOAC certainly covers what constitute legal and therefore probably morally sustainable reasons for the use of force, lethal or otherwise. Prisoner abuse, for instance, is clearly unlawful as well as immoral. Fortunately, the Adjutant General could report with some satisfaction that, 'as at 8 May 2006, not one single soldier has been tried for firing his weapon, in a tactical context, on operations in Iraq' (Viggers 2006).

The Royal Navy's and Royal Air Force's training must also be taken into account. They do not have to consider Operational Ethics in as much detail as the Army, because there are fewer occasions in which their non-commissioned and junior rates/ranks come into contact with adversaries or civil populations. The RAF conducts routine training in elements within their published Ethos, *Core Values and Standards*, much of it conducted by unit padres based on the acronym 'RISE' (see above). The Royal Navy are currently reviewing their training on the factors which constitute their Institutional Ethics in the context of shipboard and naval bases. The Royal Marines pay much attention to training in their codified *Ethos*: each man, being doubly selected (on entry and for commando qualification), perhaps brings higher and more certain technical standards, motivation and self-discipline, than in mainstream infantry battalions in the Army. Militaristic tendencies, however, can easily develop in Special Forces unless sensibly controlled. 'Humility', the Marines remind themselves, is a cardinal personal and corporate virtue.

No Absolutes

From the start, this chapter has drawn attention to the current state of flux in education and training in military ethics in the British armed forces. Rather like compulsory church parades, moral philosophy has in the past been treated disdainfully by too many officers for comfort. Some complain its inclusion in a taught syllabus is naïve, patronizing and even insulting. It has to be learnt through experience, guided and taught by officers, not by professional educators. What do the armed forces want: commonsense or intellectual rigour? The answer must be both.

One senior officer, who has written extensively on the moral component, has stated that he personally had to take a 'long journey' intellectually in order to begin to simplify military ethics in his own mind without becoming simplistic. Good leaders on occasions need the ability to simplify complexities of circumstance, relationships and events, otherwise effective action may be made difficult or impossible by indecision or risk-averseness. Britain needs more officers who have taken this journey in understanding moral philosophy and its application, as well as consciously understanding their role of exemplifying 'good faith'.

The lessons from the above is that a distinction must be clearly made between 'Moral Dynamics' and 'Military Ethics', and between 'Operational Ethics' and 'Institutional Ethics'. If codified as theory one can take note of what US philosopher William James said: 'There is nothing more practical than good theory'. The study of ethics, however, can never achieve absolute answers. Just as 'right and wrong' are not the same as 'good and bad', nor is 'truth' the same as 'reality'; debate and argument are the only effective methods leading to both knowledge and understanding. One hopes firmer guidance will promote and sustain the resources of 'moral imagination', 'moral identity' and 'humanity' in whatever operations the future holds for Britain's armed forces.

Bibliography

Bett, M. (1995), *Independent Review of the Armed Forces Manpower, Career and Remuneration Structures. Managing People in Tomorrow's Armed Forces* (London: HMSO).

Bird, W.D. (1925), *The Direction of War*, 2nd edition (Cambridge: Cambridge University Press).

Britannia Royal Naval College (1999), *Britannia Guide to Military Ethics* (Dartmouth).

Davies, L.H.J. (1979), *The Theory of Action* (Englewood Cliffs, N.J.: Prentice Hall).

Deakin, S. (2006), 'Ethics and the British Army's Values and Standards', *British Army Review* 140, 39–46.

de Lee, N. (2004), 'The British Approach to Military Obedience: Pragmatism, Operational Necessity and Moral Dilemmas', *British Army Review* 135, 97–105.

Hackett, Gen Sir J. (1983), *The Profession of Arms* (London, Sedgwick and Jackson).

Keegan, J. (1994), *Daily Telegraph*, 13 August.

Kiszely, Sir J. (2006), 'Learning about Counter-Insurgency', *Journal of the Royal United Services Institute* 151:6, 16–21.

MacIntyre, A. (1999), 'Social Structures and their Threats to Moral Agency', *Philosophy* 74:289, 311–29.

Mileham, P. (2003), *The British Army Officer. Thematic Report and Literature Review*, for Directors of Army Personnel Strategy.

Mileham, P. (ed.) (2004), *War and Morality*, Whitehall Paper no. 61 (London: Royal United Services Institute).

MoD (1989), *British Military Doctrine*, A.C. 71451.

MoD (1996), *British Defence Doctrine*, 1996, Joint Warfare Publication 0–01.

MoD (2000), *The Values and Standards of the British Army*, Army Code 63813 and 63812 respectively.

MoD (2007), *British Defence Doctrine*, 3rd edition.

MoD (Army) (1993), D/AG/415/1, October.

MoD (Army) (2000), *Soldiering. The Military Covenant*, Army Doctrine Publication No. 5, (ADP5) Army Code 71692.

MoD (Army) (2002), *A Soldier's Guide to the Law of Armed Conflict*, Army Code 71130.

MoD (Army) (2004), *Soldier Management*, Army Code 64286.

MoD (Army) (2005), *Land Operations 2005*.

MoD (Army) (2007), *Military Annual Training Tests, Values and Standards No. 6*, Current Policy Statements.

MoD Army Training and Recruiting Agency (2000), *Code of Practice for Instructors*.

MoD Army Training and Recruiting Agency (2006), *Basically Fair, Respect for Others in the British Army*.

MoD (Navy) (2004), *Royal Marines, Ethos*.

MoD (Navy) (2006), *Royal Navy Ethos. The Spirit to Fight and Win*.

MoD (RAF) (2004), *Ethos, Core Values and Standards of the Royal Air Force*, Air Publication 1.

Montmarquet, J. (2003), Moral Character and Social Research', *Philosophy* 78:305, 335–69.

Moskos, C. (1990), 'Armed Forces after the Cold War: The Personal Implications' in *Seminar Proceedings of the British Military Studies Group* (London: Centre for Defence Studies, King's College).

Moya, Carlos J. (1990), *The Philosophy of Action* (Cambridge: Policy Press).

Royal Military Academy Sandhurst (2004), *The Queen's Commission*, MoD (Army).

Snell, R. (1993), *Developing Skills for Ethical Management* (London, Chapman and Hall).

Sun Tzu (1963), *The Art of War* (Oxford: Oxford: University Press).

United Nations and University of British Columbia (2005), *Human Security Report* (New York: Oxford University Press).

Knaap, C. van der (2006), Opening speech at the Netherlands Conference, 'The Moral Dimension of Asymmetrical Warfare', Amsterdam, 4 October.

Viggers, Gen. F.R. (2006), 'The Military Criminal Justice System', an article by the Adjutant General MoD (Army).

von Clausewitz, C. (1968), *On War*, Rapoport, A. (ed.) (London: Penguin).

von Clausewitz, C. (1984), *On War*, Howard, M. and Paret, P. (eds) (Princeton: Princeton University Press).

Wallace, Lt Gen. Sir C. (2004), in Mileham (ed.), *War and Morality*.

Chapter 5

Ethics Education, Ethics Training, and Character Development: Who 'Owns' Ethics in the US Air Force Academy?

Martin L. Cook

I doubt there is any other organization in American life that talks so constantly, openly, and unabashedly about the importance of 'ethics', 'professionalism', 'integrity' and 'core values' as the US military. Furthermore, many in the US military openly state that the military and its culture is in many ways morally superior to the civilian population it ostensibly serves – and, in the most extreme form, that the military itself offers a kind of moral light to a nation lost in a morass of moral relativism and decay (as such speakers would put it).

Given the amount of moral talk in the US military, it is perhaps surprising to observe the confusion about the meaning of central terms of this discourse (such as 'integrity' and 'professionalism'). Even more surprising is the balkanized approach to the teaching/training of cadets and officers in this area. Is ethics the province of the chaplains? The lawyers? The leadership trainers? The behavioural scientists? The 'character development centre'? Or (least probably in the minds of many) of the philosophers?

In fact, all the groups I just mentioned conduct activities that, at least in their own minds, are a part (and not surprisingly, in the opinion of each group, their part is the most important part) of the ethical and moral development of cadets and officers. The activities these various groups think central to the enterprise vary widely in their content, approach, and even subject matter. This paper deals specifically with the US Air Force Academy (USAFA), because that is the institution I know best by daily work and observation.

My many conversations with colleagues at the other US pre-commissioning academies give me strong reasons to believe that most, if not all, of what I will say pertains to them as well. All have functional equivalents to most, if not all, of the institutional structures I will be describing at USAFA. All have the same division of labour between the 'academic', 'military training' and 'character development/honour system' (plus, of course, the highly overemphasized athletic programmes).

When the ethics programmes at places like the US Air Force Academy are briefed to outsiders, the PowerPoint slides suggest a seamlessly coherent, multidisciplinary and comprehensive approach to moral development of cadets. From the inside, however, what one really sees is a fundamentally incoherent and confused welter of programmes justified, if at all, by the belief that if ethics is important, throwing lots of resources at the subject from any number of angles and approaches must somehow be doing some good. One is tempted to think that the discipline most likely to explain USAFA ethics programmes is archaeology. I say this because different programmes are begun, often in response to a specific issue, scandal, or initiative, only to be followed by additional ones in response to the next crisis. What one finds in the end is something close to a complex stratigraphy problem in archaeology where one has to reconstruct the layering process that produced the site one finds today.

Given this diversity, some analysis of the fundamental problems and issues that need to be addressed in a comprehensive ethics education programme may help determine the fundamental tasks to be accomplished and the disciplines best qualified to perform the essential tasks. So with some trepidation, I will attempt a sketch of what I consider the essential tasks.

The first and foundational component of military ethics is the formation of habits and bearing that occurs in core military training. From basic cadet training through the entire four years of the Academy experience, great attention is given to the formation of the habit, military bearing, customs and courtesies that distinguish the professional military officer from his or her civilian counterpart. This aspect of cadet life is governed by what at the Air Force Academy is called the Training Wing. Other 'mission elements' – and especially the faculty, since we have the most frequent and extended contact with cadets – are expected to know and enforce the standards inculcated and reinforced by the training programme. Ideally, cadets receive a consistent and uniform message about the institution's expectations of their behaviour and military bearing across the institution.

Most of this training in habit formation is grounded more on long military experience and tradition than on theoretical foundations (not to diminish the scholarly efforts of colleagues who work in the fields of leadership studies and military sociology). But as a philosopher who reflects on what is going on in this foundational level of military formation, it is rather obvious that Aristotle is the intellectual father of the enterprise. The core of the effort is the formation of habits through the application of pleasure and pain to the cadet. The specific habits being formed are justified functionally: the resultant consistent and reliable patterns of behaviour are believed to be essential for a well-disciplined and reliable officer corps.

The aspect of Aristotle that is largely, if not entirely, neglected, however, is the role of *phronesis* (practical wisdom) – the ability to reflect on *why* the habits being formed and the pains and pleasures the institution uses to regulate behaviour do indeed serve important functional requisites of military behaviour. One might argue that this reflective component is unnecessary, and perhaps even unhelpful, since we are preparing officers to be persons of action more than reflection. On the other hand, the relative absence of attention to this aspect of character can result in cadets' experiencing their military training as an elaborate but apparently arbitrary set of rules. Perhaps doing a better job locating their formation in a broader sense of the essential habits of officers would alleviate this issue. The recently developed (three years ago) Officer Development System is an attempt to do precisely that (see USAFA Defense Technical Information Center website).

Core aspects of Academy culture such as the Honor Code (in the case of the US Air Force Academy, 'We will not lie, steal, or cheat, nor tolerate among us anyone who does' (United States Air Force Academy website) and the Air Force Core Values ('Integrity First, Service Before Self, and Excellence in All We Do' (US Air Force Core Values website) provide baseline expectations that are learned by rote. They are also suitable for posting on walls. Cadet leaders fairly routinely conduct 'honour lessons' as part of their unit training programmes that attempt to give specificity and concreteness to the Honor Code. The Core Values are invoked regularly, although seldom if ever subjected to any critical thinking regarding their meaning – not to mention the possibility of conflict between them in difficult cases. Central terms are often ill-defined, or defined circularly in terms of one another.

In the case of the Honor Code, there is a corresponding apparatus of discipline and expulsion for violations of the code, in theory (and to a large degree, in practice) operated by cadets themselves. I believe it is a fair generalization that all the US academies are dissatisfied with the actual operation of their honour systems for several reasons. The primary one would be the steady and perhaps unavoidable encroachment of the lawyers into the entire honour hearing process. Since cadets' careers and futures are on the line in these hearings, it is perhaps inevitable and even necessary that their rights be scrupulously protected and that the integrity of the process be unquestionable. But it has the unfortunate effect of providing incentives for cadet defendants to adopt very defensive and legalistic postures rather than to honestly disclose their conduct and allow an honest judgment of their peers. Also, cadets on the honour boards, who are often friends of the defendants or afflicted with 'there but for the grace of God go I' concerns, are reluctant to follow the evidence rigorously to its logical conclusion. The standard that a cadet must be found in violation to beyond a 'reasonable doubt' is often stretched to a degree that reasonable doubt can always be found.

The practical results of these factors are that the results of honour hearings appear wildly inconsistent across cases, and confidence in the fundamental integrity of the system is threatened with a pretty pervasive cynicism on the part of cadets, faculty and commanding officers. Surveys of our cadets indicate that they take pride in the idea of living under an Honor Code, unfortunately coupled with cynicism about the actual realities of the honour system and its functioning.

In any case, the core belief of this portion of military ethics training is that cadets will acquire a subtle set of habits and dispositions. To reiterate, the approach is broadly Aristotelian: repetition, coupled with allocation of pleasure and pain, cumulatively bring about the desired result.

The Training Wing also presents a wide variety of activities that can in general be called hortatory and exemplary. Cadets are routinely lectured on the importance of values and honour. Frequently, retired officers and war heroes are brought in to serve as 'role models' for cadet behaviour. About 13 years ago, USAFA created a Character Development Center in addition to the Training Wing. The other academies have Character Development programmes and, in the case of USMA and US Naval Academy, ethics centres as well. The USAFA Character Development Center supplements the hortatory approach by taking cadets out of class time for day-long retreats at least once a year. Perhaps the best (and most highly rated as effective by cadets) element of the day are the small group discussions in which experienced officers and civilians discuss with cadets their own real-world moral conflicts and hard cases they have encountered in their professional lives (USAFA Center for Character Development website).

To my surprise, cadets pretty routinely report that they find these days valuable and enjoyable. Whether they result in substantial improvement in the moral thinking and behaviour of cadets is debatable, and I am unaware of any substantive evidence that they do.

The Center also conducts an annual National Character and Leadership Conference which brings together cadets and college students from across the country to hear football coaches, successful business executives, beauty queens and so forth, to speak on issues of character and leadership. Essentially, these day-long events are extended versions of the hour-long lecturing on the importance of character and putting 'role model' exemplars before the audience (USAFA National Character and Leadership Symposium website).

All of these events experience a tension between genuinely thoughtful analysis and discussion, on the one hand, and 'motivational speaker' style emotional appeal on the other. It is fair to say the latter generally receives pride of place.

If one examines the underlying assumptions of this approach, one must conclude that the belief is that by being spoken to frequently about the importance of ethics, honour and character, cadets will thereby be made more honourable and more ethical. Certainly there is something to be said for having the subject matter so routinely a part of a culture that it is inescapable. At a minimum, no cadet can claim that he or she did not understand that the institution's expectations were for high character and honourable conduct.

On the other hand, for the very reasons Aristotle was worried about Plato's approach to this teaching of ethics, one must wonder about the efficacy of mere lecturing to cadets about these matters. As Aristotle put it, 'The many ... do not do these actions [i.e., the ones that actually produce virtuous habit]. They take refuge in arguments, thinking that they are doing philosophy, and that this is the way to become excellent people' (Aristotle, 1105b15).

Especially for the very young people we are dealing with at the Academy, one suspects the issue is less that they do not know what is expected of them, than that they have not formed habits and disciplined their appetites sufficiently to resist temptation in practical ways – precisely the kind of formation of virtuous habit Aristotle championed over the Platonic view that moral virtue could be attained by means of verbal discussion and insight. On the other hand, if one takes seriously Plato's ideal academy as a practical proposal for the education of Guardians, perhaps the distinction is overdrawn (Plato, *The Republic*, Parts III and IV). Indeed, one might argue that the 'total environment' of USAFA where cadets work, play, and study entirely within the framework of military discipline is the closest approximation in the modern world possible to Plato's ideal. But unlike Plato's model, we get cadets at 17 or 18 years of age when many of their habits are already well formed and the job of attempting to retrain them is central to the enterprise. Whatever the success of those efforts may or may not be, the actual form of many of these 'character development' efforts amounts to 'ethics education' by means of discussion and lecture.

One might think that the best foundation for discussions of professional ethics is precisely the fact that cadets are junior members of the profession of arms and need to learn their professional obligations. In fact, cadets vary widely in the degree to which they see themselves as members of the profession of arms at the cadet stage of their careers. Indeed, one of the perennial surprises to me is that when I teach them military ethics in their third or fourth year of a four year programme, I realize that few of them have reflected deeply if at all on the moral meaning of the military career upon which they are about to embark.

This is perhaps especially true of Air Force cadets. Often they are motivated to 'fly jets', but few have reflected on the fact that these are *military* jets they are to fly, and that their purpose in the end is to kill people and break things. I suspect this is much less a problem at West Point, where the reality of being in Iraq or Afghanistan a few weeks or months after graduation is palpable.

Appeals to the importance of maintaining high professional standards as an element of sustaining the trust of the civilians they are sworn to defend works for some of the more mature and thoughtful cadets. But many still see themselves as teenagers and very young adults attempting to act as much like civilian college students as they can within the constraints of the Academy system.

Here is an area where the Academy's impulses are in tension with each other. On the one hand, it is unreasonable to expect cadets to mature and begin to see themselves in terms of responsible professionals if they are micromanaged and infantilized by the rigid system of Academy discipline and time management. On the other hand, because the Academies are so carefully scrutinized by the press and government, there is a great fear of anything that would generate bad press as a result of cadet misconduct. Hence the response of cadet conduct failures is usually to tighten the micromanagement still further. One common complaint about newly graduated cadets is that their social skills and ability to function practically in the world are actually well below those of their civilian counterparts, precisely because they have been in a system that removes a great deal of decision making from their lives for four years.

Ideally, this would be the proper foundation for serious ethics education at the Academy level: the emphasis on the fact that cadets are not merely college students with an element of military training and discipline, but are, in fact, attending a professional school and being formed as young members of a profession with high and reasonably well-defined professional obligations.

I turn now to the various ways in which the specifically academic elements of the Academy's educational programme contribute to, or bear on, overall cadet exposure to ethical and professional obligations.

One major academic component of ethics education is offered by the Department of Behavioral Sciences and Leadership. They describe their Core (i.e., required of all cadets) course as follows:

> This course explores leadership and the development of high moral character – leaders and followers accountable and responsible – as a scientific study. A historical examination of the empirical basis for the scientific study of leadership will be combined with experiential exercises, case studies, and student projects that allow students to form a deeper understanding of leadership – styles and strategies. Students will also gain practical knowledge and skills that will have direct benefits as cadets and future officers. Students, through action, observation, and reflection, will learn to discern the situations and contexts within which leaders with character can flourish.

This course does very little to articulate a *normative* ethical framework for leadership discussions. Instead, it largely remains within the *descriptive* and social science approach of articulating the empirical fact that a leader's values importantly influence his or her style of leadership and ethical issues of how they choose to exercise the power their positions give them.

There is also a small ethical component to the required Military Studies course all cadets take. The course they take in their first year has lessons on the Officer Development System – the Academy's explicit model of the cumulative process by which cadets are to be formed over their four years careers as cadets into well-developed officers. There are also lessons on the Prisoner of War Code of Conduct and the Return with Honor expectations of the US military. There are discussion of the Air Force's Core Values, and case-study discussion of the classic Second World War movie 'Twelve O'clock High'.

There is, of course, an aspect of the ethical development of cadets that is the province of the law. Cadets experience this in two ways. On the academic side of their development, every cadet takes a core course in law. That course includes four lessons on Law of Armed Conflict, including cases dealing with torture and targeting of ordnance. They also deal with law for commanders and issues of command discretion in enforcement of the Uniform Code of Military Justice.

The other way cadets encounter law is in punishment for improper behaviour. Cadets can receive Article 15 non-judicial punishments and, in extreme cases, courts martial for their behaviour. In this way, the law defines the moral 'floor' for their conduct, beneath which they will be legally punished. Further, the same offence can treated through both the legal punishment system and the honour system. Beyond the Academy, the law instrumentalizes 'ethics' by regulating conduct in war in accordance with the Law of Armed Conflict. Also, proper conduct as a servant of the Federal government is regulated by 'ethics' regulations which set out standards of conduct and specify judicial punishments for infractions (Joint Ethics Regulation website).

At least at the US Air Force Academy at present, there is a very high degree of intense religiosity among cadets. Many cadets spend a good deal of their time in religious activities (Bible studies, worship services, and so on). Some do this through the military chaplaincy offerings and services, but increasingly they engage through civilian churches – often the nondenominational mega-churches that are coming to characterize much of American religious life. Indeed, one major shift in the culture of the US military generally is the decline in the role of the chaplaincy in influence over the religious life of military members, and a decreased sense in the minds of many chaplains of their responsibility to meet the spiritual needs of all military members rather than to advance their own personal religious convictions.

In terms of emotional power and influence, for many cadets (perhaps even the majority), these ties are perhaps the most important influences on their day-to-day ethical choices. This reality is a mixed blessing. Obviously, it is of great value that young people in the course of their individuation from their families and the formation of their adult identities find a powerful support for those changes in a religious community.

On the other hand, it has been my experience that the kinds of independent and nondenominational Evangelical churches many cadets choose to attend (Colorado Springs being 'the Evangelical Vatican') tend to instil a resistance to critical thinking and complexity in ethical reflection. Many begin an ethics course articulating a view that there are no hard ethical questions requiring exercise of human reason because 'the Bible is the guide to my life', or 'God will lead me'. Whatever one makes of such claims religiously, they inculcate a kind of anti-intellectualism when it comes to ethical reflection that is often quite difficult to penetrate in a classroom.

Furthermore, the almost exclusive preoccupation of much of Evangelical culture with the salvation of individual souls provides little ethical perspective on larger real-world issues and questions involving use of military power, just war, and political responsibility – especially if (as it often is in modern US Evangelicalism) it is coupled with a fervid apocalyptic expectation of the imminent return of Christ and the end of this world. Little if anything in the life and teaching of these churches connects cadets to the Christian theological-ethical tradition that might help them make sense of their profession (such as the writings of Augustine, Aquinas, Luther and Calvin). For example, Focus on the Family is one of the largest nondenominational Evangelical ministries in the US. It owns and operates a bookstore which is almost entirely devoid of any serious historical systematic theological or ethical writings. In its place, the offerings consist largely of Christian self-help literature, Bible commentaries, and apocalyptic novels and 'prophecy' writers.

For many not in the orbit of passionately held religious ideals, often the problem is the opposite. Many have absorbed a very lazy kind of moral and cultural relativism that makes them as resistant to normative moral claims and analysis as their religious peers. The particular version of relativism they typically advocate is so philosophically shallow that it is easily countered – *if* they are willing to engage in philosophical analysis at all, which, in the extreme version, they often are not. Such cadets often conform to the 'rules' of the USAFA system well, but not for any normative or deeply held reason. Indeed, conformity is easily justified in light of the very relativism they espouse: these are the local rules, obedience to which gives rewards, and disobedience punishment.

Lastly, there is the explicitly normative and reflective component of each cadet's education provided by the required Philosophy course. This course at USAFA incorporates philosophical classics (Plato, Aristotle, Kant and Mill) as well as extended discussions of just war theory, civil military relations and the nature and demands of professional ethics (United States Air Force Academy website).

Cadets consistently rate this course as one of the very best in their Core Curriculum. Often they comment that its relevance to their future careers is quite obvious to them.

We believe the Core Philosophy class accomplishes two central developmental purposes: 1) it is the one place where they engage in sustained normative reflections and learn some skills for doing so; and 2) it is one of the few points in their Academy education where they engage in sustained critical thinking about complex problems.

My major negative criticism of the course would be that it comes later in the curriculum than it should. In terms of course numbering, cadets should take the course in their third year (already too late in my judgment); in practice, however, many do not take it until their last year, often the last semester of their last year. Many comment that they wish they had had the course much earlier so that they could have reflected deeply on the moral meaning of the commitment they are making to military service before they were already committed to a number of years of service. There is no in-principle reason why the course comes as late as it does. That reality is driven entirely by internal bureaucratic exigencies.

This completes the factual summary of the disparate approaches to ethics education at USAFA. What conclusions might one draw from these realities? First, there is no question of the centrality of ethical development to the Academy's vision of its mission. On the other hand, there is little coherence to the approaches and, in the case of some activities, little evidence and little prima facie reason for thinking that they are notably effective. On the other hand, one might well argue that the mere fact that ethics is so routinely a part of so many activities creates a culture where at least the awareness of the importance of the issues is inescapable for cadets.

The central challenge is developmental. We know cadets are very young adults, very much in the process of formation of their adult identities. We are very successful, by and large, in regulating, rewarding and punishing the proper *behaviours* of cadets. Are we thereby actually inculcating the proper habits? To some degree, yes of course, but could we do better? Probably. But that would require taking more risks by allowing cadets more discretion about their choices.

Second, the intellectual component of ethical development – careful and critical thinking about complex ethical issues – is key to development of mature and subtle ethical reflective ability. The fact that we have a required philosophical ethics course is central to that developmental question. But the fact that so much of what passes for 'ethics' in other aspects of the Academy's culture is formulaic, hortatory, and slogan driven conditions cadets to not understand the importance of this aspect of their development until very late in the typical cadet experience. One has to wonder about the efficacy for the average cadet of this one component of critical ethical reflection against a backdrop of so much rote learning and uncritical sloganeering.

At root, much of the problem is related to the cluster of problems Aristotle identified a long time ago. Youth is not the best stage in development for the serious study of ethics for all the reasons he identified. Youths lack experience in life and in the profession that would lead them to fully realize the importance of the issues. They are not fully prepared to let reason regulate their lives, as they are still struggling with passions and appetites which are not yet regulated. So what can one realistically hope for at this stage?

First, one can still work on the formation of habits. As Aristotle so well argued, if we can form strong habits and beliefs about what is right and wrong, even if the reasons are not well understood, that is an invaluable and necessary foundation for later development and more explicitly rational ethical analysis. Second, we can motivate cadets and inculcate high moral ideals by means of the non-rational appeals to emotion and role models to emulate which, at its best moments, the Character Development Center's efforts provide. Lastly, we can begin laying the foundation in a core philosophy class which, if effective, at least demonstrates that a method of systematic and rational analysis of ethical matters exists, and perhaps motivate them to explore those questions further as they gain the experience of mature officers.

The views expressed in this paper are solely those of the author. They do not necessarily reflect the policy or position of the government of the United States, the United States Air Force, or the United States Air Force Academy

Bibliography

Aristotle, *Nichomachean Ethics*.
Joint Ethics Regulation (updated 1 March 2007), <http://www.dod.mil/dodgc/defense_ethics/ethics_regulation/> (homepage).
Plato, *The Republic*.
United States Airforce Academy, <http://www.usafa.af.mil/index.cfm?catname=AFA%20Homepage> (homepage).
USAFA Center for Character Development (updated 1 March 2007), <http://www.usafa.af.mil/34trw/cwc/cwch.cfm?catName=cwc>.
USAFA Defense Technical Information Center, <http://stinet.dtic.mil/oai/oai?&verb=getRecord&metadataPrefix=html&identifier=ADA428315>.
USAFA National Character and Leadership Symposium (updated 1 March 2007), <http://www.usafa.af.mil/34trw/cwc/cwcx/ncls/?catname=ncls> (homepage).
US Air Force Core Values, <http://www.usafa.af.mil/core-value/> (homepage).

Chapter 6

Canada's Defence Ethics Programme and Ethics Training

Colonel Yvon Desjardins

Introduction

Leadership engagement is the key to creating and implementing a successful ethics programme in any organization. It is perhaps even more important within a military organization where subordinates look to their leaders for guidance and support. The primary objective of the Defence Ethics Programme (DEP) of the Canadian Department of National Defence (DND) is to promote the values shared by the majority of Canadians. As such, the programme provides a framework to help Canadian Forces (CF) leaders and DND civilian managers to further improve the ethical behaviour of all the people working within their respective groups.

The establishment of an effective ethics training and education programme is one of the key elements of success in evolving the ethical behaviour of personnel, thereby contributing to the creation of an ethical work environment within any organization. Some will argue that it is difficult to change the values of individuals, especially when people join an organization at an age where their values are already set. Indeed, it is a challenge. Nevertheless, it is a challenge that we must accept to ensure that the men and women who dedicate their life to the service of their country can do so in an ethical environment that will ensure they can perform to the level expected of them.

This paper will briefly describe the Canadian DND and the CF to set the stage for a more in-depth analysis of the DEP. As ethics training and education are key element of the programme, we will conclude by detailing the methods and tools used to influence the men and women of the DND and the CF to adopt the ethical principles and obligations of the DEP.

The Department of National Defence and the Canadian Forces

DND is the largest department of the Government of Canada. It currently employs approximately 25,000 civilian employees whose primary purpose is to support the CF, which has about 64,000 active duty members in the Regular Force and some 23,000 part-time members in the Primary Reserve Force. The department is divided into some 20 functional areas or groups led by Associate Deputy Ministers (ADM) and Environmental Chiefs of Staff, also referred to as Level One Advisors.

The DND and CF missions are to defend Canada, its interests and values, to contribute to the defence of North America in partnership with the armed forces of the United States, and to play a major role in maintaining international peace and security. To this end, since 1947, the CF has completed 72 international operations. That figure does not include current operations, or the many CF operations carried out in Canada. At present there are more than 3,000 Canadian soldiers, sailors and air force personnel deployed around the world on peace support operations, including some 2,300 with the NATO-led International Security Assistance Force (ISAF) in Afghanistan. On any given day, 8,000 CF members – one third of the CF's deployable force – are preparing for, engaged in or returning from an overseas mission.

Rules and Regulations Governing Ethics

The DND civilian employees and CF members, who work side by side in meeting the objectives of the government, are subject to a number of rules and regulations pertaining to the values-based DEP. These represent the compliance component of the DEP. These rules and regulations address matters such as behaviour, discipline, harassment and conflicts of interests.

The Defence Administration Orders and Directives (DAOD) 7023 outlines the DEP and explain the policies, expectations, responsibilities and authorities of various groups and individuals within the departmental hierarchy, from Level One Advisors down to new employees and young recruits. Civilian employees are also subject to the *Values and Ethics Code for the Public Service* (Code). However, the Code does not apply to CF members. Nevertheless, the DEP's principles and obligations go hand in hand with the Code. And since adherence to the Code is a condition of employment for civilian public servants, DND further increases the promotion of high standards that would result in improving ethical decision-making both at the individual and the collective levels. Moreover, the Director Defence Ethics Programme maintains an ongoing relationship with the Office of Public Service Values and Ethics of the Public Service Human Resources Management Agency of Canada. Such a relationship allows for a healthy exchange of information and practices that generally benefit all federal government departments.

Development of the Defence Ethics Programme

The DEP is relatively new. It was officially established in December 1997 when the DM and the CDS outlined the objectives of the programme and provided the focus, framework and processes that were required to guide, assess and improve the ethical conduct of DND employees and CF members (see Deputy

Minister of National Defence 1997). The aim was, and still is, to ensure that all individuals perform their duties to the highest ethical standards. It is noteworthy that the Department had initially set up in February 1994 a precursor Protection of Resources and Ethics Programme and established a number of activities to promote ethics, including a first DND and CF conference on ethics held in Ottawa in October 1996 (for a report of that conference see Ministry of Public Works 1997a).

In March 1993 a critical event sent a clear signal to the CF's leadership and highlighted the need to create an ethics programme within Canada's military. Indeed, as stated in the Somalia Commission of Inquiry report (Ministry of Public Works 1997b), Canadians were shocked when they heard that soldiers from the now disbanded Canadian Airborne Regiment had beaten to death a 16-year-old Somali during the deployment of a CF Battle Group to Somalia, as part of a United Nations peace enforcement mission. Although the publication of the report in 1997 was not the initiating event leading to the development of the DEP, since the programme was already active at that time, the significant media coverage of the Somalia mission, the military boards of inquiry that followed, and the Somalia Commission of Inquiry hearings themselves were certainly strong motivators for maintaining the momentum and further developing the DEP.

The Tait report published in December 1996 was also one of the important factors that shaped the DEP. John Tait, a former Deputy Minister of Justice, led a study team on *Public Service Values and Ethics* and published in 1996 a revolutionary report entitled *A Strong Foundation* (Tait 1996). The report provided an in-depth analysis of many essential aspects related to values and ethics, and challenged the federal government to create values-based environments in all federal departments and agencies. Tait argued that senior managers had the responsibility to exercise leadership and take active measures to identify and preserve corporate values and ethical conduct within their respective organizations. The report continues to this day to generate discussions and concrete actions pertaining to public service values and ethics.

The Defence Ethics Programme

The DEP is a values-based programme that fosters the practice of ethics in the workplace and in operations. It guides CF members and DND employees in performing their duties to the highest ethical standards. The DEP's expectations are briefly laid out in a *Statement of Defence Ethics* that explains the three core ethical principles governing the manner in which the Department wants its members to carry out their responsibilities. They are: respect the dignity of all persons; serve Canada before self; and obey and support lawful authority. These principles are supported by six obligations related to professional behaviour: integrity, loyalty, courage, honesty, fairness, and responsibility (see DND 2001). The principles are stated in order of priority, meaning that when challenged with a decision, one must answer the first principle first. The last principle also addresses in a specific manner the compliance element of the programme.

The DEP therefore strikes a balance between judgment based on values and absolute compliance. Indeed, with a values-based programme, the focus is set on identifying the essential ethical values and developing the environment and tools to support them. As such, the Code and the DAODs help individuals in dealing with hard issues and increasingly complex and difficult environments. A pure 'compliance with rules' approach would require a high number of rules, regulations and codes that would stipulate what is right and wrong. But since it is somewhat inconceivable that all the members of an organization would know all the rules, a values-based programme allows individuals to make the right decisions when they are not able to spend a significant amount of time with legal advisors. In crisis situations such as those found on modern battlefields, soldiers will rely more on their training, experience, education, good judgment, and values, than on unfamiliar or unknown rules. DND therefore believe that a values-based approach, with a compliance component, is perhaps the best way to increase ethical practices in an organization. A pure values-based approach that cannot accommodate all the values of all people, or a pure compliance-based approach that requires the drafting of additional rules every time something new happens, have not been preferred orientations for the DEP and are not likely to be implemented in the future.

In the information age, where public scrutiny is a reality that we all must live with, DND employees and CF members have high expectations placed upon them to maintain the highest levels of ethical behaviour. The media constantly monitors members of the armed forces, and to a certain extent civil servants, to a point where they are not allowed to do what ordinary citizens may be able to. When organizational values and compliance mechanisms come into conflict with one's personal values, one must give priority to the public values, as public interest must prevail. If a member cannot agree to that, we believe that he or she must leave the military or the civil service.

Implementation and Delegation

As DND and the CF are large and complex organizations, the implementation of the DEP is decentralized. As such, Level One Advisors, or the Environmental Chiefs of Staff and Group Principals, are responsible for promoting ethics within their respective organizations and for setting up, with the support of the DEP Directorate, education, awareness and training programmes tailored to their specific needs. The DEP Directorate, with a staff of approximately 12 civilian employees and military personnel, oversees implementation of the programme and provides support to the Level One Ethics Coordinators. These coordinators serve as the principal advisors to their respective Level One.

To support the implementation of the programme, the DEP Directorate developed a Defence Integrity Framework that describes seven ethical processes that must be integrated within the programme to make it comprehensive and effective. They are: leadership, dialogue, training, decision-making, expectations, ethical risk and improvement. Of those, leadership, training and ethical risk assessments are the processes that require the most attention.

It may be an old cliché, but leadership by example is still a key element to implementing the DEP. Leaders at all levels are expected to behave ethically and make ethical decisions in a complex and often contradictory defence environment, and in turn to enable and encourage their subordinates to make the right choices. It is also important to influence members of the organization so that they choose to make the right decisions. Without effective leadership, there are risks of losing credibility, reputation, and strong morale.

In 2000 the Auditor General of Canada reported that DND had one of the two most comprehensive values and ethics programmes within the federal government. That statement was also reiterated in the Auditor General's 2003 report, and is supported by the results of a DND and CF-wide Ethics Survey conducted in 2003. This indicated good progress in terms of the ethical climate within the defence organization, when compared to the first survey done in 1999 ('ethical climate' being defined as 'the shared perception of what is ethically correct behaviour and how ethical issues should be handled'). The 2003 survey was distributed to 7,000 civilian and military DND employees, of whom 1839 responded. The major weakness revealed was a perception that 'organizational fairness' within the department was not as strong as it should be (Dursun 2003). The results of a further survey conducted in 2007 were still being awaited at the time of writing. Some work clearly remains to be done. Full implementation of the programme is still not complete, especially at the lower echelons of the organization.

Training

One of the roles of the DEP Directorate is to ensure a common approach in the implementation of ethics training throughout the DND and the CF. The fact that most of the department's ethics practitioners share similar opinions about ethics training has made the task much easier.

There is a fundamental difference between taking a formal course in ethics and being involved in a discussion group or a case study session with colleagues. We tend to call the latter 'learning and awareness activities' as they focus on getting people to think about the decisions they would make, before getting involved in making them 'in the heat of battle', while discussing the ethical elements with colleagues, co-workers and brothers in arms. The DEP offers these types of learning activities in a vast number of fora to both civilian employees and military members, and also conducts formal training. Some of the activities are compulsory while others remain optional.

Officer Training

Training in the field of ethics, whether formal or informal, is found in all elements of the CF's officer development from basic training to senior officers' courses and seminars.

The Royal Military College of Canada (RMC) is a recognized military university that confers degrees in Arts, Science, and Engineering. As part of its four-year undergraduate curriculum, all RMC officer-cadets must take one of two courses in ethics delivered by the Department of Military Psychology and Leadership. The two courses entitled *Military Profession and Ethics* and *Leadership and Ethics* (see Royal Military College of Canada website) have essentially the same syllabus and cover ethical theories, moral philosophy, ethical decision-making processes, moral and ethical dilemmas and codes of conduct pertaining to military service. They also focus on leadership values and obligations required of officers such as personal integrity and respect for human dignity. Cadets have the opportunity to familiarize themselves with the ethical dimensions of the profession of arms, the DEP and the Codes of Conduct for CF personnel which apply to all military operations conducted abroad by the CF. The RMC courses provide the basic and necessary ethical tools to prepare junior officers to fulfill their responsibilities, especially in the early years of their career. As they progress, other ethics training and educations fora will supplement their initial education.

It is important to point out that only a certain percentage of CF officers are RMC graduates. The others officers are subsidized to attend civilian universities, and already have a degree when they join the CF, or in certain cases obtain a degree through a part-time education programme at a regular university or through distance learning at RMC. Therefore, to supplement basic training and ensure that all officers reach a similar level of military education, the Officer Professional Military Education (OPME) Programme was established. Developed and delivered by RMC's Division of Continuing Studies, the programme is mandatory and all junior officers must complete it early in their career. As part of the OPME curriculum, junior officers take the Leadership and Ethics course, the same course offered to RMC Cadets. RMC graduates receive OPME credits and do not have to take the course again. The OPME's ethics component then provides the same basic ethics education to non-RMC graduates, and therefore ensures that all junior officers have a common knowledge.

Ethics has also been included in some of the curricula of junior officers' basic occupation courses. The objective is to eventually incorporate an ethics component into all classification training. Pilots, armoured officers and ships' navigators, for example, would be exposed to ethics as it applies to their respective occupations. Such endeavours represent a significant challenge for many reasons. The number of training days is limited and officers must concentrate on learning the basic skills they need to perform in their respective occupations. Ethics also competes with other common fields that are an integral part of an officer's modern-day realities such as media relations, law of armed conflict or financial management. A possible approach would be to insert ethical dilemmas in field exercise scenarios. The time required to deal with a situation would not increase the length of a course and would allow officers to exercise their judgment and ethical decision-making skills, as they would have to do once they joined their unit after their training was completed.

As officers progress through their career, they undergo advanced development periods that will expose them to more advanced education.

Canadian Land Forces Command and Staff College

The Command and Staff College's Joint Command and Staff Programme syllabus focuses, among other things, on operations, leadership, the law of armed conflict and ethics. The roughly one-year-long course prepares selected senior officers, normally at the rank of major and naval lieutenant-commander and a few lieutenant-colonel and naval commanders, for command and staff appointments. It instils the need to avoid improper behaviour and reinforces an attitude that fosters ethical conduct of senior officers. The Ethics and the Military Profession 15-hour module covers various ethical models and theories that the students would apply in fulfilling their responsibilities as senior officers. They familiarize themselves with some of the ethical thinking concepts and examine a number of contemporary thoughts on ethics and on the nature of morality as they apply to the military profession. They also look at the concepts of *jus ad bellum* and *jus in bello* and how they relate to the conduct of military operations.

The Advanced Military Studies Course (AMSC) and the National Security Studies Course (NSSC) are part of the last formal development period for senior officers. While the AMSC prepares selected colonels and naval captains for operational-level command and senior staff appointments, the NSSC prepares generals and flag officers, selected colonels, naval captains, and civilian equivalents for strategic leadership responsibilities. Both courses examine the influence of ethics and morals on decision-making and decision-making processes. However, NSSC students review in more detail the fundamentals of moral philosophy and ethical reasoning and examine the relationship between ethics and the military profession. They also discuss the challenges of inculcating ethical behaviour in their subordinates, peers and superiors.

Briefing Base Commanders

In 2006, we started briefing on the topic of ethics and conflicts of interest at the Base and Wing Commander and Base and Wing Chief Warrant Officers Fora that are held twice a year. The objective was to sensitize these senior officers and their chief warrant officers to the ethical risks which they could potentially encounter during their assignments, and to make them aware of the actions they need to take to regularly inform base and wing military and civilian personnel to avoid unethical situations. We are planning on continuing to provide such briefings as they help move away from lectures on ethical theory or on the DEP *per se* and discuss real-life scenarios encountered in the day-to-day work on a military base.

General and Flag Officers

Once at the rank of general or flag officer, officers must continue learning and assimilating information that will help them perform their duties and responsibilities to the highest standard. Leadership is a key element in a successful ethics programme. It is therefore of the utmost importance to engage these highest elements of the hierarchy in promoting the DEP and in reflecting on the ethical dilemmas encountered by CF members at all levels of the chain of command. In the first few years following the creation of the DEP, seminars for general and flag officers were organized to meet that objective. For some reason, they stopped taking place three years ago, a lapse which raises some questions. As we believe such fora to be extremely useful, we intend to put them back on the agenda during fiscal year 2007–2008. The focus of the one-day seminars would be on CF operations abroad. For example, the CF has been involved since 2002 in a vast spectrum of military operations in the Arabian Gulf region and in Afghanistan, including offensive combat missions. This involvement will allow general and flag officers to reflect on the dilemmas faced by the deployed men and women of the CF. Among themselves, they will have the opportunity to discuss ethical behaviour and decision-making in operations, and therefore contribute to raising the ethical awareness at the strategic level of the CF. Of note, we are also thinking of holding similar fora for the most senior elements of the civilian component of the Department.

Non-commissioned Members

As we have seen, officers are exposed to ethics throughout their career. Non-commissioned members (NCM) also receive ethics training and will soon be exposed to more practical elements pertaining to the field of ethics.

During basic training, recruits get a brief introduction to the DEP as one of the their key leadership development objectives. During the Primary Leadership Qualification Course, students spend two hours on the topic of ethics, while on the Intermediate and Advanced Leadership Courses they dedicate two to three 45–minutes periods to the issue. This includes a lecture and group discussions on the ethical behaviour of CF members of all ranks. Some trade-specific courses also have introduced a brief ethics element that pertains specifically to their trade. However, the long-term objective is to ensure all courses have an ethics component that will have a direct application to the topic of the course. This will remain a challenge, since ethics is competing with other important topics while the lengths of the courses cannot be extended.

Unit Ethics Coordinators

The training component of the DEP is far from being complete, and much more needs to be done. One of our projects is to develop a two-day Unit Ethics Coordinator's (EUC) Course. The objective of this project is to train junior officers and NCMs, and civilian employees, to be effective as ethics coordinators at the unit level. As a secondary duty, these people will be able to provide advice and guidance to their commanding officer, or civilian manager, and will be well prepared to lead group discussion and case study sessions with the members of their unit or organization. The course is an altered version of a qualification course developed for the Army UECs. The Army conducted a trial course in

April 2006 and we should be able to distribute the generic version of the course to Level One Ethics Coordinators in 2007.

Learning Activities and Group Discussion

It is well known that repetition and reinforcement of any topic is good, but too much could have the reverse effect. We must therefore exercise caution and perhaps avoid overtraining CF members and DND employees. Frustration could result in 'ethics fatigue', which would be counter-productive and may risk leading people to avoid all ethics discussion. It is also important to make people understand that all DND employees and CF members come from a multicultural society, and that they must adapt to reflect the common values of that society. We cannot compel individuals to endorse something they do not agree with. And since these people are all volunteers, they may choose to leave the Department or the CF if they are unable to adapt to the principles and obligations of the DEP.

The UEC course should ensure that the majority of the training focuses on learning activities where group discussions and case studies become the main method for discussing and promoting ethical behaviour in the organization, especially at the lower echelons of the chain of command. Of course, we will continue teaching ethical theories, but at different levels depending on the audience. The leaders, the Level One Ethics Coordinators, will receive more theoretical information and will be encouraged to pursue some reading of the important philosophers and applied ethics practitioners.

We believe that spending time, in small groups, with the people one works with is possibly a better approach to instilling good ethical principles in the younger DND audiences. It would indeed be somewhat utopian and perhaps naive to believe that young sailors, soldiers and air force men and women would enjoy spending time in class being lectured on the teaching of Socrates or Kant (although, no doubt, some individuals would love it). As responsible leaders, we must design our training activities and learning sessions to optimize the little time available while ensuring our personnel get what they need to do their job better and learn to think about their actions. We have always tried to develop among our junior staff the ability to think, exercise judgment and take the initiative, allowing them the latitude of being responsible individuals, accountable for their actions and those of their subordinates. A good understanding of applied ethics can only increase their skills and thus ensure that not only the senior leaders and managers make the right decisions and do the right things, but all military and civilian personnel understand the need to act ethically at all times.

CF Operations

At times, individuals involved in combat operations face competing values, or even a perceived inconsistency between the theatre rules of engagement and the *Statement of Defence Ethics*. Recently, for example, some junior CF combat team leaders were seen on television exercising judgment and leadership. After temporarily detaining alleged Taliban fighters, CF soldiers about to transfer them to local Afghan authority, in accordance with the mandate of the coalition forces in Afghanistan, seemed concerned for the personal safety of these people. They had heard that the local Afghan security forces were intent on killing the detainees. Therefore, to ensure the personal safety of these detainees, the CF soldiers made the ethical decision to keep them under their custody a little longer and to transfer them later to other Afghan officials. This quick decision under extremely stressful circumstances showed to the world that the soldiers were doing the right thing. This example also demonstrates the need to further the training and continue to better prepare soldiers before they deploy to a theatre of operation. We will therefore promote the inclusion of various ethical dilemmas in the scenarios of the pre-deployment training. Also, the ethics survey that will be done in 2007 will have a special section specifically targeting CF personnel returning from operations abroad to see if the 'working environment' is as ethical on operations around the world as it is at home. The results will then allow us to better understand individual and group behaviours in complex and perhaps chaotic situations, and take the appropriate measures to better adapt the pre-deployment training to suit.

On-line Introduction Course

A few years ago, we developed the *Introduction to Defence Ethics* course. Aimed at preparing the Level One Ethics Coordinators, but available to all DND staff, the course rapidly became very popular. In its classroom format, the one-day course touches on the basic philosophy and ethics theories to give the students the basic knowledge necessary to recognize ethical dilemmas as they apply to National Defence while running them through real case scenarios. The delivery of the course is contracted out to ethics practitioners. The current instructor is a university professor with a PhD in ethics. The course is voluntary and attended by many individuals who are not involved in ethics per se, other than having a personal interest in the subject. In 2006, one Level One Advisor mandated all his staff, more than one thousand people, to take the course over the next two years. This has created a situation where the demand for the course exceeds by far the delivery, especially given that the course is mainly offered in Ottawa about twice a month and in two other locations in Canada about once a month. To alleviate the problem, we will be creating an on-line version of the course, therefore allowing all CF members and DND employees, whether in Canada or abroad, to take the course. It is expected to be on-line by the end of fiscal year 2007–2008. As about 30 percent of DND staff does not have access to a computer on a continuous basis, a CD-ROM version of the on-line course will also be offered to ensure that all have access to the course. It is understood that taking such a course will not have the same value as a course taken in a classroom. Nevertheless, we believe that it will satisfy a demand and solve the current restricted availability of the classroom course.

Conclusion

In this chapter, I have explained why we believe that it is important that the DND's values-based DEP continue to encourage ethical behaviour in the work environment and in operations. As the Canadian public expects a high standard of conduct from its military and from its civil servants, we must foster the conditions that will develop and maintain a healthy ethical culture in DND. We have therefore focused on briefly describing the training and education mechanisms currently in place, or soon to be, because we think that they can significantly contribute to raising the level of awareness and knowledge of the DEP, which will lead to making the Department a better place. Ultimately, we want all DND employees and CF members to behave ethically and make ethical decisions not only because they have to, but because they choose to and know that it is the right thing to do.

General Ray Henault, a former CDS and now Chairman of the NATO Military Committee, once said:

> CF members have unique obligations that make us distinct from the rest of Canadian society: for example, we can be lawfully ordered into harm's way – that is, ordered to work in conditions in which we might have to kill or be killed. We perform the dangerous tasks involved in implementing the domestic and international policies that support Canadian values and interests around the world. This duty includes the obligation to use carefully applied deadly force when necessary to achieve the mission and, on operations, CF members sometimes find themselves in morally ambiguous situations. Throughout, we serve the government and people of Canada, but we are individually and collectively responsible for abiding by the military ethos, obeying the law, and complying with our professional standards. (DND 2003–4)

Bibliography

Deputy Minister of National Defence and Chief of the Defence Staff (1997), *Terms of Reference – Defence Ethics Programme*, Ottawa, Canada, 21 December, <http://ethics.mil.ca/documents/mandat_e.pdf>.

DND (2001), Defence Administration Orders and Directives 7023-1, Annex A – *Statement of Defence Ethics*, <http://admfincs.mil.ca/admfincs/subjects/daod/7023/form/a_e.asp>.

DND (2003–4), *Making Choices, Annual Report of the Chief of the Defence Staff 2003–2004*, <http://www.cds.forces.gc.ca/pubs/anrpt2004/intro_e.asp>.

DND (2005a), *Backgrounder BG-05.017*, Canada Command, 28 June.

DND (2005b), *Backgrounder BG-05.024*, Canadian Expeditionary Forces Command, 13 September.

DND (2005c), *Backgrounder BG-05.025*, Canadian Special Operations Forces Command, 13 September.

DND (2006), *Backgrounder BG-06.003*, Canadian Operational Support Command, 31 January.

Dursun, S. (2003), *Individual Values and Ethical Climate: an Empirical Study of Canadian Forces*, <http://www.internationalmta.org/Documents/2004/2004038P.pdf>.

Minister of Public Works and Government Services Canada (1997a), *The Many Faces of Ethics in Defence, Proceedings of the Conference on Ethics in Canadian Defence, Ottawa, 24–25 October 1996*, <http://ethics.mil.ca/archives/documents/conf1996_e.pdf>.

Minister of Public Works and Government Services Canada (1997b), *Dishonoured Legacy – The Lessons of the Somalia Affair, Report of the Commission of Inquiry into the Deployment of Canadian Forces to Somalia*, <http://www.forces.gc.ca/site/Reports/somalia/index_e.asp>.

Royal Military College of Canada website, <http://www.rmc.ca/academic/registrar/programmeme/courses/milpsyc/mlpsy4_e.html>.

Tait, J.C. (1996), *A Strong Foundation: Report of the Task Force on Public Service Values and Ethics* (Ottawa: Canadian Centre for Management Development).

Chapter 7

What Ought One to Do? Perspectives on Military Ethics Education in the Australian Defence Force

Jamie Cullens

Introduction

Ethical failures have occurred in Western militaries over the past few decades and in the twenty-first century they continue. In recent Australian Defence Force (ADF) experience some serious operational incidents have highlighted ethical problems. These have ranged from Operation Morris Dance off Fiji in 1987 where an infantry rifle company was ordered to load and unload their machine guns seven times in 24 hours as assessments were made as to how a heavily armed intervention might appear to Fijians; to Operation Lagoon in Bougainville in 1994 where the question asked was how 'ethically sound is it for troops that have been deployed to establish a presence and create a deterrent to be permitted to shoot in protection of life and property?' (Breen 2003, 2–7) The fact that the ADF has performed to a high ethical standard on recent operations can be attributed to the quality of leadership, training and a degree of luck. There have been only a handful of casualties on Australian operations since East Timor in 1999 and most of these have been training related incidents. A higher rate of casualties would change many perceptions and perhaps also raise the number and nature of ethical dilemmas encountered by Australian forces.

This chapter examines the state of ethics education in the ADF but does not enter into a philosophical discussion about ethical theory. The St James Ethics Centre, a Sydney-based independent not-for-profit organization which provides a non-judgmental forum for the exploration of ethics, promotes the phrase 'What ought one to do?' as the central question of ethics. The author asks whether the contemporary approach taken by the ADF in military ethics education is the right thing to do and suggests things that need to be done to develop better and more relevant military ethics programmes.

Some Historical Context

Australia's military history suggests that the nation's armed forces have generally conducted themselves well in fighting overseas and, with exceptions, have generally 'done the right thing' on military operations and in training since the first deployment of the New South Wales contingent to the Sudan in 1885. Exceptions include the shooting and bayoneting of German prisoners at the Battle of the Menin Road on the Western Front in September 1917 (Carlyon 2006, 451–2) and stories of atrocities against Japanese prisoners in the South West Pacific campaigns. Australia has also had its fair share of infamous commanders who are worthy of consideration in the military ethics education process. Three of them are worth highlighting as examples.

Lieutenant Harry Harboard 'The Breaker' Morant was born in England and migrated to Australia in 1883. In 1901 in South Africa he was commanding a detachment of the Bushveldt Carbineers at the age of 37 and was arrested and charged with the shooting of 12 Boer prisoners and a German missionary. He was tried by court-martial, found guilty and subsequently executed along with Lieutenant Peter Handcock. He is arguably Australia's first war criminal.

During the Second World War, Major General Gordon Bennett was the General Officer Commanding the Australian Imperial Force in Malaya and Singapore in 1941 and early 1942. Following the Japanese invasion and subsequent surrender of the Allied forces, Bennett left his 8th Division after the surrender was signed on 15 February 1942, and returned to Australia in order to inform the Government of Japanese fighting capabilities. His Division went into captivity at Changi and many were involved in building the Thailand-Burma railway where they suffered appalling deprivations, disease and death over several years. A Royal Commission was convened in November 1945 to investigate matters relating to Bennett's departure from Singapore, including 'Whether in all the circumstances Lieutenant General Henry Gordon Bennett was justified in relinquishing his command and leaving Singapore'. The debate continues to this day as to whether Bennett had 'done the right thing' (see Lodge 1986).

Finally, Captain Duncan Stevens, Royal Australian Navy, was the Commanding Officer of the destroyer *HMAS Voyager* when it collided with the aircraft carrier HMAS Melbourne in February 1964. He lost his life along with 81 members of his crew. The subsequent Royal Commission found him to be abusive, a chronic alcoholic and unfit to command. The investigations also revealed attempts by the Navy to engage in a cover-up campaign and it cast unfavourable light on the behaviour of some senior officers. In his book on the disaster, the former executive officer of *Voyager*, Peter Cabban, remarked on the impact of the disaster on personal relationships in the Navy: 'the scandal that followed placed loyalty, friendship and respect under sometimes unbearable pressure. Embedded in these conflicts was the ancient moral dilemma of having to choose between personal conscience and the common causes: the expendable individual against the greater good' (Cabban 2005, 90). To this day survivors of the disaster are still seeking compensation.

In addition to these individual examples, Dr Bob Hall, in his seminal work *Combat Battalion*, has examined the ethical behaviour of an infantry battalion on operations in Vietnam in 1969–70. He remarks that the war in Vietnam 'placed young Australian soldiers in positions of impossible moral ambiguity and expected them to cope alone. Still, the number and extent of moral or ethical failures was probably no larger than in earlier wars' (Hall 2000, 214). These examples serve to remind ADF personnel engaged in twenty first century warfare that the ADF is fallible and that leaders at all levels need to remain vigilant in the complex environments in which they operate.

Contemporary Perspectives

Over the past two decades the nature of ADF operational experience has raised ethical dilemmas for commanders and personnel, the challenges in Rwanda, East Timor, Afghanistan and Iraq coming immediately to mind. There was also extensive commentary in the media about the ADF's ethical deficiencies in the 'Children Overboard Affair' in 2001 (concerning false allegations by government ministers that children had been thrown overboard by asylum seekers on a boat intercepted by an Australian naval vessel), and it continued into 2007. The Preface of the Inquiry into 'the effectiveness of Australia's military justice system' by the Foreign Affairs, Defence and Trade References Committee of the Senate, tabled in June 2005, included the following comments:

> A decade of rolling inquiries has not met with the broad-based change required to protect the rights of Service personnel. ... This failure to expose such abuse means the system stumbles at its most elementary stage – the reporting of wrongdoing. ... Complaints were made to this inquiry about recent events including suicides, deaths through accident, major illicit drug use, serious abuses of power in training schools and cadet units, flawed prosecutions and failed, poor investigations. (The Senate 2005)

The Senate report highlighted ethical areas of concern which need to be addressed in the professional military educational environment. The volatility, uncertainty, complexity and ambiguity of our operating environment suggests we need to prepare our leaders for the challenges of the future by educating them in the ethical issues that have emerged in recent conflicts, deployments and barracks incidents. The ADF recognizes that it can no longer afford to be reactive in this regard.

In January 2002 one of the first tasks given to the Centre of Defence Leadership Studies was to investigate a proposal from the Deputy Chief of Army that the ADF should establish some sort of research capability in military ethics which would focus on the importance of ethical decision-making in contemporary operations. At the same time Dr Hugh Smith from the University of New South Wales prepared a discussion paper on the need to establish a centre for military ethics (Smith 2006). The proposal recommended an Australian Defence Force Academy-based centre with academic and military staff and with a budget of over $300m per year. The proposal did not receive widespread support but the idea is still alive.

As debate developed regarding an appropriate course of action, discussions with the Chief of the Defence Force (CDF) confirmed that military ethics 'were the ethos that binds the organization together' and that the topic needed to be built into the leadership development framework. The Secretary of the Department of Defence also believed that military ethics expertise should reside at Australian Defence College (ADC). In July 2002, the ADC planned and hosted the first military ethics forum in the ADF. Speakers included the Anglican Archbishop to the ADF, the Inspector General, and the Executive Director of the St James Ethics Centre. The forum attracted more than 50 people from ten groups in the defence community. The attendees proposed that the Centre for Defence Leadership Studies (CDLS) take the lead in developing military ethics programmes at the ADC and should continue to investigate the requirement for dedicated research in this field.

In August the need outcomes from the forum were discussed with the Chief of the Defence Force who posed the questions 'do we have a problem?' and 'what is it that we would give up to fit military ethics?' into extant professional military education programmes.

In order to generate debate on the development of military ethics education CDLS published a research paper by Rachel Rees-Scott, entitled *Ethics in Defence: Organizational DNA* (Rees-Scott 2002). The paper concluded that the ADF could not justify a stand-alone centre at this stage but that we should establish a research officer position to further investigate the organizational requirement.

In 2003 CDLS delivered the first military ethics packages to the Australian Command and Staff College and the Centre for Defence and Strategic Studies. Up until this stage little was being done on a holistic basis in the ADF beyond the initial education at Australian Defence Force Academy (ADFA), the service colleges and the various service training institutions. The following year, the ADC cleared with CDF the military ethics topics for discussion by the courses during that year's programme. CDF directed that ADC hold off on the parachute battalion issues, the fire on HMAS Westralia, and 'Children Overboard' because of ongoing legal and media sensitivities related to the incidents and the forthcoming Senate Inquiry into Military Justice. These case studies were eventually delivered in 2005 (see appendix for details).

Australian Defence College Programmes

The ADC is the flagship joint educational institution in the ADF and consists of the Australian Defence Force Academy (ADFA), the Australian Command and Staff College (ACSC) and the Centre for Defence and Strategic Studies (CDSS). Education in the sphere of military ethics is a key component of the ADC focus on achieving the necessary balance of 'how to think' and 'what to think'. The ADC ethics programmes are examined in some detail because they set the standard for the ADF as a whole.

Australian Defence Force Academy

The Charter of ADFA includes the requirements to provide midshipmen and officer cadets with: military education and training for the purpose of developing their professional abilities and the qualities of character and leadership that are appropriate to officers of the ADF; and a balanced and liberal university education within a military environment (ADFA 2004). Cadets and midshipmen complete three and four year degrees in Sciences, Engineering, Humanities and the Social Sciences.

In addition to the academic study there is an extensive common and single-service military training programme which includes weapons training, physical training, leadership and management training, military communications, defence studies, and drill and ceremonial.

Recent comments from specialist staff at ADFA suggest that the teaching of ethics is not done well. Over the three year standard undergraduate period, officer cadets and midshipmen receive about 18 hours of instruction on character and moral decision-making in a military environment. The curriculum development is haphazard and there are critical gaps in the programme. Recent proposals include the requirement for a clear, coordinated, cross-disciplinary curriculum (ADFA 2007). The problem is exacerbated by a posting tenure of key staff of only two years, meaning that there is little time to build corporate experience in such a complex field. There are also concerns about the self-awareness of the staff and their ability to teach military ethics. At the Academy there is now recognition of a need for an interdisciplinary and multidisciplinary approach to military ethics education and a review process is underway this year.

On the academic side at ADFA, Dr Stephen Coleman, lecturer in ethics from the University of New South Wales, explains that there are three ethics courses taught by the School of Humanities and Social Sciences, two of which specifically focus on issues in military ethics. The three courses are: 'Introduction to Military Ethics' in the General Education (GE) programme; 'Practical Ethics in the 21st Century' in the undergraduate programme (which examines practical topics selected by the students themselves, which may range from abortion and euthanasia through to issues of truth in advertising and bias by the media); and 'Legal and Moral Problems in International Violence' at the postgraduate level. Dr Coleman points out that military personnel are often required to make ethical decisions of different types. The more difficult decisions can be classified into two types; ethical dilemmas and tests of integrity. Ethical dilemmas are situations where a member of the military is faced with a number of options, often all of them bad, and the difficulty arises out of the fact that it is not obvious which of these options is the ethically correct one to follow. Tests of integrity are situations where a member of the military is faced with a decision where they know which is the ethically correct option to choose, but where there is considerable pressure on them (in one form or another) to choose the ethically wrong option. It is the ethical dilemma that is the main focus of discussion in courses taught by the university.

Topics examined in the GE course include: just war theory and ethical problems involved with humanitarian interventions; issues of weapons and targeting, including collateral damage and discussion of permitted and prohibited weapons; ethical issues of military life, such as giving and following orders, problems of medical treatment in combat zones, and issues raised by religious beliefs; ethical issues involved with prisoners of war, especially during the War on Terror; and ethical decisions faced by students during their time as cadets or midshipmen at ADFA.

The postgraduate course first examines the relationship between law, morality and politics, and then explores issues such as just war and self-defence; armed intervention in the affairs of other states (from assassination through to humanitarian intervention); laws of armed conflict; terrorism, the role of the United Nations, and enforcement of law by international courts; and whether individuals, civilian and military, can conscientiously object to violence by their state (Coleman 2007).

These courses commenced in 2006 and are proving popular with students.

Australian Command and Staff College

The ACSC programme is discussed in detail because it is the jewel in the crown of ADF military ethics education. This is appropriate as the course members invariably go on to command most units in the ADF. The Staff College opened in 2001 and is the result of the collocation and integration of the previous three single Service Staff Colleges. It educates officers from Australia and 22 other countries at the Major (equivalent) and Lieutenant Colonel (equivalent) levels in a comprehensive 12 month course. Conducted in a joint and integrated environment, and promoting a vision of excellence in warfighting, the course aims to develop future leaders who can better contribute to the ADF's warfighting capability.

The military ethics programme is conducted as a two-day workshop early in the year and as part of the command and leadership module. The workshop is unique for several reasons. First, it is conducted as a partnership with the St James Ethics Centre. The Centre's Executive Director, Dr Simon Longstaff, is a moral philosopher who has been working with the ADC for five years, and he has built his military knowledge through working with other militaries in Asia. Second, the workshop uses a case studies approach that includes presentations by the individuals, including many commanders, who were involved in the incidents in question. Third, students are encouraged to discuss in detail, under the Chatham House rule, ethical dilemmas that they have had to face in their careers. Some are administrative or of a barracks nature, but increasingly operational ethical issues are emerging. This approach has proved to be a powerful learning medium and its success is supported by the workshop evaluation process.

The programme uses some of the principles suggested by the Harvard Business School:

• ethics is as much an attitude as it is a set of skills and knowledge;
• outstanding leaders, organizations, and practice are emphasized;

- the focus is on decision making with all its complexity and ambiguity, not on issues of ethics or social responsibility in isolation;
- early instruction is important to allow course members to reflect on issues throughout the year.

The Defence Values of *professionalism, loyalty, innovation, courage, integrity and teamwork* are used as the basis for discussion. Although the individual services and the Australian Public Service retain their values, these specific Defence Values were established to provide a common and underlying thread for all people working in the defence community. Integrity is defined as 'doing what is right'.

The programme contributes to the development of operational and strategic leaders by:

- recognition of the centrality of ethical values in the context of individual and organizational effectiveness and national support of the ADF;
- recognition of the breadth of responsibility of the modern military, as well as the constraints and trade-offs attending the exercise of that responsibility;
- encouragement of reflection on the value and constraints of members' own approaches to military ethics.

The theme of the workshop is taken from a statement by Dr Longstaff in 2002; 'the truth about ethics and the human condition is that there is no prescriptive answer. It is judgmental and there are no assurances of certainty.' With this in mind the presenting teams offer little in the way of solutions but a great deal of material for reflection. A critical part of the workshop process is the active participation of the students with their unparalleled collective experience.

The presenting team recognizes that delivering workshops on military ethics is a tricky business and accept that with an international audience some are bound to be offended. They also recognize that the workshop will raise more questions than can be adequately answered in the available time. The workshop focuses on practical issues as opposed to debating abstracts. Many of the students still struggle with the fact that so many of the issues are not black and white, and there are always a handful who miss the point of the discussion. Although many contemporary issues are discussed the workshop is not interested in laying blame and James Reason's perspective is used as a guide:

> First, most of the people involved in serious accidents are neither stupid nor reckless, though they may well be blind to the consequences of their actions. Second, we must beware of falling prey to the fundamental attribution error (i.e. blaming people and ignoring the situational factors). (Reason 1990)

The course members are also asked to write down a recent ethical dilemma that they have faced, either of an administrative or operational nature. Few struggle with this activity. They are then asked to discuss the nature of the dilemma with a colleague and debate some of the 'shades of grey'. This has proved to be a challenging and successful exercise.

Centre for Defence and Strategic Studies

CDSS is the senior course at the Australian Defence College and it is charged with providing 'officers of the ADF, the Australian Public Service and overseas participants with the knowledge and skills required by commanders, strategic leaders and managers engaged in national security issues' (CDSS 2007). The students are predominantly at the Colonel (equivalent) level. Early in the 12-month accredited study programme, course members examine the moral and ethical imperatives that influence and drive strategic and operational decision-making. The Principal of CDSS, Dr Alan Ryan, points out that much of this work is embedded within the course curriculum, but specific units of study address the ethical and legal aspects of military service in the twenty first century and those peculiarly Australian imperatives that shape decision-making in the security sphere. A key issue that is examined is the extent to which ethics in a military environment are universal. The ethics component of the course is of a general nature and involves presentations and syndicate discussions. Ethical issues are also discussed through the medium of the law of armed conflict and international humanitarian law.

An additional area of ethics education is delivered to CDSS by the Myer Foundation through the one-day Cranlana Programme. This intervention provides the opportunity for the course members to participate in unique programmes of reading, study and discussion, directed at enhancing their understanding of the philosophical, ethical, and social issues central to creating a just, prosperous and sustainable society in Australia and beyond (CDSS Exercise Cranlana 2007). Course members address the '… vision and perspectives of great thinkers of the past and present. These discussions help strengthen their decision-making and leadership roles and reinforce and enhance their skills in practical reasoning, analysis and debate' (ibid.). The writings for analysis and discussion include Thucydides, Machiavelli, Hobbes, Rousseau and Mill. The syndicate exercise examines the concept of going to war for an idea and the concept is applied to the invasion of Iraq. Over the years this programme has been extremely successful and it challenges the students, amongst other things, to examine ethical decision-making at the strategic level.

The CDSS military ethics programme could be further enhanced with the consideration of Australian case studies and discussions with strategic leaders who have had to tackle major ethical issues. CDSS students should also be encouraged to discuss ethical challenges they have faced in their careers and be given the opportunity to reflect on real-world ethical issues. In the CDSS electives programme there is also the opportunity to include a detailed study of Thucydides' *History of the Peloponnesian War* as developed by Dr Martin Cook at the US Army War College (Cook 2006).

The ADC has developed a comprehensive knowledge-base in the field of military ethics and indeed some similar US institutions have remarked that the ADC is taking a bold and innovative approach to raising awareness of military ethics because the ADF is willing to debate contentious contemporary issues. It has also been suggested that the nature of Australian culture allows the ADF to examine sensitive and contentious issues in a way that other militaries are reluctant to consider.

The ADC firmly believes in Jonathan Glover's view that if we think about ethics in the context of past disasters we can learn from what we have been lucky enough to avoid. This is one reason why the programme tends to focus on organizational *mea culpas*. The workshop process recognizes that much more is to be learned from organizational failures than organizational successes and this is particularly so for a high performing organization like the ADF. Most training in the ADF focuses on 'good' examples and exposure to Australia's proud military history is a key foundation of all ADF training. There are very limited opportunities to debate the 'bad' issues in a non-threatening environment, but we are able to do this at length on the ADC courses.

Other ADF Perspectives

At the Army's Recruit Training Battalion, Chaplain Dave Hosking (March 2007) points out that the character training and ethics focus is on introducing the recruits to critical thinking about themselves, their military and social environment and the moral and ethical decisions needed to survive in an operational environment. The course complements the instruction on values given by platoon staff. The moral and ethical framework that is offered attempts to create a personal framework in the individual soldier that will allow the soldier to make ethical judgments in the heat of battle without having to resort to a 'situational ethic' where no previous ethical process has been considered. It is something that the Australian soldier has done well in the past and it is maintained through the character training process. The Recruit Training Battalion believes that the Australian soldier should be a 'thinking' soldier. The programme, run over two separate days, includes consideration of what makes a good soldier; an analysis of social pressures and internal value systems and how they determine reactions to a situation; Defence Values; ethical decisions; the Geneva Conventions; an analysis of the events at My Lai; and small group work on ethical situational problems using real examples from operations in Iraq and East Timor.

The RAAF Officer Training School programme includes two periods on ethics delivered by the chaplains. The theory lesson includes revision of the definitions of values, morals and ethics; just war theory; an outline of the process of ethical decision-making; an outline of the need for ethical conduct in the Air Force; and a discussion of ethics in the military environment. The second lesson focuses on the examination of case studies. These include fictional administrative and operational dilemmas which ask the students to decide on a course of action and then justify their decision using ethical principles.

The Royal Australian Navy's Commanding Officer/Executive Officer Course is run twice each year and a military ethics programme is included in the Sea Command and Leadership module. Students consider a series of case studies including that of the *USS Vincennes* (see appendix), and the St James Ethics Centre facilitates discussions on ethical intelligence and fitness for command. The students also have the opportunity to debate ethical dilemmas that they have encountered and syndicates are asked to come up with solutions to the issues presented by other students. The course evaluations reveal that this approach is very successful although it is disconcerting that for many it is the first ethics education opportunity they have had since their initial training.

There is clearly some good work underway in the field of military education but it arguably suffers from a lack of coordination and a common philosophy.

An Appropriate Approach?

In recent years there has been considerable discussion at the executive level in the ADF concerning the future of military ethics education. Senior Defence personnel agree that the current approach is *ad hoc* but there is little agreement as to how to improve the situation. Some favour the trial of a military ethics research position whilst others do not believe that the proposal should be supported because the case is not sufficiently robust. Another perspective from a three star officer suggested that there was no evidence of contemporary ethical shortcomings in the defence community. However, it is recognized that the nature of contemporary operations is placing increased ethical challenges on ADF personnel at lower rank levels and that although the ADF has done well to date, it needs to sustain and enhance its efforts in the delivery of military ethics education. It is further acknowledged that military ethics education is difficult and invariably sensitive work, as should be expected when 'War – the business of killing in the name of the state – is an activity where the very existence of ethics is often disputed' (Smith 2006).

The current approach to the delivery of military ethics programmes could be summed up as containing some good ideas and appropriate intent but lacking in focus and cohesion. There is no agreement as to what is to be achieved by the various programmes other than a rather vague notion of ensuring that the ADF has 'good people' who will 'do the right thing' when faced with an ethical dilemma. A twenty-first-century military has to do better than this.

What Ought the ADF to Do?

As the St James Ethics Centre points out, 'the use of case studies, as the foundation for reflection, and in particular, the incorporation of the live testimony of those most intimately involved with the events in question – must surely rank as world's best practice in this area' (Longstaff 2004). At the ADC, the military ethics programmes are well established on some courses but require more work in other areas. Across the ADF the approach is more *ad hoc*. Other than at the University of New South Wales at ADFA, there are no moral philosophers or ethicists involved in the delivery of military ethics programmes. As a contrast, in the US, each military academy has teams of appropriately qualified professionals. This is not to say that the chaplains and ethicists need to take over but rather that the delivery of ethics training requires a multidisciplinary team that includes people with specific, recent operational experience.

The ADF can and should develop a strategy for the delivery of military ethics at all stages of its single service and joint professional military programmes. The resources required, when compared to the huge outlays on capital expenditure over the next decade, are miniscule. But an ethical failure could have drastic consequences.

It is worth thinking of professional military education as a capability, just like the Joint Strike Fighter, special forces, or air warfare destroyers. The ADF needs to ensure that its people, and particularly its leaders, are ethically equipped for the operational challenges of the twenty first century. Dr David Cox and Dr Andrew O'Neil suggest that leadership and 'ethics should form the core' of professional military education, and that:

> For a truly professional military, ethics incorporate a fundamental set of guiding principles that go beyond the laws of war and international legal obligations. These principles provide an enduring moral compass that supports complex problem solving and effective decision making that underpins operational success. (Cox and O'Neil 2006, 64)

Conclusion

This chapter has examined a broad range of issues and themes relating to the delivery of military ethics education in the ADF. The new military ethics programmes at the Australian Defence College have been running for five years and when benchmarked with other militaries it is apparent that the ADF has taken a bold and innovative approach which appears to suit the Australian culture. The ACSC delivers the jewel in the crown of ADF military ethics programmes and it can be used as a model for the organization. Time pressures should not be an impediment to the development of robust, intellectually and ethically challenging programmes that meet the needs of ADF personnel at all levels. The central issues remain a lack of appropriate resourcing and a single service *ad hoc* approach to curriculum development. At a time when the ADF is espousing Network Centric Warfare and joint operations, we are not placing an appropriate focus on the development of military ethics programmes that present our future leaders with the range of dilemmas that they will encounter in their careers, either on operations or in the staff.

The programmes at the ADC, which have evolved each year as a consequence of participant feedback, are displaying a degree of maturity. The focus should remain on operational issues and where possible use should be made of Australian examples. It is also important to recognize that there 'is no best single method of education and training in ethics. Debate, character development and leadership must all play a part' (Smith 2006, 19).

A critical component of ADC programmes has been the willingness of individuals involved in the actual incident to talk under the provisions of the Chatham House rule about their experience. This should continue and indeed be actively encouraged. The ADF is well ahead of our coalition partners in this regard.

The ADC believes that the case study approach with the students doing the bulk of the work is the most effective delivery method. This becomes particularly interesting given the international composition of the courses. The engagement of the St James Ethics Centre in the programmes has also been critical. It provides the professional philosophical balance to the practical military problems. It is important to note that, unlike in the United States, there are few Australians who are recognized as academic experts in the field of military ethics. Australia has been blessed with the luxury of being able to reflect and learn from the ethical failings of other militaries. It is important to align and embed military ethics as a central component of all the ADF's professional military education.

Our sense, developed over more than five years and backed by data from the course evaluation process, is that the students want to spend time discussing ethical issues. The feedback we are getting is certainly positive. We have had enough ADF incidents over the past few years to provide us with a solid base for reflection and we have people in the system willing to talk about their experiences so that the issues are really brought to life. The world press continues to highlight on a regular basis how important these issues are to the profession of arms. The Chief of Air Force remarked in 2004 that, 'I consider that we could do more to prepare our future leaders in this vitally important area'. What is needed now is action to develop the organizational strategy, a modest allocation of resources, and a continuing run of good luck on operations.

Note

This chapter reflects the views of the author and not the Australian Department of Defence or the Australian Defence Force.

Bibliography

Australian Defence Force Academy (2004), *Handbook* (Canberra: ADFA).
Australian Defence Force Academy (2007), paper on the teaching of ethics, March.
Breen, B. (2003), *Ethical Dilemmas on Operations*, a presentation to ACSC, 11 March.
Cabban, P. (2005), *Breaking Ranks* (Random House: Australia).
Carlyon, L. (2006), *The Great War* (London: Macmillan).
CDSS Exercise Cranlana, 2 March 2007.
Centre for Defence and Strategic Studies (2007), *Handbook* (Canberra: CDSS).
Coleman, S. (2007), *Ethics Teaching at UNSW@ADFA*, notes provided to the author, 16 March.
Cook, M.L. (2006), 'Thucydides as a Resource for Teaching Ethics and Leadership in Military Education Environments', *Journal of Military Ethics* 5:4, 353–62.
Cox, D. and O'Neil A. (2006), 'Professional Military Education in Australia: Has it All Gone Terribly Right?', *Australian Defence Force Journal* 171, 57–74.

Hall, R.A. (2000), *Combat Battalion: The Eighth Battalion in Vietnam* (Sydney: Allen and Unwin).

Lodge, A.B. (1986), *The Fall of General Gordon Bennett* (Sydney: Allen and Unwin).

Longstaff, S. (2004), letter to author, May.

Niell, D.A. (2000), 'Ethics and the Military Corporation', *Canadian Military Journal* 1:1, 27–40.

Reason, J. (1990), *Human Error* (New York: Cambridge University Press).

Rees-Scott, R. (2002), *Ethics in Defence: Organizational DNA*, DLS Leadership Paper 2/2002.

The Senate, Foreign Affairs, Defence and Trade References Committee (2005), *The Effectiveness of Australia's Military Justice System* (Canberra: Commonwealth of Australia).

Smith, H. (2006), *The Profession of Arms and the Promotion of Ethics*, draft (UNSW@ ADFA).

Appendix

Military Ethics Case Studies Developed and Used by the Centre for Defence Leadership Studies (CDLS)

The ADF Experience in Rwanda 1994-95 – leadership, ethical decision-making and trauma with the Kibeho massacre and the leadership of the Canadian Lt Gen. Romeo Dallaire. The session uses the film *Shake hands with the Devil* and incorporates the perspectives of Australians who witnessed the killings at Kibeho. Conducted at Australian Command and Staff College.

Black Hawks Down – the leadership, ethical, risk and cultural issues relating to the Australian Army's loss of 18 men in the crash of two Black Hawks in 1996. Conducted at Australian Command and Staff College.

The Brutal Battalion? – Command and leadership challenges in 3 RAR, the Army's parachute battalion, 1998-2000. ACSC each year.

A Certain Maritime Incident 2001 – tactical, operational and strategic leadership in the children overboard affair. An examination of the Select Committee report of October 2002 and discussions with a panel of key players. Conducted at CDSS in April 2005.

Columbia and the Pig – the cultural, risk management, ethical and leadership issues associated with NASA's loss of the Space Shuttle Columbia in 2002 and the RAAF F-111 fuel tank deseal/reseal programme that ran for more than 20 years until 2000. Conducted at CDSS in April 2005.

Friendly Fire: Tarnak Farm – the outcomes of the bombing of Canadian troops by USAF F-16 aircraft in Afghanistan in 2002.

The HMAS Westralia Fire 1998 – reflection on the Board of Inquiry findings and the Western Australian Coroner's Report. Presentation by the ship's Commanding Officer. Conducted at Australian Command and Staff College each year.

Khobar Towers (Professor Eliot Cohen) – leadership, accountability and duty of care in relation to the bombing of the USAF barracks in Saudi Arabia in 1996.

The Loss of Shark 02 – the Board of Inquiry into the crash of the RAN Sea King helicopter on the island of Nias in Indonesia on 2 April 2005. The report will be released later in 2007 and the case study is to be developed from that report.

Madeleine's War – strategic and operational leadership, strategic decision-making and friction in the NATO Operation 'Allied Force' against the former Yugoslavia in 1999. Legal or illegal under international law? Coercive diplomacy and the challenges of a 19-member coalition. Conducted at CDSS in 2005.

Operation Bali Assist – exemplary ADF leadership in the evacuation of the Bali bombing victims in 2002. Conducted at CDSS in April 2005.

Operation Tsunami Assist – an examination of the Sumatra relief effort following the 2004 tsunami. Under development.

Project Wedgetail – innovation, risk management, culture and leadership in the development of Australia's pocket AWACS to 2007. This case study is under development.

RAAF Aircraft Losses in the 1990s – reflections on the RAAF leadership and safety culture of the early 1990s.

The Seasprite – an examination of the controversial Navy helicopter project and the lessons learned to 2007.

Senate Inquiry into Military Justice – reflection on the parliamentary inquiry into inappropriate behaviour in the ADF. The report was tabled in Parliament on 16 June 2005. Defence has established a Military Justice Implementation Team to implement the recommendations from the inquiry under a Navy two star. Considered by ACSC in 2006 and 2007.

Somalia and Dislocation: Ethics and the Canadian Forces – the fallout from the murder of a Somali youth by the Canadian Airborne Regiment in 1993. Conducted at CDSS in 2005 and at ACSC in 2006 and 2007.

Tailhook – US Naval aviators and inappropriate behaviour; the suicide of Admiral Jeremy Boorda in 1996 and a service 'struggling for its soul'. This case study uses the documentary 'US Navy Blues'. Conducted at the Navy Commanding Officers' designate courses.

The US Marine Corps and the Italian Cable Car Disaster – an examination of the aircrew conspiracy to destroy evidence after the Aviano incident in 1998.

The Use of Torture in the Long War – reflections on the Afghanistan (2002) and Abu Ghraib (2004) experiences. Australian Defence Force perspectives. This case study uses the Frontline documentary *The Torture Question*. Conducted at CDSS in April 2005 and at ACSC in 2006 and 2007.

USS Vincennes – the shooting down of the Iran Air Airbus in 1988. As the ADF decides on an Air Warfare Destroyer, the case study focuses on the command decision cycle and the complexity of the Aegis system. This case study uses the documentary *The Other Lockerbie*. Conducted at the Navy Commanding Officers' designate courses.

War Crime: Srebrenica – the UN Dutch Battalion and the massacre of Bosnian civilians by the Serbs in 1995.

Chapter 8

Ethics Training in the Norwegian Defence Forces

Tor Arne Berntsen and Raag Rolfsen

When an earlier version of this chapter was presented at a workshop in military ethics at the University of Hull, the content of the presentation below was not picked up in the ensuing dialogue. The fact that the persons making the presentation were chaplains was, however, mentioned by several of the participants. Some questioned the expediency of such an arrangement and argued that in their defence forces it was an important and distinct point that ethics, in increasingly multicultural societies, should not be linked to any religion.

This, of course, is a pertinent observation. It has been given close consideration in the development of the ethics training programme in the Norwegian Defence Forces. The programme, at all levels of education, is careful not to push a particular set of values onto the soldiers, but it rather strives to make the soldiers reflect on the consistency and applicability of their own set of values. Being vigilant concerning this aspect of the programme is one of the fundamental points in the training of chaplains for their role as instructors.

Against this background, the following questions can be asked: Can there be a completely secular ethics? Is it possible to define ethics without relating oneself to some kind of transcendence; to something ungraspable, something that by definition is not part of the structure to which the ethical is speaking? Is an academic, military or political professional identity sufficient in order to prevent the properly ethical dimension of military ethics from collapsing? It could be argued, in opposition to the evident truths of secularism, that ethics necessarily carries with it a religious dimension.

These questions have not yet been not answered. They merit additional discussion, in which the more fundamental challenges facing military ethics in our times could be addressed.

Background

How do we teach ethics in the Norwegian Defence Forces? And, why do we do it? These questions could be developed at length, especially the question of 'Why'? When does ethics go *from* being ethics proper, i.e. from constituting something that comes from without the military system to direct and critically address it, *to* the point of having become just another tool in the military toolbox, repairing a dysfunctional machine and enabling it to work as smoothly as possible? Since we have been asked to answer the specific question of *how* military ethics is taught in the Norwegian Defence Forces, and not of *why*, we are not going to develop at length here the question of when military ethics stops being ethical in the proper sense of the word and starts becoming just oil lubricating the machine.

However, we cannot entirely avoid the question 'Why?', because it is this question that keeps us awake and aware of the constant danger of treating ethics as being of solely instrumental use. The *primary, fundamental* motive for teaching ethics in the military is neither to clean up the act of military operations under the gaze of the media, nor to make military operations more efficient. We teach ethics in the military because we want to *promote good and prevent evil*.

On our way from the question of why we teach ethics in general to the question of *how* we teach military ethics in particular in the Norwegian armed forces, we will pause at another and more recognisable 'Why?'.

During the last decade or so, the status and importance of military ethics in Norway has improved considerably. In 2006 and 2007, *The Basic Values Document* of the Norwegian Defence Forces was revised and rewritten (the document has been finished and sent to the Chief of Defence for approval; it includes, after some debate, the expression 'The Norwegian Defence Forces grounds their ethos in Christian and humanistic basic values' and not the broader 'on the values of our tradition', which was proposed at one point). At the same time, the Department of Defence has also finished its *Plan of Action on Moral Attitudes and Leadership* (the document was presented by the Minister of Defence on 18 September 2006 in Oslo: Norwegian Ministry of Defence 2006).

During the last couple of years, and in parallel with this ongoing programme, the Norwegian media have been full of headlines, articles and commentaries focusing on the relation between the military forces and moral standards and questions.

This renewed and strengthened focus on the relationship between the military and ethics comes as a result of two developments. The first is the development *from* a situation during the Cold War, when military forces were seen almost solely as defence forces, not needing any moral justification beyond the right to self-defence, *to* a situation where the armed forces were perceived, to a growing extent, as an instrument available to the state in the pursuit of its own interests.

This approach to the use of military force demands a much stronger moral justification than the one that defines armed forces solely as an instrument of self-defence. This approach has resulted in a sharp distinction being made between the political and the military spheres of influence, and consequently between questions *ad bellum* and questions *in bello*. But this increasing demand for ethical justification has resulted in a situation in which the *ad bellum* dimension of war, i.e. the justification of when to go to war, is no longer solely the province of the politicians. The moral justification for the war *per se* now plays an important role 'on the ground' for the soldier, who will have to live with his or her participation in the war; for the media, who will interpret the successes and failures of the war in light of its moral legitimacy; and for the population in the area of operation, who will resist or cooperate according to its view of this legitimacy. A too rigid separation between *jus ad bellum* and *jus in bello* can endanger the success of the operation as such.

The second development that has strengthened the focus on the need for military ethics is a more long-term development, namely the slow but decisive change in the field of anthropology as to how we view the moral agent, and, it has to be added, how the moral agent sees him- or herself. Armed forces can in many respects be perceived as the last remnant of social structures where desirable ends are achieved through hierarchical and command-based means. While society at large and its various subgroups have, through democratization, departed from this way of organizing themselves and from the anthropology supporting it, the military forces have preserved the old structure; they are the last remnant of this paradigm.

There is no way, however, that the organization of military forces can, in the long term, resist change. The old paradigm was supported by a homogeneous society: one state, one national culture and identity, one religion, one set of values, and one mass of people needing to be castigated and brought into line within this homogeneous society. When these pillars start to crumble away, the military organization can no longer build upon them.

Change has indeed slowly crept into military culture. In Norway, the transition from what has been called command-based leadership to leadership through task assignment and intention, and even network-based leadership, reflects efforts to ensure that soldiers are viewed both by society and by themselves as more independent and as morally integrated agents. Put crudely, military ethics is necessary to fill the accountability-gap created by this transition.

Education for Conscripts and Lower Level Officers

It is in light of these developments that we should view the 'how' of the teaching of military ethics in the Norwegian Defence Forces. In our teaching we try to activate and engage the moral feelings and values of soldiers who come from a pluralistic society. We challenge these values and feelings by presenting, for study and critical analysis, dilemmas arising from the military setting and from war. We therefore utilize the pedagogical approach called *dilemma intervention*. In order to activate the soldier's own values, they are confronted by between six and ten dilemmas during a session and are challenged, both as individuals and in small groups, to react to or solve these dilemmas. The responses are recorded on the whiteboard, and the consistency of the ethical approach is tested as new dilemmas question the general validity of the values recorded. Each lesson ends with the teacher summing up all the responses recorded, and, based on the soldiers own values, he or she will try to sketch out a consistent ethical approach relating to the theme of the session.

The programme includes six double lessons, and the themes that are covered range from entry into the military system, via how to deal with diversity and the use of force, to how we tackle crisis and death. This programme of ethical education is based on the core values of the Norwegian Defence Forces; Respect, Responsibility and Courage. All the conscripts go through it, and, when they take the next step on the military educational ladder, the ones aspiring to become officers are faced by new lessons focusing on the dilemmas of leadership.

Ethics Training at the Military Academies

At the Norwegian Military Academies, military ethics is at the core of the officers' training programme. This came about because of the above-mentioned developments in attitudes to the use of military force, as well as an increased awareness, both within the military and on a political level, of the importance and relevance of military ethics training in the Norwegian Defence Forces.

In their first year at the military academies the cadets undergo an introductory course in military ethics. The purpose is to give the cadets a basic understanding of the moral foundations of the military profession and of the use of military force. Some of the topics that they are introduced to are: ethical theory, professional ethics, the use of force, the legitimacy of the military institution, ethics of war, cultural challenges in international operations and post-war ethics.

In other words, this course has as its main objective instilling in the cadets an ethical 'language', so that they can relate to the different ethical problems and dilemmas they are faced with as military officers, both from an individual and societal perspective. The cadets are encouraged to apply the different ethical theories and principles to real-life military challenges. Although this part of the ethics training programme is based on a theoretical approach, the cadets are encouraged to relate these issues to their own military experiences. This is stressed as particularly important in a context in which the very premises for the use of military force are changing.

However, to become an officer you need more than just theoretical knowledge and the ability to reflect critically upon ethical issues. The military needs officers who themselves are morally integrated and capable of performing leadership not only by command but also through task assignment. On the battlefield, moral integrity will also function as a shield against the demoralising consequences of war. This is probably the most important, and at the same time, the most challenging aspect of the ethics training programmes at the military academies. An officer must be able to make critical decisions when needed, and at the same time have the integrity and endurance to live with unsolved paradoxes and dilemmas. The cadets are therefore guided, through practice and reflection, in exploring and shaping their own values and practical behaviour.

The pedagogical model used in this ethical training programme is one that brings together both theory and practice through a dialectic of reflection, exercise and mentoring. As a result of this practical approach to ethics training, military ethics is not only seen as an isolated course with its own traditions and sources; it is also integrated into the other courses and subjects at the military academies, such as political philosophy, psychology, history and military doctrine.

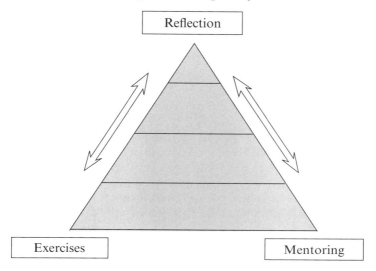

Figure 8.1 Pedagogical model

Research, Publications and Academic Progress

Due to a determined effort to visualize the importance and relevance of ethics training among soldiers and officers in the Norwegian Defence Forces, the Norwegian military chaplaincy has gained a position as one of the leading institutions in military ethics in Norway.

The military chaplains have always had a strong position in the Norwegian Defence Forces and have been responsible for ethics training. However, as a result of a number of social and political changes both within the military and in the society at large over the last years, focus has gradually shifted from teaching Christian ethics to teaching military ethics. Teaching military ethics has thus been established as one of the chaplain's basic functions. This has particularly been highlighted through the implementation of the newly developed ethics training programme for conscripts.

To gain such a position, academic progress and development have been seen, and are still seen, as strategically important for the Norwegian chaplaincy. To coordinate the ethics training programmes, the Norwegian chaplaincy has developed an ethics department, which also functions as an ethical adviser to the military dean. Although all military chaplains are responsible for ethics training, the chaplains at the military academies and at the Defence College have been dedicated to ethics training. At each of the three military academies there is a chaplain who is responsible for the ethics training programme. There is also a chaplain at the Norwegian Defence College, who is the point of contact within the military education system.

The chaplains at the war academies and the Defence College as well as the chief of the ethics department have 50 per cent of their work set aside for research.

There is also a senior researcher in the chaplaincy dedicated to more independent research and development projects. Altogether there are two chaplains with a doctoral degree in theology in the chaplaincy, while five chaplains are currently working on, or are about to complete, their doctoral degree.

Today, within the military chaplaincy, there is research on important topics such as just war theory, the philosophical foundations of military ethics, virtue ethics, and the ethics of peace and reconciliation.

In addition to individual research and publishing, the Norwegian military chaplaincy edits two journals on military ethics; *Pacem* and *Journal of Military Ethics*. *Journal of Military Ethics* was in fact the first international journal on military ethics, and the editorial board consists of a number of leading international scholars.

Over the years the Norwegian military chaplaincy has published several books and studies on military ethics and related subjects. One of the most debated books was Bård Mæland's *Adventurous Expeditionists: Reconstructing Moral Reasoning and Agency of Norwegian Platoon Commanders in Kosovo* (Mæland 2004). Another book worth mentioning is *Military Ethics*, which was written by the chaplains at the military academies and the Defence College, and published in January 2006 (Lunde and Mæland 2006). This is a basic introduction to military ethics for the bachelor degree programme at the military academies.

Altogether the Norwegian military chaplaincy contributes extensively to the development of ethics training programmes and plays an important part in emphasizing the role and relevance of ethics training in the Norwegian Defence Forces.

Challenges

The challenges arising from teaching military ethics are both many and complex. We will neither name them all nor explore them in depth. Some deserve to be mentioned nevertheless.

First, the general challenge: How do we prevent military ethics from being swallowed up by the system it is set to serve and critically analyse? When ethics is reduced to becoming just a means of character development, leadership training and the securing of unit morale, ethics disappears in its supporting disciplines: psychology, sociology, theories of organisation, and so on.

The second challenge is to go from a situation where ethics to some extent is only the propping up of the façade of what is going on anyway, to a situation where ethics are owned by the soldiers and officers in such a way that it effects real change in conduct. Connected to this challenge is the question of how to triangulate ethical theory with both military exercises and mentoring. How do we get into a self-enforcing 'good circle' where hands, hearts and minds inform one another in a continuous development, as a result of which not only the communication of military values but also the integrity of the soldier are ensured? How do we balance the necessities of war with the predominant independent self-image of modern man and woman? How do we prepare people to, in some situations, willingly disregard their own desires? And, finally: how do we secure the resources for research and further development of military ethics, so that it can follow the rapid development in military skills, technology and operational effectiveness?

These are some of the challenges facing us in the work of developing military ethics in Norway, and we probably share most of them, if not all, with those responsible for ethics training in the military across the world. To engage in critical and constructive dialogue with each other across national boundaries is an important step towards confronting, and perhaps even resolving, the dilemmas inherent in these challenges.

Bibliography

Lunde, N.T. and Mæland B. (eds) (2006), *Militæretikk (Military Ethics)* (Trondheim: Tapir Akademisk forlag).

Mæland, B. (2004), *Skadekutt Idealisme: Norsk offisersmoral i Kosovo (Adventurous Expeditionists: Reconstructing Moral Reasoning and Agency of Norwegian Platoon Commanders in Kosovo)* (Bergen: Eide forlag).

Norwegian Ministry of Defence (2006), *Plan of Action on Moral Attitudes and Leadership*, <http://www.regjeringen.no/upload/kilde/fd/nyh/2006/0097/ddd/pdfv/290388-handlingsplan_forsvarssektoren_holdninger_etikk_ledelse_korr.pdf>.

Chapter 9

Ethical Education and Character Development in the Armed Forces of the Federal Republic of Germany

Stefan Werdelis

Innere Führung – Leadership and Civic Education

With the creation of the Bundeswehr in 1955, and in the context of past military excesses, it was necessary to provide reassurance that the reestablishment of military power in Germany was compatible with liberal democracy. As a result the concept of *Innere Führung* was established as the ethical foundation of the German armed forces. This chapter examines the meaning of *Innere Führung* and the methods which the Bundeswehr uses to instil it into its members. Although the concept is unique to Germany, its principles may be equally valuable in other societies.

According to Joint Service Regulation ZDV 10/1 of the German Federal Ministry of Defence, 'the principles of *Innere Führung* serve as a basis from which general requirements of all soldiers and special requirements for the leadership behaviour of superiors are derived' (Federal Ministry of Defence 1993, 2). This document describes the purpose of *Innere Führung* in the following terms.

First, while giving due consideration to ethical aspects, *Innere Führung* aims to convey the political and legal justification for military service and make the purpose of the military mission transparent and intelligible. Second, it aims to promote the integration of the Bundeswehr and the service member in the state and society, and to awaken an understanding of the tasks which fall to the Bundeswehr within the Alliance and in mutual collective security systems. Third, it should strengthen the willingness of service members to fulfil their duties conscientiously, to assume responsibility and to cooperate with others, as well as to preserve discipline and cohesion among the troops. And finally, the purpose of *Innere Führung* is to create an internal order for the armed forces which is humane, conforms to the law and provides the necessary efficiency for mission performance. (Federal Ministry of Defence 1993, 8)

The German expression *Innere Führung* is hard to translate into English. Literally it means 'inner command', 'internal guidance' or 'self-rule'. I do not think there is a directly equivalent English expression which captures its meaning exactly (although 'autonomous self-determination' comes very close), but here is a brief attempt to explain the background to what possession of *Innere Führung* entails (for further details, see Federal Ministry of Defence 1993, German Bundestag, and McGregor 2006):

First, the organizational structure of the armed forces, the soldier's rights and duties and the way he sees himself must be brought into line with those normative principles which guarantee a certain level of 'democratic adequacy' of the armed forces. Second, the armed forces must be integrated into the system which separates powers in such a manner that civil control or primacy of political authority is guaranteed and self-rule within the armed forces (i.e., 'praetorianism') will have no chance of gaining a foothold. Third, the legal status of the soldier must be a protection against infringement of his human rights. Restrictions on these rights – in case of military necessity – will be determined in accordance with the law. It is not within a commander's province to either grant or limit the fundamental rights of his subordinates. And fourth, every soldier is and remains a 'Citizen in Uniform' or, better, a 'Citizen under Arms'. This description fits the model of a soldier who acts responsibly, demonstrates both competence of moral judgment and the ability to act accordingly, and who sees it as part of his duties to honour established human rights and to show fairness, tolerance and loyalty towards those who take decisions in the name of democracy.

This democracy-orientated model of professional ethics, combined with an ethically reflected soldierly self-image, cannot be guaranteed to work in practice simply through the giving of orders or by threats of sanctions and punishment. The free recognition of, and moral loyalty to, the values and principles of the democratic order constitute the aim of educational processes with the German Forces. Moral loyalty and moral competency of the soldiers cannot be brought about by decree, but are the result of ethical development and a process of ethical reflection.

Since the European Union (EU) adopted a common security strategy at the end of 2003, the question that needs to be answered has been: Can we create a 'European security and defence identity'? In this respect, it seems an obvious first step to draw up a common leadership philosophy for the Union's armed forces, which could be based on *Innere Führung* and the model of the 'Citizen under Arms'. It goes without saying that, if this were to be done, it would be necessary to take account of the different historical backgrounds and political realities in individual EU countries. The development of a common leadership concept should be moved up the agenda for the creation and development of a common Europe. The concept of *Innere Führung* and the model of the Citizen in Uniform or under Arms need to be retained as central elements in the culture of the Bundeswehr and should not be sidelined at a time when it is facing a new range of tasks and when the armed forces of Europe are growing closer to each other.

Ethics Training in the Bundeswehr

The training facilities of the Bundeswehr – the career training courses for officers and NCOs – include no specific subject called 'ethics'. Topics with an ethical content are imparted under the heading of 'Leadership and Civic Education' which is taught as a compulsory subject within officer and NCO training. Instruction on what is understood as the legal basis of the service, the binding rules of law to which all military action must conform, plus historical and political education – these are the central subjects taught under this heading, as detailed below.

The legal education class is concerned with the legal status of the soldier, the limitations set to the authority of command, the soldier's duty of obedience to the existing legal regime and the most important legal requirements of international humanitarian law.

From a moral point of view, and as far as the soldier's obedience to the law is concerned, the law has a subsidiary function; sanctions will be applied only after the agent has failed to abide by the law. Legal sanctions are a last resort, imposed after serious violation of the law. But the imposition of sanctions does not guarantee that the soldier will then start to respect the law and continue to do so. The soldier must also have respect for the *moral* principles which underpin the legal regime. This is particularly important in the area of international humanitarian law. The soldier whose answer to the question 'Why should non-combatants not be killed?' is 'Because this is forbidden by the law' will hardly act in accordance with the law when placed in critical situations. It is important, therefore – and especially during the legal class – to discuss clearly the moral basis of international law insofar as it imposes restrictions on the use of military force. Norms and standards in international law are not just based on mere convention and arbitrary definition, and are not to be upheld and obeyed for purely instrumental reasons.

Historical and political education is aimed at developing and promoting individual willingness to reflect on basic issues of the soldiers' profession, including its political and moral dimensions. Historical education is centred upon a value-orientated and conscious examination of the historical development of military forces in Germany. Political education in the Bundeswehr is compulsory for all soldiers regardless of their rank. The Leadership Development and Civic Education Centre, where I teach, is in the process of developing patterns for instruction along with methodological aids for adult-oriented education projects that deal with subjects like 'Intercultural Competence', 'Dealing with Stress', and 'Dealing with Death and Wounding'.

Apart from the legal classes and the historical and political education, which are the responsibility of military commanders, the establishment of the 'new' German armed forces in 1956 brought about the creation of the so called *Lebenskundlicher Unterricht* ('Character Guidance Training') which has since been in the hands of the military chaplaincy.

In this class, moral aspects and issues regarding service in the armed forces are examined and discussed from a perspective of Christian tradition. The instruction takes place on a regular basis and encompasses enlisted men, NCOs and officers without distinction of rank. For the class, a special curriculum was developed covering a range of topical issues in the field of professional ethics. By dividing up these issues by courses, the idea is to ensure that, during their training, NCOs and officers are given a comprehensive grounding in professional ethics.

The curriculum has four core elements. The first is entitled *Ethics of Peace*. Military leaders should learn how to judge the use of military means from a both ethical and political point of view. The second element is *Leadership Responsibility*. This consists of creating a sensitivity and ability to conduct command and leadership in a responsible and effective way, including virtues like tolerance, fairness and effective communication. The third element is *Conscience and Obedience*. The tension between the two is made clear, ethical limitations regarding obedience are drawn up, and the responsibility of the soldier, regarding both obedience and his disobedience due to the dictates of conscience, are focused on. The fourth and final element is *The Soldier's Profession*. This is characterized by a number of specific moral, physical and psychological 'threats'. Not only is the soldier subject and object for the use of force, but he is also called upon to justify – from the moral point of view – why military force is being used. The possibility of non-justified use of force is something that the soldier must at all times be aware of.

Is it Possible – Anyway – to Teach Ethics?

Ever since the days of ethical reflection in Ancient Greece – up to our own times – moral philosophers have underlined the need for 'ethics' and/or 'virtues' to be taught, whilst knowing at the same time the limitations of the lecture as a means of imparting moral education.

Ethical education is directed towards morally based action, but not in the sense of making or producing it. Moral knowledge cannot be utilized in a technical manner. Many think it is not compatible with the needs of an organization that strives for efficiency and functionality while, at the same time, aiming at a morally worthy objective.

It is these very limits set to the ethical education effort which, in my view, would make it appear reasonable to deal with ethical education and instruction in conjunction with education in other fields, such as law, history and politics, as above.

Quite a few soldiers express a self-image or self-concept, that makes them look upon professional soldiering as 'a dirty business'. Such a self-image is the result of a strictly 'deontological' conception of one's duties that prohibits, without exception, the performance of certain acts. Situations in which the very violation of such commandments would appear necessary and appropriate will then be interpreted as an ethical 'Catch 22' (whatever you do, it will be the wrong thing). You will be guilty regardless.

Professional ethics as a field of instruction must not just provide an introduction into ethical theories, and in no way should it focus or dwell in detail on the intricacies and complexities of competing deontological and teleological justification theories. Instead, the purpose of ethics education is to offer a theoretical understanding of what morals is all about in a way that meets our moral intuitions and at the same time provides help in working out reasonable decisions in times and cases of conflict. All our moral and ethics education is accordingly directed towards developing and promoting abilities, skills, attitudes and personal qualities; all soldierly ethics must be based on inculcating the virtues necessary to be 'a good soldier'.

An ethics of virtue does not ask 'Which action is right?' or 'What should I do?' but rather 'Who should I be?', 'What kind of soldier should I be?' When asking questions like these, we are looking at the soldier's character.

In the individualistic so-called modern world and its societies, questions like 'Who do I want to be? What am I going to do with my life? What is good for me? What am I going to invest my money and my lifetime for?' can be answered in many different ways. One should not conclude from this self-chosen plurality of personal values, virtues and life plans, however, that from now onward normative expectations with regard to professional action are no longer desirable or needed. An ethos tailored to the soldier's profession does not represent an all-comprising value collection that covers all aspects of life, but it is rather a means of orientation, whenever and wherever military action is called for. This in no way contradicts modern-day pluralism. Even in an open and pluralistic society, the picture of the 'good soldier' is by no means vague. And for this reason it must be acknowledged that not every individual conception of what a 'good life' might consist of will be consistent with the soldier's profession.

In the past, soldierly professional ethics have been regularly defined and laid down as a canon of soldierly virtues such as bravery and the willingness to make sacrifices, which are aimed at for their own sake. Military ethics understood in this sense can hardly be distinguished from, say, that of a gang of Mafiosi. For Mafiosi (or terrorists?) may have to show courage in pursuing their criminal or ideological aims and may, in order not to jeopardize group cohesion, adhere to principles of justice and fairness when it comes to distributing the stolen goods.

Virtues are necessary preconditions for correct action but they often do not tell you what is correct, from the moral point of view, in a given situation. The inculcation of competence in moral judgment, expressed in the ability to act in accordance with general moral principles in a purposeful, correct manner constitutes another indispensable aim of ethics education in the military. Imparting an ethics of virtues, along with competence in morally correct judgment – these two go together, complementing each other.

In order to instil and cultivate this competence in ethical decision making, the use of so-called dilemma cases has proved a helpful training aid during ethics classes. From my experience I can say that those cases in which are there are clear conflicts between values and duties are the most useful, as a lead in to consideration of more complex situations in which, under pressure of time or in the face of a dangerous turn, decisions have to be taken quickly. But pedagogical problems are apparent here. A great number of our soldiers are gifted with moral intuitions, allowing them to assess situations and actions from a moral point of view, yet they are seldom able to articulate a justification for their intuitions and judgments (this problem is not, of course, one which affects soldiers alone; it is common in all walks of life). Usually they look upon moral convictions as being more in the nature of religious confessions, and therefore as something of individual concern only; something rather private and beyond the demand of justification.

Yet, in situations of conflict – under conditions of insecurity and uncertainty – soldiers are called upon to accept full (moral) responsibility for and to justify their actions. Thus the commander who has to take an important strategic and tactical decision, whose consequences are often not completely predictable, must abide by and justify his decision. Similarly, the private on guard at a camp, observing a stranger approaching the camp within unknown intentions, has to decide for himself whether or not to use his weapon. He must likewise abide by and justify his decision.

There are and will always be situations where 'acting morally' entails accepting the risk of mistakes and errors of judgment since otherwise no action would be possible in the first place. It is typical of the soldier's profession that such risks, at times, cannot be avoided.

Conclusion

Ethics education in the German military is built upon two core concepts, 'Civic Education and Leadership Development' and its moral image of the 'Citizen under Arms'. Teaching professional ethics is necessary, because the democratic state and democratic society (and, indeed, many soldiers themselves) have certain expectations regarding compliance by soldiers with moral and legal standards and norms. A programme of ethics education which is focused on the acquisition of virtues and the ability to make sound moral judgments will only work in practice if we accept the inevitably contingent nature of our moral lives and the limitations of any attempt to instil morality into those who lack the necessary integrity attendant upon possession of *Innere Führung*.

Bibliography

Federal Ministry of Defence (1993), *Innere Führung: Leadership and Civic Education*, Joint Service Regulation ZDV 10/1 (Bonn: Federal Ministry of Defence).
German Bundestag, *The Principles of Innere Führung*, <http://www.bundestag.de/htdocs_e/parliament/03organs/06armforce/armfor05_2.html>.
McGregor P. (2006), 'The Role of *Innere Führung* in German Civil-Military Relations', *Strategic Insights*, 5:4, April. Available online at <http://www.ccc.nps.navy.mil/si/2006/Apr/mcgregorApr06.asp>.

Chapter 10

Reshaping the Ethical Training of Future French Commissioned Officers

Henri Hude

The Coëtquidan Military Academy in Brittany teaches and trains, on a 20 square mile camp, all future officers of the French land forces, both regular and reserve. Coëtquidan consists of two major units, the Ecole Spéciale Militaire de Saint-Cyr and the Ecole Militaire Interarmes (there is a third, smaller and more recent unit, the Ecole Militaire du Corps Technique et Administratif, whose very name describes its function). At any one time there are about one thousand future officers under training and each year 3,000 more go on training courses elsewhere.

Two-thirds of the Saint-Cyriens (cadets of Saint-Cyr) have been selected through a competitive exam taken after two or three years of hard preparation following successful completion of the baccalauréat, the French equivalent of the English A-Level. They go through two semesters of intensive military training and toughening in the first and last years of their three-year course. It is worth noting that about the half of the ethical training takes place during the first semester, when they are working virtually full-time in the field. There are four academic semesters interspersed between the two military semesters. Two of them are not very different from what would be an ordinary university teaching course; the third is dedicated to writing a long dissertation; the fourth is an international semester, during which cadets are dispersed around the world.

One-third of Saint-Cyriens already have BA or MA degrees. These are exempted from the academic modules but undertake the two military semesters along with their younger comrades. It is also worth noting that within one week of their arrival at the Academy, cadets enter into a contract of service with the Army and are paid €1,000 for the first year. On completion of the second year of their training they cease to be cadets and become commissioned officers, with the rank of second lieutenant.

The cadets of the Ecole Militaire Interarme are former young NCOs, aged 22 to 30 years, who have been selected to receive a commission after two years military and academic training. Most of them only arrive with only A-levels. On the one hand, it may appear inappropriate to deliver the same ethics training to both categories of cadet. On the other hand, all French teenagers who get their A-levels (about 60 per cent of the cohort) have had a one year philosophical training module at school, with a schedule of two to eight hours a week. This is compulsory for all school children. If the work has been done correctly upstream (which is not always the case), the cadets are not completely devoid of any philosophical frame of mind, which can help them greatly when they are faced with ethical problems.

So, what does our ethical training and teaching consist of at Saint-Cyr Military Academy? I will first briefly review the situation as it obtained until 2002: then I will sketch our present system, still a tentative one, incomplete and hardly satisfying. I will conclude by sharing some plans for the future.

The Past

At Saint-Cyr, until 2000, there was no formal teaching or training in ethics. Nevertheless, some subjects, such as 'The Military within the Nation', or 'The Ethics of Serving the State', used to be studied as part of the leadership training, known as FEXA (*Formation à l'EXercice de l'Autorité*).

The example of leaders, the memories and traditions handed down from the elders in Academies (and later on in regiments), and the good form and atmosphere of the group, were supposed to impregnate the young individuals with the due code, standards and values they had to imbibe as warriors of the French Republic. Obviously, life in the community is and will be always an irreplaceable means of cultivating conscience and of handing down values and traditions. Documents regularly issued from high military command reminded the military at large what ideals and norms should be held by 'the moral warrior'. We also had many rows in the past (and they burst out into public debate from time to time) about how to handle insurgencies and terrorism, in Indochina and then in Algiers. Yet a formal training in ethics was not deemed necessary, even if there were sometimes seminars on more specific ethical subjects. For a long time family and school had been permeated either with Christian, mainly Catholic, values, or with strong secular philosophical values, mainly of the Kantian type. In France, both religious and secular people basically agreed about the contents of morality, in spite of referring to different ultimate foundations for morals, and in spite of being often at issue with each other about politics. This situation changed in the 1960s and since then the driving force in French culture has been liberal ethics, tending towards moral relativism, scepticism or even nihilism. Over a span of one generation, a great deal of the religious faith and the greater part of the deep and serious convictions of republican humanism have been wiped out. There is in today's France neither a significant neo-conservative movement, nor any other serious challenge to what could be called dogmatic relativism or sceptical orthodoxy. Or at least, such a movement has not yet begun to emerge, even if in many quarters and in ever greater numbers people are becoming increasingly dissatisfied with the continuing refusal to address important questions about self-regulation and moral education.

In the armed forces, a particular situation has prevailed: France has almost always been willing to play a significant part in world politics, especially as a permanent member of the United Nations Security Council. This has entailed the setting up of significant permanent armed forces, which hold those strong values and virtues without which there cannot be an efficient military. Standards and values which have come to count for little or nothing in civil society have continued to be cultivated, and have to go on being cultivated, in the sphere of the armed forces. Examples of such standards and values are: the primacy of the common good upon the individual; discipline; respect for traditions; selfless commitment; frugality and self-sacrifice. Many cadets, even if they often come from different backgrounds, share a positive appreciation of these values, and enlist in order to live in an institution which embodies such values.

Given the prevailing balance of cultural, social and political forces in France, her political centre of gravity has for many years been situated more leftward than in many other European countries. The military used to arouse suspicions among the left wing, and although anti-militarism has mostly faded away in ordinary people, especially since the suspension of conscription, it still endures in large sections of politically committed people. Those in the military have found it hard to gain acceptance from all their fellow citizens unless they display morally exemplary behaviour and a strong commitment to republican values, as a pledge of their ability to control their supposedly violent tendencies, (curiously, moral laxity in society does not imply moral laxity in the military; the very reverse may be true).

Awareness of the ongoing and unacceptable tensions inherent in such a situation led the heads of the French professional army to address the problems. They undertook a comprehensive review during the years 1998-99 and their findings and recommendations were published in the 'Green Book' report, *L'exercice du métier des armes dans l'Armée de terre: principes et fondements* (*Military Professionalism in the Army: Principles and Foundations*) (État-major de l'Armée de terre 1999).

Two main objectives were identified by the authors of the report. The first was to preserve the fighting power of the armed forces. Since cadets are coming from the civilian world and the values which are necessary to preserving such fighting power are somewhat fading away in civilian society, it was recommended (and the recommendation was subsequently implemented) that there should be additional formal teaching and training specifically aimed at cultivating these values among the cadets. The latter very often subscribe to them theoretically, but fall short of a commitment to putting at least some of them into practice, and they are also very confused about the ethical aspects of practical decision-making.

The second objective was to resurrect and improve communication between society at large and the armed forces. Achieving this objective required two correlative strategies.

The first was aimed at bridging the gap between the military and the civilian, in line with French traditions and the general mood of society, through a sort of *aggiornamiento*, or updating, of the perception of the role of the military profession and the consequent shift in emphasis on the underlying values. This strategy involved emphasizing, for example, the peace enforcing, or peace making, or reconstructing, or state building roles of the military. This, in turn led to a consideration of the relationship between leadership and brotherhood, and between resorting to controlled force and respecting and enhancing human rights.

The second strategy was aimed at exerting an influence throughout society at large, and especially among universities and *grandes écoles* (the French equivalent of competitive universities). The stated aim of the authors was in many ways no more than a reasoned response to the pre-existing needs and requirements of society. We in the military had become increasingly aware of the fact that civilians were (and still are) calling for help from the armed forces (and especially the military academies) in order to assist in the moral education (or re-education) of the nation's youth. After the 2005 autumn riots, President Chirac was prominent in supporting these ideas and policies. Recently, and much more surprisingly, the (then only probable) socialist candidate for the presidential election, Ségolène Royal, added her own support. But this does not necessarily entail putting the soldier on a pedestal and treating him as the best embodiment of citizenship; that might be a self-defeating ploy, leading to a modified version of that same French militarism which caused the problems in the first place.

The Green Book on military ethics was not welcomed by everybody. It became the target of much criticism, mainly from two quarters. Technicians and realists laughed it to scorn, and traditionalists feared it smacked of hard liberal or secular ideology; both suspected it of being infected with the supposed utopianism and impotence of the United Nations.

The Present

Eventually the polemics died away. The new superintendent of Saint-Cyr Military Academy, Major General Bruno Cuche (at the time of writing, Chief of the General Staff (CGS)), in line with the January 2000 CGS directive, decided by the end of 2001 to set up a formal ethics training and teaching programme at Saint-Cyr. From the beginning of 2002, we began to put in place the elements of the present ethics curriculum.

The first element was a full day colloquium on 'human dignity', attended by all cadets of all grades and all academies. The speakers, both military and civilian, did their best to introduce the cadets to the richness of this vast and profound topic, which has proved itself appealing to young consciences. This colloquium was composed of a series of 40-minute seminars, each on a specific topic within the general syllabus. Each conference was followed by a discussion session (also lasting about 40 minutes) in which free questions were posed by the cadets and answered by the speaker. For instance, in April 2005 the topic was 'Human Dignity in Violence and Distress'. We listened, among others, to navy Captain Marin Gillier, from the Special Forces Command, on 'The Officer Facing his Choices', about his experiences in Afghanistan; to Françoise Sironi from the University of Paris on 'Torture: its Mechanisms and Effects on Victims and Torturers'; to the great French reporter Michel Scott on 'The Media and Human Dignity'; and to the famous novelist, now deceased, Vladimir Volkoff, who spoke on 'The

Concept of Victim Abuse: Examples of Disinformation'. Overall, the colloquium worked very well.

The second element, for all the first year cadets, as soon as they had signed their contract with the Army, was a half-day symposium on 'The Meaning of the Military Profession', with a conference, a movie (usually Pierre Schondorfer's excellent *L'honneur d'un capitaine* (*A Captain's Honour*), telling the story of a French captain in Algeria, or the heart-rending Terrence Malick film *The Thin Red Line*), a workshop on questions centred on the idea of their commitment, and briefings in lecture halls in front of the whole year. We used this opportunity to stress the importance of virtues of commitment and sacrifice, to comment on the values expressed by the motto 'liberty, equality, fraternity', and to present and explain the theme and objectives of the Green Book.

The relative success of these first attempts led us to set up, from the 2002–03 academic year, an annual course of five *journées d'éthique*, or 'ethics days', on the following five leading subjects:

- the military within the nation;
- the military character;
- leadership and management;
- moral dilemmas;
- to be faced with death.

This selection was a tentative one, but it shows that we do not sever political issues from ethical ones. Moral values are inextricably linked to the body politic; a society keeps united because the people share at least some basic values and put them into practice. We are concerned to make clear the position of the military within the nation as a whole but under the authority of the political power.

No war waged by a democratic state can be won if the people do not understand what it is all about and if they do not believe that the ensuing sacrifices are worthwhile. The answer to the question 'Why do the strong lose?' (Record 2005–6) is that no technical or logistical superiority can ever be enough to promise and grant victory to a democracy if this democracy cannot make her case – her moral case – in the political international debate. And a critical point for that is to treat the officers, when they are still cadets, not as nobodies but as responsible individuals and citizens, who need to know what their country stands for and what they are really being trained (and training themselves) to fight against. If officers truly believe their country is in the right, not because they just want to do so or because they do not think about it and are not yet under too great a strain, but because they know the cause is just and the argument cogent enough, or even definitely cogent, then the soldiers will follow; their phone calls to the civilians at home will support the morale of the people at large. The ethical value of a fight is a critical element for this public political approval of the war, which is the key point for victory.

Let me return to the 'ethics days'. We prepare them in conjunction with the officers in charge of cadet groups. There is one captain for each group of 25 cadets and each group is led by the same young captain for two years. These young officers are usually among the best, and they are carefully selected. Many apply for Coëtquidan, and most of the few who are accepted have a fine future ahead of them. The cadets admire them and willingly follow their examples. Their role is critical to the fine quality of the training.

During the two weeks before the 'ethics days', I typically hold meetings with ten or 12 of these young captains in a row. They are given a dossier with articles, cases to study, lists of questions, and so on. They ask their questions. They focus on the aim of helping the cadets, developing their understanding of the ethical dimensions of their chosen profession to the point where they become deeply involved with and concerned by the subject.

Then the captains find opportunities for short discussions, make points and suggestions, and encourage reflection. Their seniority and frequently their field experience help them to make cadets understand and appreciate that this is not just an exercise in playing with abstract ideas, but that it has serious and important practical consequences when they are 'in the field'; the success or failure of their future missions might well depend on it. They have to overcome prejudices and to sweep aside clichés in order to clearly conceive what today's operations really are, how complex they are and how the moral element and the ethical side of the matter are crucial for victory. Through this process, the whole group is given a fairly thorough grounding in the subject, the better for the coming 'ethics day'.

During this important day, in the morning, the cadets of the first year are split into groups of eight or nine. Each group discusses a specific problem which has been entrusted to it. They usually talk among themselves, for two hours, from time to time in the presence of their captains (who rarely interfere). They choose a leader, who moderates the discussion, writes key words and leading ideas on the blackboard, and a speaker who will summarize their conclusions when they gather in the lecture hall in the afternoon. I can testify from personal experience that it is working quite well. The cadets realize they are talking about very serious questions with which they are, and will be, concerned and they improve together their resolution to become self-possessed and self-sufficient 'moral warriors'. After the morning debates and before lunch and the afternoon briefings, they gather in the huge lecture hall and listen to a talk delivered by a senior speaker, for instance the coach of the French basketball team, or General Gobillard, who tells of his time in Sarajevo when he was many times blackmailed, facing the threatened shooting of 15 of his men who had been taken prisoner, or the even more callous threat to kill his nephew, the son of his sister, who had been kidnapped by the Serbs. Cadets confidently ask questions of these speakers, and do not mince their words, even with the CGS or the Minister of Defence, who come, not necessarily for the 'ethics days', but often for reasons related to ethics training, as happened during the 2005–06 academic year. These leaders usually address a crowd of about 1,000 cadets.

The end result is that five and a half days during the first semester are devoted to ethics. This means about 40 hours. Apart from these days there are no formal classes for ethics, nor are there exams or grades for this ethical training. Each month, the cadets are supplied with a copy of one dossier on a complementary topic: courage, justice, authority, citizenship, friendship, democracy, liberty, and so on. The cadets are supposed to read and study it, and to write a one or two page commentary, to be read and corrected by the captains. But as everybody is very busy and tired during the demanding first military semester, rarely getting a full night's sleep, the inevitable consequence is that most of them do not do this work. Sanctions are rarely imposed; the captains do not see the work as a top priority. Some of these dossiers have been collected into one volume (Hude 2004), which has been awarded the French Academy Montyon Prize, but this volume is too difficult for the boys and girls and wisely it has been shifted into a textbook for more advanced readers, including candidates applying for entrance to the war college. Would it be possible and fruitful to propose a teaching plan more structured, compulsory, and controlled? The pro and cons of this question are still being discussed.

When Major General Cuche left Saint-Cyr, his successor, Major General Coulloume-Labarthe acted with great vigour in pushing for reforms along these very lines. He kept the same basic lesson-plan, but decided to reshape the whole curriculum completely. His audacious plan was to start with the ethics training element and then build up the remainder of the curriculum around it. In fact, the major flaw of the Academy was a divorce between the academic teaching and the human and military training. Too many cadets hated academics at large, not because they were dumb, but because it was difficult for them to see the link between their studies and their living interests, their future missions or their ideals. As a result, many officers got out of the Academy with a mix of prejudice against intellectual work and an inferiority complex. Major General Coulloume-Labarthe undertook to cure these ills. He decided to reorganize the whole curriculum around three core areas (ethics, politics and tactics) and to produce a fully integrated whole. He saw these three core subjects as embodying the following values and having the following functions:

- *Politics*: a good and effective officer involved in a military operation abroad has to see clearly what the political aim of such an operation is. He must be able to explain it to his men even if he is not always completely in agreement with such a policy.
- *Ethics*: a policy means little or nothing for a soul if it is all about material assets. A citizen and an honourable person will not willingly commit himself to his duty and put his life at risk if the issue is not about values and the common weal of mankind. Enthusiasm disappears if we feel called only to serve a cynical state and a selfish people. Moreover, the military profession is hard and complex. The officer in puzzling and stressing situations must find out and know the right thing to do, and has to call up all his or her inner strengths to be able to do this right thing. Ethics, according to us, means the study, meditation and cultivation of the values which are the end of a good or well framed society, the rules of right action and the moral forces making it possible to know and to do the right thing (in days gone by such forces were called virtues).

- *Tactics*: in spite of such ethical and political preparation, the officers will obviously not be completely prepared for their job unless they have been physically, technically and tactically trained.

In our Academy, therefore, careful and reflective employment of the social sciences should help us to clarify what our French policy was, is and should be. Ethics is not taught as an academic discipline, but as the art of building one's character and of becoming strong enough to decide upon and do the right thing in any situation.

Major General Coulloume-Labarthe has founded two centres: the 'Centre for Military Ethics' and the 'Centre for European Politics'. Our Centre for Military Ethics is a very recent creation, founded 14 October 2004, after two years of informal operation. Major General Coulloume-Labarthe's successor, Brigadier General de Lardemelle will in due course found the third centre (the 'Centre for Tactics').

The Future

What I have outlined so far has certainly progressed beyond theory, but is still far from being a fully worked out reality. Our primary concern, for the next academic years, is to complete our programme.

We are not able to afford both a numerous military staff for supervising the cadets and a civilian one for teaching a complete course of ethics. We have therefore deemed it advisable to train the trainers. We will try to reach an agreement with a French university to grant the captains trained in ethics a master's degree in 'ethics, strategy and management of human resources'. This will be useful for their further careers, whether military or civilian, and no doubt will strongly motivate them and give them, when dealing with the cadets, the qualification and confidence to supplement their example, experience and conviction with knowledge and arguments.

Today, the ethics training is concentrated during the first year, half of it during the first military semester. We hope to provide in coming years more such training, during the second military semester, i.e. the sixth and last one in the cadets' course at the Academy. This last semester would be more centred on the study of particular cases. I am not really satisfied with the way these 'ethics days' are contrived today. Without losing the positive aspect of the present formula, we should also help the cadets to build a more structured body of basic concepts and principles, such as the logic of decision making and just war doctrine. In order to achieve such results, we need to train the captains and to find some workable scheme of study and of production of written work, the better to control and monitor the student's progress in the acquisition of skills. Otherwise, I fear many cadets will only half listen and any lessons learned will soon be forgotten.

We also need handbooks fit for the captains, both anthologies and casebooks. When I attended the Joint Services Conference on Professional Ethics in Springfield, Virginia in January 2006 and visited the US Naval Academy, I was very pleased to find existing books (e.g. Lucas and Rubel 2006), quite good examples to imitate, taking into account the difference of policies and traditions.

This work cannot, and should not, be a nationally self centred one; we have to work closely with the military training establishments of other countries. The paradox of the life of any just warrior is that he claims to fight for peace. World peace is the first element of the common weal of mankind. That is why there is no just war without an intention to prudently use force in order to keep or to make peace. The problems our common humanity has to cope with are dreadfully difficult to solve even in peace, and are probably insoluble in or through war. The military today is, at least in a reasonably just country, a means for producing world peace, in cooperation with the militaries of other countries; such peace is an unavoidable prerequisite of human development and progress. But this international military cooperation requires us to reach an international understanding of, and harmony on, ethical issues. Creating awareness of, and respect for, such harmony is probably, after the training of our young people, the most valuable contribution we can hope to make to the common good.

Our centre for military ethics is therefore primarily concerned with international cooperation, first with our traditional allies but also with other nations; we would be delighted to send each year perhaps six cadet-officers, for their semester abroad, to the centres for military ethics of other countries. I suggest we could also take advantage of video-conferencing to organize from time to time fruitful conversations between cadets of various academies.

As a pledge of our commitment to international cooperation, we managed to hold in Saint-Cyr last November an international conference on military ethics ('The Ethical Problems posed by Asymmetric Conflicts') with senior speakers coming from the UK, the United States, Israel, Palestine and Hungary.

Apart from undertaking the improvement of the training and education in the Academies, our centre has been called to play a part in the life of the military institution as a whole, or at least as an educational institution. This came about through an issue I would like to briefly summarize.

When formal ethical training was introduced I heard criticisms from various quarters in the armed forces, as if ethics was only a brake on a heavy fighting machine which had already to overcome many frictions, such as fear and human weaknesses. Did not this machine really need an accelerator rather than a brake? It did indeed. Ethics was therefore to be welcomed; it is not a burden holding the military back, but a force, a moral force, pushing it forward. ('The moral dimension of fighting power', as Major General Sebastian Roberts put it (Roberts 1998)). Resolution, efficiency and toughness are required, not complexes and inhibitions.

Both sides in this argument were in fact partly right; the common interest required a synthesis. 'Man is neither an angel, nor a beast', as Pascal wrote. We therefore republished an old 1922 textbook on *les forces morales* ('moral force'). An informal dialogue then took place around this text. The outcome of the reflection was a conclusion that ethics is traditionally about virtue and that moral force can be an important factor in the inculcation of virtue.

Another task has therefore just been entrusted to the Saint-Cyr centre for military ethics. We have been called to carry out a fresh study of *les forces morales*, the inculcation of which is important in society at large, not just in the military. We have a mandate, given by the COFAT (Land Forces Military Training Command), to prepare a text on this topic for the new CGS.

So what is it all about? As the reflection on ethical training in the military was going on, we were becoming increasingly aware of the fact that ethics was not only an item of the whole curriculum, let alone a marginal one, but was at the very core of the military profession, an essential part of the architectonic structure of military education. We perceive ethics as being centrally involved with the cultivation of the moral forces, including the cultivation of what tradition called 'prudence', i.e. the strength, both intellectual and moral, to find out 'the right thing to do'.

This mandate to study moral forces – moral powers – is a mandate to formulate the basics of an ethically based philosophy of military education. The mandate stipulates that we should do this job as far as possible in close cooperation with civilian experts and also foreign experts and institutions dedicated to such topics. Such will be the contribution of the Saint-Cyr Academy centre for military ethics to military doctrine. Is it not the duty of any responsible country to cooperate in shaping common rules for the common fight for the common weal?

Bibliography

Bachelet, J.-R. (2006), *Pour une éthique du métier des armes: vaincre la violence* (*Towards an Ethic for the Military: Vanquishing Violence*), preface by Max Gallo (Paris: Vuibert).

Canto-Sperber, M. (2005), *Le bien, la guerre et la terreur: Pour une morale internationale* (*The Good, War and Terror: Towards an International Morality*) (Paris: Plon).

Brodeur, J.-P. (2000), 'Ethique policière, militaire et pénitentiaire' ('Police, Military and Prison Service Ethics'), *Revue Ethique Publique* 2:1, 157–76.

Écoles de Coëtquidan, Pôle d'éthique/ILO-Universitas Program (2006a), *Ethique et Sports; Dignité au travail et forces morales* (*Ethics and Sport: Dignity at Work and Moral Force*), seminar held 15 December 2006.

Écoles de Coëtquidan, Pôle d'éthique (2006b), Military ethics conference, *Les problèmes éthiques posés par les conflits asymétriques* (*Ethical Problems in Asymmetric Warfare*), 24/25 November 2005.

Écoles Militaires de Coëtquidan, DFE, FEXA (late 1990s), *Prise en compte du facteur humain dans le relation de commandement, Séminaire de psychosociologie* (*Taking Account of the Personal Element in Positions of Authority; Seminar on Social Psychology*).

État-major de l'Armée de terre (1999), *L'exercice du métier des armes dans l'Armée de terre: fondements et principes* (*Military Professionalism in the Army: Foundations and Principles*), <http://www.ac-versailles.fr/defense/pistes_ethique_fondements.pdf>.

Hude, H. (2004), *L'éthique des décideurs* (*Ethics for Decision Makers*) (Paris: Presses de la Renaissance).

Lucas, G.R and Rubel, R. (eds) (2006), *Ethics and the Military Profession: The Moral Foundations of Leadership* (Boston, MA: Pearson and Longman).

Record, J. (2005–6), 'Why the Strong Lose?', *Parameters* 35:4, 16–31.

Roberts, S. (1998), *Soldiering, the Military Covenant*, <www.army.mod.uk/servingsoldier/usefulinfo/valuesgeneral/adp5>.

Chapter 11

The Ethics Curriculum at the Netherlands Defence Academy, and Some Problems with its Theoretical Underpinnings

Peter Olsthoorn

Introduction

The question of what someone would do if he or she were invisible has been a recurring theme from Plato's tale of Gyges' ring to Paul Verhoeven's movie *Hollow Man* (2000). Both Gyges and the main character of the movie, scientist Sebastian Caine, seem to prove the truth of John Locke's words from the seventeenth century: 'View but an army at the sacking of a town, and see what observation or sense of moral principles, or what touch of conscience for all the outrages they do. Robberies, murders, rapes, are the sports of men set at liberty from punishment and censure' (Locke 1971, I: ii, 9). Locke's belief that man has no innate moral principles made him value something that we today would call a conventional ethic: people generally behave well, but mainly because they are sensitive to peer pressure and concerned about how their behaviour might look in the eyes of others. This visibility that conventional ethics depends on is also its Achilles heel: morality is potentially reduced to a matter of not being caught.

Most ethicists today are therefore probably not too upset that conventional ethics gave way to more demanding forms of ethics, giving central place to the notion of autonomy. People are to be just from a love for justice, not from a fear of losing face, and it is therefore generally seen as a moral improvement that we, contrary to our predecessors, live in a 'guilt culture' rather than in a 'shame culture'. In most military ethics training and education programmes, and the ethics curriculum at the Netherlands Defence Academy (NLDA) is an example, it is virtue ethics and deontological or rule-based ethics, both requiring some form of 'right intention', that are used most often, while there seems to be a general 'agreement that utilitarian ethics do not work well in the military setting' (Bonadonna 1994, 18).

This chapter serves two purposes. The first is to outline ethics education at the NLDA, starting with a few words on the changed context, and then turning to the ethics curriculum. The second is to focus on some problems that follow from a precept shared by both virtue ethics and deontological ethics (probably shaping the ethics education in most military institutions, including the NLDA, as its underlying predisposition is common to most ethicists): namely judge by the intention, not by the action.

The Context of the Ethics Curriculum at the NLDA

As at other institutions, the ethics curriculum of the NLDA has in recent years adjusted to the changed environment the Dutch armed forces are working in, and some remarks on this altered context are appropriate. As happened to most militaries in the West, the core tasks of the Dutch armed forces were redefined after the collapse of the Soviet empire and the diminished threat of a large-scale conflict in Europe, shifting from the classical task of the defence of the home territory and the NATO-treaty area to the control of international crises in the broadest sense, from peacekeeping to peace enforcement. This dual task of peacekeeping and peace enforcing operations, as well as contributing to Europe's safety, provided the direction for restructuring the armed forces: the organization had to be adapted to be able to participate in peacekeeping operations, resulting in the rejection of military hardware in favour of a greater capacity for deployment. The Dutch armed forces have to be capable of participating for a limited time in a peace enforcement operation with a brigade or its equivalent (e.g. a maritime task group, three squadrons of fighter aircraft, or a combination of these units), or in a maximum of three sustained, simultaneous, peace-related operations involving contributions at battalion level or its equivalent (e.g. a squadron of fighter aircraft or two frigates). At the same time, the Netherlands wants to maintain sufficient reserve strength to defend the NATO-treaty area in a major conflict.

In spite of these ambitions, the Dutch armed forces have had to face several reductions, leaving them with roughly half the amount of personnel compared to the heyday of the Cold War. Notwithstanding these reductions, the armed forces are now better prepared for peacekeeping operations, and they can sustain them for a considerable time. The downside to this structural change is that it is now even more difficult to contribute to a traditional force capable of fighting a major conflict.

Threats like a large-scale war are not considered likely to happen in the near future. In the meantime, the other tasks – humanitarian assistance, peacekeeping, peace enforcing (advancing international rule of law and stability) and assisting civil authorities – have gained importance. As a result, it is to a large extent uncertain where, when, with whom, under what circumstances and for what task the units of our armed forces will be deployed in the future. What is certain, however, is that the tasks of protecting territorial integrity and of promoting international law are beginning to merge into each other because of the emergence of terrorism. Hence, operations are being conducted further from home and often last for years; units must be prepared for operations across the entire spectrum of possibilities (see in particular Wijk 2004).

When conducting peace support operations, the Netherlands armed forces try to practice something labelled (by the Dutch themselves) as 'the Dutch approach' (see also Onishi 2004), that is to say: non-threatening, culturally aware, transparent, making minimal use of force, mutually respectful, and firm but friendly with the local population. This approach is thought to yield better information and more cooperation from the residents, and thus increased security for the troops. The ethics curriculum is designed within the framework of this approach.

Ethics Education at the NLDA

The NLDA trains officers for the Royal Netherlands Army, Air Force, Constabulary (*Marechaussee* in Dutch) (all in Breda) and Navy (in Den Helder). Students, who in most cases just left high school and are about 18 years old, can opt for either the short (one year) or long (four year) curriculum, the latter one possibly perceived as enhancing the chances of a long career, ending in the higher strata. The four-year curriculum consists of about six months of military training at both the start and the end, and three years of academic education in the middle. As for the academic part, the Academy switched to the bachelor-master degree system in 2003, in line with civilian higher education. As a result, part of the curriculum enjoys academic recognition; the complete curriculum should have academic recognition by 2008 or 2009. The cadets and midshipmen, as the trainee officers who take the longer route are called, study for bachelor's degrees in Management, War Studies, or one of three technical majors (the major 'chosen' depends to a large extent on the chosen branch; most Army and Air Force cadets choose Management or War Studies, the Constabulary always follows Management, while Navy midshipmen in most cases choose the technical majors). After finishing their studies at the NLDA, the students can enrol in a university to obtain their master's degrees.

The courses given and the textbooks used at the NLDA are in general designed in support of the expeditionary task of the military, and the same holds true for the lectures, courses and dilemmas in the ethics curriculum. Aims, assumptions and basic outlines of the ethics education are laid down in *Military Ethics* and the accompanying *Practice Book Military Ethics* (both have appeared in English in a single abridged and updated volume (van Baarda and Verweij 2006)). These two books are primarily aimed at those responsible for training in military training centres and the NLDA. In them, it is stated that the ethics curriculum aims to contribute to the future officer's moral competence (assumed it can be developed) at cognitive, affective and volitional levels. More specifically, this means that moral questions should be recognized as such, and not merely as practical problems; this requires the ability to recognize and analyze moral problems. It also means that military personnel should be open-minded, being able to see both sides of the situation. Finally, moral convictions should be so central to one's identity that one also acts upon them (ibid., 14–18).

Ethics is not a course in itself, but part of different courses taught at the NLDA, and, in combination with a course on the philosophy of science, adds up to a programme called 'Philosophy and Ethics'. As a starter, a three day Academic Introduction for the first-year students has recently been developed, and it is now given at the very beginning of the academic curriculum in both Breda and Den Helder (as the first year for every aspirant-officer taking the academic route is the same). It should mark the transition from military training to a more studious life and proves the importance attached to ethics, in that it has a major ethics component of about one and a half days, which integrates the different elements of ethics that used to be given in the first year. In this Academic Introduction, students are given lectures on 'the importance of ethics' and on 'courage'. Subsequent to these two lectures, students are presented with a dilemma based on a real-life incident in a military context and are asked, in groups of about seven, to write a short paper applying the appropriate theory (Kohlberg, virtue vs. deontological ethics, etc.) to find a resolution of the dilemma. In a subsequent course on Management, about two months after the Academic Introduction, students are lectured on, and read a chapter on, organizational ethics.

In their second year, students majoring in Management or War Studies attend the course 'Military Leadership and Ethics', the *pièce de résistance* of the ethics curriculum. The first part of the course is mainly (but not exclusively) on leadership, although ethical issues are addressed; the course starts, for instance, with a meeting at which the television documentary *Four Hours in My Lai* (1989) is shown and discussed. The remainder of the first part of the course consists of seven meetings (in classes of about 15 students), discussing the compulsory reading for that week, sometimes using some video material. The second part of the course, mainly devoted to the subject of military ethics, involves a lot more in the way of student participation than the first part. At each meeting a group of three or four students has to give a presentation on the required reading. Areas under discussion are, among other things: obedience, courage, moral disengagement, leadership vs. management, and responsibility (see appendix for the set readings on these topics). At the end of the course, they have to submit a paper applying what they have learnt on the case of Srebrenica. For instance: was the mission in Srebrenica realistic, and what should a commander do when he gets an impossible order? Did Dutch military personnel show (a lack of) courage when the Serbs invaded Srebrenica? Were there instances of Dutch military personnel misbehaving in Srebrenica, and what can a commander do to prevent his men from committing war crimes? Was the leadership in Srebrenica effective, and what can the organization do to improve the quality of leadership? To what extent are political and military decision-makers responsible (in the juridical and moral meaning of the word) for what happened? On the whole, the course seems to work, the second, interactive part probably somewhat more so than the first part. In the near future, this course will be updated, with the Srebrenica case probably dropped in favour of a more recent one drawn from events in either Afghanistan or Iraq.

In the third year, students majoring in Management have a meeting on 'integrity', as a part of a course on Human Resource Management (comparing a narrow 'compliance strategy' with a broader 'integrity strategy'). In addition, those majoring in Management and opting for the minor Accounting and Control must follow an 'integration ethics course' in which students have to undertake a small research in the field of organizational ethics, aimed at enhancing both methodological skill and knowledge of the subject of organizational ethics. Independent of their major of choice, all students take an optional subject in the final phase of their education, one option being the course 'Perspectives on Violence' that includes literature on the history of warfare, causes of aggression (with literature by Freud and Fromm), and human rights.

As a general rule, students at the NLDA are interested in ethics, and they hold the topic to be important, especially as they expect to be sent abroad after their education, possibly getting some first hand experiences with ethical dilemmas. This probably explains why they have a preference for discussing real life problems, preferably leading to one best solution. They are often somewhat less interested in abstract ethical theory, for instance going into the relative merits of virtue ethics and deontological ethics, and do not want to be bothered too much with long-dead thinkers such as Aristotle or Kant. Nonetheless, the ethics curriculum consists not only of discussing practical problems, but also of studying ethical theory to underpin these discussions.

Theoretical Underpinnings

It is not always completely clear who, to borrow Martin Cook's phrase, 'owns the curriculum'; most courses are given by ethicists and philosophers, but some parts (for instance the Integration Course Business Ethics) are given by lecturers from the management department. Nonetheless, the curriculum does seem to have a 'focus': although students have to be familiar with different approaches in ethics, the emphasis is on virtue ethics.

This should be no surprise: parallel to the renewed interest over the past two decades in virtues in ethics literature, military virtues are now more in the spotlight than they used to be in military ethics (see e.g. Toner 2000; Bonadonna 1994; French 2003; Osiel 1999; Westhusing 2003). A virtue is usually described as a trait of character, not to be understood as an inherited or god-given quality, but as something that can be acquired, mainly through training and practice. References are often made to Aristotle's *Nicomachean Ethics*, where a virtue is defined as a disposition of character, to be developed by practising virtuous acts, and occupying the middle ground between excess and deficiency, springing from a noble intention, and serving a morally just cause. This latter element is important for Aristotle: by definition, a virtue cannot serve an unethical end, nor can it be motivated by the desire for money or glory, or by the wish to avoid punishment or disgrace. Virtue should be its own reward. In other words: courage is defined as the middle position between rashness and cowardice, to be developed by practising courageous acts, and springing from the right attitude concerning feelings of confidence and fear in the pursuance of (and motivated by) an honourable cause. This Aristotelian view on virtues is still pivotal in many texts on military ethics dealing with the subject, and it has been argued that Aristotelean virtue ethics, with its emphasis on character building, provides a better basis for military ethics than rule-based, deontological ethics or utilitarian ethics, stressing self-interest, even though the Aristotelian requirement that virtue should serve a noble end is problematic, an issue which will be dealt with in the next section.

In the literature used at the NLDA, virtue ethics is presented to the students as being better suited to the military profession than rule-based ethics. The reading material used in the Academic Introduction is for instance more generous to virtue ethics than to deontological ethics. In line with this, the literature for the second-year course 'Military Leadership and Ethics' contains a text on virtue ethics vs. rule-based ethics, which expresses a preference for the former, mainly on the ground that rule-based ethics aims at no more than the ethical minimum, whereas virtue ethics asks for a lot more. In a chapter from the same course, the authors of *Military Ethics* present virtue ethics-based formation of character as the best way to prevent war crimes by military personnel. International law, standard operating procedures and values imposed by the organization are for different reasons deemed less optimal instruments, mainly because these try to condition behaviour, leaving less room for personal integrity. The chapter on courage in the same book follows Aristotle's account of courage quite closely and, in general, the chapter stresses the importance of virtue ethics for the military profession.

It is not all virtue ethics, however. The works of Lawrence Kohlberg and John Rawls are deemed important and useful, especially on the topic of moral development, and *Military Ethics* covers them quite extensively, yet at the same time the book is realistic about both the level of moral development most personnel are on, as well as the progress that can be made.

Both Kohlberg and Rawls are adherents of rule-based ethics, the main alternative to virtue ethics, inspired by the works of Immanuel Kant, and do not see much of a role for traits of character. Rule-based ethics stress the importance of universal, categorically binding moral norms. It asks us to follow these moral rules against our natural (selfish) inclinations, where virtue ethics call for the development of good inclinations: we are virtuous when doing the right thing gives us pleasure. The philosophy of autonomy is sometimes considered less apt for the military because, with its emphasis on rules and duty, it supposedly does not invite the kind of supererogatory acts the military depends on. Rule-based ethics allegedly aims at no more than at the ethical minimum, whereas virtue ethics asks for a lot more. However, although asking no one to go beyond the call of duty, this main alternative to virtue ethics does require quite a lot of military men and women: moral duties are to be followed, not because they are imposed from the outside and are backed by sanctions, but because they accept them by choice, requiring quite an amount of altruism and an universalistic outlook. Despite the popularity of virtue ethics, this view still has its advocates: in a recent plea for educating military personnel to be morally autonomous, based on the work of Kant, Susan Martinelli-Fernandez states that 'it is the mark of a morally mature agent to conform to moral principles voluntarily and for their own sake' (Martinelli-Fernandez 2006, 55–6). Normative rules that are followed because of rewards and punishment will often not suffice, because rules are then not followed when no one is around.

Lawrence Kohlberg's influential model of moral development (Kohlberg 1981) is paradigmatic for this line of thought and widely used by military ethicists, including in Dutch curriculum. According to this three level (and six stage) model, people are egoistic and calculating at the pre-conventional level, the one thing keeping them from misbehaving being their fear of punishment. Once at the conventional level, they are also sensitive to peer pressure (at the first stage of this level) and the norms of society (at the second stage), and concerned about their reputation. Adherence to universal principles is deemed the highest, post-conventional or 'principled' level. Kohlberg (who, by the way, denounced virtue ethics as a 'bag of virtues approach') mentions Gandhi and Martin Luther King as examples of the post-conventional level.

One military ethicist recently described Kohlberg's model, with its emphasis on the morally autonomous individual, as 'troublesome' in the military context (Toner 2000, 56–7). Inside the military, as is the case elsewhere, most individuals are stuck at the second, conventional level, but most soldiers perhaps function often at the first stage of this level, possibly more inclined to conform to the norms of their peers than to the norms of society. This seems not to have diminished Kohlberg's popularity among military ethicists; the same author who called the Kohlberg model troublesome for the military maintains that the moral education in the armed forces should nonetheless aim at reaching a higher 'Kohlberg stage' (cf Gerhard Kümmel: 'The soldier will have to develop ... some sort of humanitarian cosmopolitanism that exists besides feelings of patriotism' (Kümmel 2003, 432)).

In line with both virtue ethics and rule-based ethics, the importance of 'right intention' is stressed on several occasions in the literature used at the NLDA: in the chapter on courage in the course book *Armed Forces and Society* students read that military personnel should study the writings of Martha Nussbaum and Amartya Sen in order to develop a more altruistic, universalistic outlook. Although this latter remark is probably a bit too optimistic, the point that a moral act should come from a right intention to deserve that predicate is probably something that is elemental in most ethics education in the military, whether the emphasis is on virtue ethics or rule-based ethics.

The remainder of this article deals with the problems that follow from a policy of judging behaviour by intention.

Two Problems

Although in many ways different, the two dominant strands of thought in military ethics, virtue ethics and rule-based ethics, both stress the importance of 'right intention', implying that good conduct should not be a result of peer pressure, fear of punishment or concern for reputation, nor of a desire for praise, esteem or approbation. There are two possible problems here. First, this might set the bar too high. The decision to join the military is, according to some, to a considerable extent motivated by post-traditional reasons such as salary and the longing for adventure, and not by the wish to further morally worthy goals, for instance freedom and democracy (see Janowitz 1960 and Cafario 2003). Similarly, in actual combat, patriotism and abstract ideals do not seem to be the motivating factor (see Stouffer et al. 1949 and Wong et al. 2003). It is probably a bit too optimistic to think that the global village will be the kind of community that soldiers are willing to run risks for.

The second problem is that military men and women actually have little to say about the causes they are fighting for. Even though Aristotle maintained, and most contemporary ethicists maintain, that acts are only laudable insofar they serve a morally just cause (see e.g. Toner 2000, 111–14), in general soldiers are instruments of politics, and do not necessarily subscribe to the causes they are fighting for. In fact, they do not have a say in what these causes are, nor do they want to have a say in such matters. In theory, it is and should be irrelevant to the professional soldier whether he is sent abroad to spread freedom and democracy, or for more base reasons such as oil or electoral success. On the other hand, '[n]o political leader can send soldiers into battle, asking them to risk their lives and to kill other people, without assuring that their cause is just – and that of their enemies unjust.' Modern princes 'work hard to satisfy their subjects of the justice of their wars; they "render reasons", though not always honest ones' (Walzer 1992, xi–xii and 39).

Clearly, there is a discrepancy here; what should motivate military men according to most military ethicists (from both the deontological and the virtue ethic schools) – i.e. working for morally just causes – is not always the same as what really makes them tick, nor is it what should concern them according to what is considered to be normal civil-military relations nowadays. In practice, armies have found a way to close this gap between theory and practice by using social cohesion and peer pressure as motivators (see also Osiel 1999, 212–13), thus making irrelevant the fact that abstract causes do little to motivate or are not of the soldier's own choosing. Working with peer pressure as a motivator, however, also means falling back on a form of conventional ethics which most of today's ethicists hold in contempt. Even so, in spite of the military ethicist's misgivings, both the training and organization are aimed at enlarging cohesion (see Keegan 1993, 53 and 72–3). Unfortunately, armed forces have thus far not paid too much attention to the drawbacks of the conventional ethics that result from stimulating social cohesion.

Drawbacks of Conventional Ethics

From the ethicist's point of view, one objection is that a virtuous act undertaken for fear of losing face hardly deserves to be called moral, and so the term seems somewhat out of place in such a case. On a more practical level we see that conventional ethics may even be reduced to a matter of 'not being caught'. In that case, when no one is around, everything is permitted – a downside already mentioned in the introduction. Another possible objection is that conventional ethics further physical courage yet do not invite moral courage (the type of courage often condemned by peers) which is in today's military is probably needed as often as physical courage.

The recent wars in Afghanistan and Iraq excluded, peacekeeping and humanitarian missions are becoming the core business of most of the militaries in the Western world, and it seems that troops who are trained for combat can experience difficulties in adjusting to less aggressive ways of working needed to win 'the hearts and minds' of local populations after major combat is over. In these new operations we sometimes see that the group cohesion this peer pressure depends on can lead to the kind of in-group favouritism that is dangerous to the people the military are supposed to protect, as well as to the conformism (or lack of moral courage) that can bring people to keep silent about any misbehaviour. Possibly, that which can be a factor contributing to the success of the initial phase of an operation might be an obstacle in stabilizing and rebuilding a country. In other words: efforts at further increasing group cohesion make sense from a war-winning perspective, but might be detrimental from a peace-building prospect. Stressing cohesion too much could be at odds with an open approach such as the Dutch military endorses.

Possible Solutions to These Drawbacks

Some solutions to these problems are now offered. First, military education should not only be aimed at group cohesion, but also at group members being able to develop relations with people outside the own group (see Soeters 2007). Although research into the behaviour of US military personnel in Somalia suggested that non-homogeneous units, i.e. including gender and ethnically diverse personnel, often do a better job in this than homogeneous groups do (see Segal and Kestnbaum 2002, 445), the need for cohesion has in fact been used over the last decades as an argument for closing the military to, respectively, ethnic minorities, women, and homosexuals.

Second, and on a more fundamental level, it is necessary that norms are internalized: the actual presence of others is no longer needed, the gaze of 'imaginary others' suffices for them to function. Although this idea of 'internalization' tackles most of the drawbacks of conventional ethics, it also brings it closer to Aristotelian and Kantian accounts of morality; it somewhat resembles the solution of the ethicist stating that moral education should aim at reaching a higher 'Kohlberg stage'. One might wonder how realistic this is. On the other hand, even in paradigmatic shame cultures, shame is to a certain degree internalized (see Williams 1993, 81–2).

Third, and most importantly, although it might look as if social cohesion fosters anything from overly warrior-like behaviour to overzealous protection, in general not the sort of behaviour that gives a central place to the interests of the local population, one has to bear in mind that social cohesion in itself does not make unethical behaviour more likely to occur; the opposite can equally be the case. It all depends on what the culture of the dominant group in question endorses (see Osiel 1999, 227–9). From this viewpoint, conventional ethics itself might be part of the solution. It only works, however, if such a conventional ethic consists in more than how the behaviour will look in the eyes of the group members, and also has some substantive content, for instance in the form of a standard or a code with do's and don'ts. Although such a standard or code makes it more demanding, it is still much less demanding than an ethic based on abstract notions such as human rights, freedom, and dignity (see Ignatieff 1997, 6).

Conclusion

All things considered, the ethics curriculum at the NLDA is fairly comprehensive for those who follow the Management or War Studies major, but the great majority of midshipmen who follow the technical majors are considerably less well off (as least as far as ethics education is concerned); for undisclosed reasons their ethics education, as part of their academic training, is limited to what happens in the first year, which is one-and-a-half days of ethics training during the Academic Introduction. Missing (and this is probably due to the wish to be practical) is anything substantial on just war theory. What is also missing is a good *student* textbook, or books, since *Military Ethics* and the *Practice Book Military Ethics* are primarily aimed at those responsible for the *teaching* of ethics (though they are nonetheless prescribed as reading material at different moments during the education at the NLDA).

On a more theoretical plane, there are some problems concerning the feasibility of what ethics training is trying to teach, both at the NLDA and elsewhere. These problems are inherent in the two schools in ethics that dominate most ethics curricula, namely virtue ethics and rule-based ethics, both stressing the importance of right intention. On the one hand, the subject matter of ethics is how people *ought* to behave, and not how they actually *do* behave; yet, on the other hand, 'any persuasive account of what makes men willing to fight ethically must be compatible with a more general account of what makes them willing to fight at all' (Osiel 1999, 202). It is a commonplace that one should separate 'is' from 'ought', but a military ethics that does not take men's actual motives into account seems a bit too academic. For the educating of ethics such an overly academic approach would, first, mean that the education would be ineffective and, second, that the above-mentioned drawbacks of social cohesion would go unattended.

So, perhaps we should be somewhat less stringent, accepting that insistence on 'right intention' is too ambitious. This would mean aiming a bit lower, no longer going for higher Kohlberg levels. This in turn implies accepting that moral rules are followed, not because they are moral, but because not following them brings disesteem, and that virtues are practised, not out of a love of virtue *per se*, but because virtuous conduct is rewarded with praise, esteem and approbation (Osiel takes this approach; see Osiel 1999 passim). Such an approach would be somewhat less demanding, and, contrary to the approach stressing the right intention, has the advantage of being consistent with military training and organization outside the ethics curriculum.

The objection that a good action undertaken for considerations of reputation does not in every respect deserve the predicate moral will not be satisfactory resolved. Abandoning the requirement of the right intention definitely falls short of the ideals put forward by Aristotle, Kant and Kohlberg; from their point of view, settling for conventional ethics would mean settling for a 'lesser' level of moral development. This objection is something probably only ethicists are bothered by; for those at the receiving end, in for instance Iraq and Afghanistan, it probably does not matter a lot. As outlined above, there are some other drawbacks that do have real consequences, and which are especially troublesome in today's missions that hardly resemble the wars of the past. The solution to these shortcomings lies not in trying to teach soldiers to rise above the conventional level, but probably has to be found within its framework. In the absence of more altruistic motives, that might be our best bet.

Bibliography

Bonadonna, R.R. (1994), 'Above and Beyond: Marines and Virtue Ethics', *Marine Corps Gazette* 78:1, 18–20.

Cafario, G. (2003), 'Military Officer Education', in C. Guiseppe (ed.), *Handbook of the Sociology of the Military*.

Deb, B. (1997), 'The Anatomy of Courage,' *Army Quarterly and Defence Journal* 127: 403–6.

de Wijk, R. (2004), 'Defensiebeleid in relatie tot veiligheidsbeleid' ('Defence Policies in Relation to Security Policies'), in E.R. Muller et al. (eds), *Krijgsmacht: Studies over de organisatie en het optreden*.

French, S.E. (2003), *The Code of the Warrior* (Lanham, MD: Rowman and Littlefield).

Guiseppe, C. (ed.) (2003), *Handbook of the Sociology of the Military* (New York: Kluwer Academic).

Ignatieff, M. (1997), *The Warrior's Honour* (New York: Metropolitan Books).

Janowitz, M. (1960), *The Professional Soldier* (Glencoe: The Free Press).

Keegan, J. (1993), *The Face of Battle* (London: Pimlico).

Kohlberg, L. (1981), *Essays on Moral Development*, vol. I: *The Philosophy of Moral Development: Moral Stages and the Idea of Justice* (New York: Harper and Row).

Kümmel, G. (2003), 'A Soldier is a Soldier is a Soldier is a Soldier', in Giuseppe (ed.).

Locke, J. (1971), *An Essay Concerning Human Understanding*, A.D. Woozley (ed.) (London: Wm. Collins Sons and Co. Ltd).

Martinelli-Fernandez, S. (2006), 'Educating Honorable Warriors', *Journal of Military Ethics* 5:1, 55–66.

Miller, L.L. and Moskos C. (1995), 'Humanitarians or Warriors? Race, Gender, and Combat Status in Operation Restore Hope', *Armed Forces & Society* 21:4, 615–37.

Muller E.R., Starink, D., Bosch, J.M.J., and de Jong, I.M. (eds) (2004), *Krijgsmacht: Studies over de organisatie en het optreden* (*Armed Forces: Studies in Organization and Deployment*) (Alphen a/d Rijn: Kluwer).

Onishi, N. (2004), 'Allies: Dutch Soldiers Find Smiles are a More Effective Protection', *The New York Times*, 24 October.

Osiel, M.J. (1999), *Obeying Orders: Atrocity, Military Discipline and the Law of War* (New Brunswick and London: Transaction Publishers).

Segal, D.R. and Kestnbaum M. (2002), 'Professional Closure in the Military Labor Market: A Critique of Pure Cohesion', in D.M. Snider and G.L. Watkins (eds), *The Future of the Army Profession*.

Snider, D.M. & Watkins, G.L. (eds) (2002), *The Future of the Army Profession* (Boston: McGraw-Hill).

Soeters, J.L. (2007), 'Bonding, Bridging and Other Contrary Demands. Why Today's Military Needs to be Ambidextrous', working paper.

Stouffer S., Suchman, E.A., deVinney, L.C., Star, S.A., and Williams, R.M. Jr (1949), *The American Soldier*, vol. II (Princeton: Princeton University Press).

Toner, J.H. (2000), *Morals Under the Gun. The Cardinal Virtues, Military Ethics, and American Society* (Kentucky: University Press of Kentucky).

van Baarda, T. and Verweij, D (eds.) (2006), *Military Ethics: The Dutch Approach* (Leiden and London: Martinus Nijhof Publishers).

Walzer, M. (1992), *Just and Unjust Wars* (New York: Basic Books).

Westhusing, T. (2003), 'A Beguiling Military Virtue: Honor', *Journal of Military Ethics* 2:3, 195–212.

Williams, B. (1993), *Shame and Necessity* (Los Angeles: University of California Press).

Wong, L., Kolditz, T.A., Millen, R.A., and Potter, T.M. (2003), *Why They Fight: Combat Motivation in the Iraq War* (Carlisle Barracks, PA: Strategic Studies Institute, US Army War College).

Appendix

Set Readings at the Netherlands Defence Academy

Set reading on 'obedience': Kelman, H.C. and Hamilton, V.L. (1989), *Crimes of Obedience: Toward a Social Psychology of Authority and Responsibility* (New Haven: Yale University Press), Chapter 4: 'The Structure of Authority'.

Set reading on 'courage': Shalit B. (1988), *The Psychology of Conflict and Combat* (New York: Praeger), Chapter 7: 'Courage'.

Set reading on 'moral disengagement': Bandura, A. (1999), 'Moral Disengagement in the Perpetration of Inhumanities', *Personality and Social Psychology Review* 3:3, 193–209.

Set reading on 'leadership vs. management': Gabriel, R. and Savage, P. (1978), *Crisis in Command: Mismanagement in the Army* (New York: Hill and Wang), Chapters 1 and 2.

Set reading on 'responsibility': Dixon, R. (1998), 'Prosecuting the Leaders', in *NL Arms: The Commander's Responsibilities in Difficult Circumstances* (Breda: KMA).

Chapter 12

Teaching and Training Military Ethics: An Israeli Experience

Asa Kasher

The purpose of the present chapter is to describe the author's experience in teaching military ethics within the framework of the Israel Defence Force (IDF). The first part of the chapter will describe the background of teaching military ethics. The second part of the chapter will put forward several insights about teaching and training military ethics, drawn from the author's personal experience and general views.

Background

Military Ethics is a conception of the proper behaviour of people as members of a military force in general and combatants in particular. Such a conception of proper behaviour is not a pile of principles and regulations, even if some codes of ethics take the form of a mere catalogue of norms. Actually, a conception of proper behaviour of members of a military force as such consists of three subconceptions: first, a conception of being a professional organization in general; secondly, a conception of having a certain organizational identity; and thirdly, a conception of operating in a certain societal setting, namely, in the more interesting cases, the civil society of a democratic state (for a related discussion, see Kasher 2005).

Whereas a conception of being a professional organization is a universal one, organizational identity varies as does the societal setting of operation. Therefore, strictly speaking, military ethics in general is not a single conception but rather a family of conceptions of the proper behaviour of combatants and other people in military uniform. Such conceptions share a lot with each other, but more often than not each of them includes some distinct elements which reflect unique historical developments, missions and visions, as well as particular national circumstances. Any discussion of a major aspect of the military ethics of a certain military force has to take place on the background of a portrayal of the unique elements of the nature of that military force and its societal setting. Accordingly, we turn now to a brief specification of several unique elements of the IDF that are relevant to the circumstances of teaching and training military ethics.

Heterogeneity

In Israel, people in military service form a highly heterogeneous group, in a variety of respects.

a) *Formal status*: Under ordinary conditions of military operation, one finds in one's vicinity career officers and NCOs as well as conscripts. Under many circumstances, people in reserve duties also take part in military operations, particularly when operations of a relatively large scale take place.

   Presumably, people of a certain formal status need teaching and training of their own, whether in military ethics or any other aspect of military life. Heterogeneous groups of people need methods of teaching and training that would be appropriate for members of each subgroup.

b) *Personal status*: People in uniform vary in their personal profiles – age, gender and marital status. Age differences are natural where there are conscripts and they are significant because they correlate with one's life experience. Gender differences are accompanied by natural and given social differences. Marital status is often significant with respect to one's attitudes.

   Again, people of a certain personal profile presumably need teaching and training that take into account their profile to the extent that it reflects experience and attitudes.

c) *Academic education*: Career development of most officers involves under-graduate studies and that of senior officers often involves graduate studies as well. Junior officers and conscripts may have no academic background. Usually, people in uniform have no academic background directly related to military ethics or even to any other professional or organizational ethics.

   Undoubtedly, levels of previous education are often of importance when appropriate methods of teaching and training or some of their ingredients are considered.

d) *Mission*: Differences between military units abound. The professional profile of a unit – mission, structure, affiliation, history, *esprit de corps* – determines the nature and the qualities of its activities, both on the collective and individual levels.

   Methods of teaching and training people in uniform are more effective the more they fit the professional background of students and trainees. In a mixed group of the latter people, *the methods have to be particularly sensitive and sophisticated.*

e) *Attitude towards military ethics*: People in uniform vary in their attitude to the very idea of an organizational conception of proper behaviour, towards the idea of a code of ethics in general or a military code of ethics in particular, or towards certain values or principles.

   Eventually, every man and woman in uniform should comply with the norms of their military ethics, on grounds of adequate understanding and sincere undertaking. The variety of preliminary attitudes must be taken into account when successful methods of presentation, explanation and persuasion are designed.

f) *Attitude towards democracy*: Since military activities are performed within the framework of a national institution, people in uniform should comply with the moral principles underlying a democratic regime, on behalf of which they operate as people in military uniform. However, there is no broad understanding of the nature of democracy, all the more so when the combination of a nation-state and a democratic regime, which is a constitutive feature of the state, is held to be of some significance.

The teaching and training of people in uniform have to inculcate the right commitment to the fundamental principles of democracy. Clearly, in order to do this, teachers of military ethics and commanders have to be sensitive to the major differences in the attitudes towards democracy which people bring with them to their military service or career.

Experience

People in IDF uniform have a very rich firsthand professional experience. Israel has experienced a major war once every decade since its independence was proclaimed in 1948. Wars took place in 1948, 1956, 1967, 1973, and 1982. The IDF has experienced long periods of military attrition conflicts (after the 1967 and 1982 wars), a period of civil uprising in belligerently occupied territories (late 1980s), a longer period of fighting terrorist organizations (2000 to present), and recently an operation against a guerrilla force (2006). Thus, every career officer and NCO has participated in intensive military activity during a war, an ongoing conflict or an operation, as have numerous conscripts and most reservists.

An additional aspect of an ordinary IDF officer's experience should be emphasized. On his way to become an IDF officer, a person serves in an appropriate unit as a subordinate of NCOs and officers. Thus, a commissioned officer will have served as an NCO, and an armour company commander as a tank commander and then as an armour platoon commander.

Consequently, officers have firsthand experience of what they instruct their subordinates to do: they did it themselves previously. They well understand their subordinates' abilities, problems, attitudes, inclinations and habits: they had them or at least witnessed them at earlier stages of their careers. Mutual trust is easier to create on grounds of shared experience.

Military Education

As much as the military experience of an IDF officer is extensive, formal military education is peculiar in the following respects:

a) *Brief*: The period a person spends in the School of Officers (of the Army) is counted in terms of months. The parallel periods at the schools of the Air Force and the Navy are longer, but still are not counted in terms of years. Consequently, some respects of an IDF officer's military professionalism are narrow, or shallow, or even hardly extant.

b) *Vertical*: Professional education is ordinarily both vertical and horizontal: it is 'vertical' when it takes place in preparation for a new stage of professional activity that involves a higher degree of professional responsibility, and it is 'horizontal' when it takes place during a stage of professional development that involves no extension of professional responsibility.

Most of an IDF officer's formal military education is vertical, taking place when a person is about to be promoted upon assuming a new assignment.

c) *Fractionalized*: Apparently, every high ranking officer should have graduated during his or her service not only from a school of officers but also from appropriate military courses (those of company commanders, battalion commanders, brigade commanders, etc.) as well as from the military colleges of Tactical Command, of Command and General Staff and of National Defence.

Many officers have graduated from only some of the courses and colleges that they should have, given their missions, responsibilities and ranks.

Qualification

IDF officers in general, and career officers and NCOs in particular, form a professional elite group not only because of the role the IDF has played in Israel's history and society, but also because they have been professionally and repeatedly determined to be the best among a certain peer group. The case of officers who are still conscripts is the clearest and most impressive. Those sent to some military professional school of junior command are the soldiers deemed best in the platoons or companies in which they served. Those sent to the School of Officers are the best junior commanders. Conscription means that the IDF has under its jurisdiction all (or at least almost all) the best qualified young persons of the whole Israeli population (strictly speaking, this holds for the Jewish and Druze populations of Israel, although quite a number of members of other ethnic groups, such as Bedouins, also serve in the IDF). If officers are the best of the junior commanders, then they are the best qualified among the best qualified of the whole population of their age group.

Decentralization

Officers of every military force are held responsible for major aspects of the professional development of their troops. However, military forces hold and implement different conceptions of commanders' responsibility for professional development.

A 'strict centralization' conception demands centralization of every aspect of delineation of professional knowledge and proficiency as well as every major aspect of the inculcation methodology of the profession. According to such a conception, a commander's major responsibility for professional development is confined to successful implementation of given doctrines of the military profession under consideration and its inculcation.

A 'decentralization' conception will have the commander responsible for parts of the doctrines, for most of the methodology of inculcation and all the implementation.

The IDF philosophy of commander's responsibility is a decentralization conception. A typical example is the delineation of the meaning of 'national defence' in the context of the IDF College of National Defence. Every commander of the college and its Chief Instructor determine for the sake of the college the current meaning of the notion. According to a strict centralization conception, or even a centralization conception that is not strict, it would have been the duty of the Ministry of Defence or at least the IDF Chief of Staff to determine the meaning of that notion for the college and its students.

Insights

Starting Point

Naturally, the first question an instructor of military ethics in a military college has to ask himself is how to introduce the field to his students.

One possible approach takes military ethics to be parallel to military history. The latter field belongs to History, which is a discipline that extends much beyond the confines of any study of wars and the history of military forces. Similarly, ethics can be presented as an independent discipline that has a chapter directly related to military affairs. According to such an approach to military history and military ethics, the introduction of each of them to students has to introduce history in general and ethics (or philosophy) in general, before proceeding to the military chapters of these disciplines.

Such an approach seems appropriate when one's students major in history or in philosophy. Such students have a 'scholastic identity', namely that of students of history or of philosophy. A general introduction of history or of philosophy is one that they either have already encountered or need to encounter. An officer who is a student in a military college, and especially an officer in a military course, has an utterly different 'scholarly identity', namely that of student of some military profession, such as command of a certain type. When this is one's 'scholarly identity', one is not assumed to have encountered, and has no self-evident professional need to encounter, an introduction to history or to philosophy or ethics in general.

An alternative approach rests on the assumption that every officer, and ideally every person, has to be 'moral' or to behave 'morally' (for the moment I disregard the crucial distinction between behaving morally and behaving ethically: I shall return to it). Thus, some conception of morality is presented as the background of which students will discuss some military affairs.

Such an approach is bound to encounter two typical reactions, when used in military colleges and courses. First, morality is considered by the ordinary philosophically naive officer to be 'relative', dependent on time, culture, religion, ethnic background, and so on. Naive moral relativism can be compellingly shown to be wrong in different respects, but in order to uproot it from students' minds and hearts, a significant amount of time is required, much beyond what is usually available. Second, and perhaps even more importantly, a philosophically naive officer, when presented with some conception of morality, with which he or she has not been familiar, will consider it to be of a heteronymous nature, not only in the sense of not being autonomous in nature, but also in the sense of being imposed and enforced on grounds of no apparent justification.

In our experience, the best way to introduce military ethics to officers in military environments is by embedding it in some project of professional development. Professionals are presumably highly interested in their own professional identity, commanders, combatants and members of other military professions not being an exception. They are usually eager to better understand themselves in their professional capacity. Talking to them about their implicit professional identity often renders it explicit, or at least much more so then it used to be, and therefore deeper, richer and more effective.

According to that approach, what one has to do, when introducing military ethics to students of a military college or course is: first, to discuss with them their being members of certain military professions; second, to inform them that they are expected to know much more about their own professions than what meets the eye or is already known to them; third, convince them that each of them is expected to develop their professional identity; and finally, show them that military ethics is directly related to their professional identities. In our experience, such an approach encounters neither resistance in terms of relativism, nor resentment in terms of allegations of heteronomy. It provides the officers with the most natural means of introducing military ethics into their professional life.

Essence

Teaching professional ethics, whether medical or military, whether in a university or a military college, often takes the form of discussing moral issues that arise during professional activities. Some textbooks do it explicitly, some do it as a matter of fact (See, for example, Fotion and Elfstrom 1986, Axinn 1989 and Toner 2000. See also French 2003 for a historical survey). We take a decision to devote a course in military ethics to a discussion of moral issues in military affairs to be misguided.

In order to see the problem created by such a decision, let us draw a distinction between moral considerations and ethical ones. In the history of philosophy, the terms 'moral' and 'ethical' have been very often considered to be interchangeable. Nevertheless, an important distinction between types of consideration has to be made and it would be best to couch it in terms of 'moral' and 'ethical' considerations.

Imagine an interaction between person Alpha and person Beta. When we ask ourselves what would be a proper interaction between Alpha as a person and Beta as a person, we use 'thin' descriptions of those persons (For a related distinction between descriptions, see Walzer 1994 and also Williams 2005 which rests on previous writings of Williams). Moral considerations pertain, first and foremost, to persons as such. Moral principles are intended to regulate interactions between persons as such. The duty to respect human dignity, for example, is a duty with respect to any person as such. Now, assume Alpha is a commander and Beta is Alpha's subordinate. A proper interaction between Alpha and Beta is not solely an interaction between Alpha as a person and Beta as a person, but rather an interaction between Alpha who is a person who is a commander and Beta who is a person who is a subordinate of Alpha. When an interaction is portrayed in terms of persons in some capacities, such a commander and subordinate, it uses 'thick' descriptions of those persons. Ethical considerations pertain to persons under some 'thick' descriptions. Ethical principles are meant to regulate interactions between persons under certain capacities, be they professional, organizational, societal or what have you.

Using our distinction between 'moral' and 'ethical' considerations, the problem of devoting a course in military ethics to moral issues that arise in military affairs is that during the discussions held in such a course, the principles to be applied are moral ones, that is to say, principles that apply to persons as such in general. The particular features of a military situation will serve as the 'input', so to speak, of the moral deliberation in terms of the moral principles. However, there is no reason to assume that a delineation of propriety in military interaction between Alpha and Beta is possible in terms of moral principles alone. Put differently, it does not seem right to hold that all the elements of propriety in military interaction are morally required. Is military discipline a moral necessity, or rather a feature of the capacity of being a military commander or a subordinate? Is unit cohesion a moral necessity? Is professionalism itself justified by moral considerations, on grounds of general principles such as respect for human dignity in general?

Military ethics is, to our mind, a conception of the proper behaviour of a person as a member of a military force. If we focus on military commanders, we are interested in a conception of the proper behaviour of persons as a military commander in that military force.

A conception one has mastered is an alternative to intuitions one used to have. A conception includes explicit principles, within an appropriate framework that clarifies their content and justifies their application. Pre-conceptional intuitions rest on tacit grounds that provide neither clear substance nor firm justification.

A conception that constitutes a certain professional ethics is a conception of proper behaviour. An interesting alternative to behaviour and the principles that should guide it could be character and the virtues that are its parts (for a discussion of military ethics in terms of virtues, see Toner 2000). We prefer principle-guided behaviour as the subject matter of military ethics in the context of IDF not only because of our philosophical inclination to prefer principles over virtues as major elements of practical normative systems, but mainly because a military force of a democracy that includes people who are conscripts and people who are reserve offices or NCOs should educate them to follow the principles of military ethics necessary for the effective functioning of the military force, but avoid any attempt to change their character in a deep and broad way of long lasting effect. Respect for the human dignity of a conscript or a reserve officer means respect for their nature and liberty to the largest extent compatible with their ability and commitment to do their best in carrying out their military missions. A change of character can take place and, we assume, often does, but it is not a necessary condition for having ability and commitment to always behaving properly.

A conception of proper behaviour under some professional capacity consists of three subconceptions, in parallel to the above-mentioned three subconceptions of any organizational ethics: first, a conception of being a professional in general; secondly, a conception of having a certain professional identity; and thirdly, a conception of operating, in our case, in the civil society of a democratic state.

Each of these subconceptions can be portrayed, on an abstract level, in terms of a family of values. In order to gain a professionally appropriate understanding of one's professional identity, one has to have a 'mini-conception' of the substance and significance of each of those values.

The first subconception includes values such as Professionalism and Integrity, as well as Understanding, to which we will return. The third subconception includes values such as respect for human dignity and rule of law. The IDF Code of Ethics includes respect for human life and restraint of force as values which can be derived from the principle of respect for human dignity.

The most complicated subconception is indeed the second one, which reflects the professional identity under consideration. In the case of military ethics it includes the values of courage and perseverance, responsibility, discipline, comradeship and others. Here is where the need is manifest to have a 'mini-conception' of each value as a professional replacement of 'pre-conceptional' intuitions. For example, a prevalent 'pre-conceptional' notion of military discipline views obedience as the gist of the value, while a proper 'conceptional' notion of military discipline will have as the core of the value relationships of mutual trust that rest on understanding and identification and maintain an inclination to obey (for a discussion of this example, see Kasher 2002).

Our views of the essence of military ethics are different from those that portray it as moral theory applied to military affairs. However, our view does not exclude moral consideration from the realm of the military ethics, but includes it in a somewhat indirect way. Recall the nature of the third subconception of the unified conception of proper behaviour that constitutes military ethics: it is a conception of operating, in our case, in the civil society of a democratic state. Such a conception rests on a conception of democracy, which in turn (see, for example, Rawls 1971 and 2001, passim) rests on moral principles such as those embodied in the above mentioned value of Respect for Human Dignity. Such an indirect incorporation of moral considerations into military ethics has the advantage of circumventing philosophical debates between different schools of moral philosophy. What are officers expected to do when they are faced with a philosophical debate between deontologists and consequentialists, or act-utilitarians and rule-utilitarians? Should they take sides? Should they be divided into Kant-orientated unit commanders and Mill-orientated ones? According to the view I have presented, officers do not have to take sides in philosophical debates, but have to apply the moral foundations of the democratic regime in which and for the sake of which they serve as officers (cf. the traditional USA officer oath which requires swearing to support and defend the USA Constitution, not allegiance to any person or office). Those moral foundations include the value of respect for human dignity and the ensuing practical principles and guidelines related to protection of human life and to constraint of force.

Understanding

Teaching military ethics in a military college involves extending officers' knowledge of certain aspects of their military activity. Much thought is being given to delineating the new knowledge officers have to acquire during their studies. However, we would like to suggest that mere knowledge is deficient to the extent it does not rest on grounds that provide understanding of what has been acquired. Therefore, understanding should be the goal of teaching military ethics whenever new professional knowledge has to be acquired or old professional knowledge has to be reinforced.

Consider, for example, the value of comradeship. I have met officers who knew that the value of comradeship is among the values of the IDF, but thought that it is emotion-oriented: the more one's troops are attached to each other, the better soldiers they become. Such a view about a correlation between comradeship and professional performance can be right, but it is not the substance of comradeship. An officer has to know that his troops will come to the rescue of a helpless wounded comrade, even when it means they have to jeopardize their lives when they properly carry out such a rescue mission. However, they should be committed to the ethical obligation to rescue their comrade whether they like him or not, whether they personally know him or not, and even when he is not a member of their military organization. To use US examples, a member of the US Army should come to the rescue of member of other defence organizations, such as the US Marines or the Canadian Forces when they fight together. Hence, the emotional relationship of attachment is not a precondition of comradeship, though when it appears it can be of some benefit.

Understanding comradeship means being able to answer the question – why is comradeship one of the values of the IDF or any other military force that nurtures it? In order to be able to answer that question, an officer should be aware of the knowledge military forces in general have acquired with respect to the motivation combatants have for participating in military fighting, even when by participating they jeopardize their lives. A major feature of their motivation is unit cohesion, which consists of firm commitments to act together with comrades and combatants of the same unit, to come to their assistance, to shoulder responsibility for what they do, and so on. Unit cohesion is a necessary condition for a unit being an effective combat organ, whether it is a platoon, a company, a battalion, or even a brigade or a division. When such understanding of comradeship is gained, one may assume that commanders will act in a variety of new ways – deeper, richer and more effective.

During the final stage of the regular presence of IDF forces in the Gaza Strip, an armoured vehicle exploded, loaded with five combatants and hundreds of kilograms of explosives intended to be used against terrorist weapon smuggling tunnels. The combatants instantly died and their bodies practically evaporated. However, their comrades looked for their traces, considering themselves to be looking for their comrades! (Note that the troops who participated in the search did not jeopardize their lives more than was required for mere presence in the area. They did not suffer any casualties, though the unit that secured them did suffer two casualties that were unrelated to the search.) To my mind, that was a clear example of understanding the value of comradeship properly and deeply, manifesting it in an exceptional and commendable way.

The requirement of understanding applies to each subconception of military ethics. We have just seen it applied to the second subconception, that of professional identity. The need to apply it to the other two subconceptions is self-evident. Most of the officers I have met held naive views of being a professional and of being a citizen in a democratic society. More often than not, officers (as well as members of other professional communities) take proficiency to be the core of being professional. They can easily be convinced that proficiency requires systematic knowledge and that both should be constantly updated. The idea that they are required to deeply understand the things that they do, such as their rules of engagement (ROEs) and other routine procedures, often comes as a surprise to them.

Similarly, the idea that the democratic nature of their society has to be reflected in all their human interactions is a novelty, mainly because their notion of democracy involves the ideas of free elections, judicial review of official decisions by the Supreme Court, and other institutional ingredients of democracy, but does not involve major individual ingredients of democracy, such as respect for human dignity.

Thus, an important goal of teaching military ethics in military colleges is to provide officers not only with understanding of their professional identity, but also with understanding the conceptual nature of being a professional in general as well as understanding the individual dimensions of being a citizen of a democracy. To be sure, understanding is here meant not as merely an additional element of professional knowledge, which is seemingly passive, but also as an additional element of professional proficiency, which is manifestly active.

An additional ingredient of understanding is involved in the nature of proper ethical deliberations. Professional arguments with respect to proper professional behaviour have to be properly presented, debated and evaluated. When people face a dilemma, in the sense of a practical conflict between two values to which they adhere, many of them think that in order to resolve the dilemma what they have to do is just to opt for one of its 'horns'. Such a view involves two grave mistakes. To see them let us consider the case of a dilemma between perseverance and protection of human life. First, facing such a dilemma, assuming that it cannot be obviated, one has to make up one's mind as to whether perseverance or protection of human life should have the upper hand under the circumstances. However, having made up one's mind, say, that perseverance should have preference over protection of human life is just a stage in planning one's activity. On the grounds of one's decision, one plans actions that will manifest perseverance in pursuits to accomplish the given mission, but among all the possible actions that manifest such perseverance, one has to prefer actions that minimize casualties, i.e. that maximize protection of human life to the extent possible when perseverance is of more importance. Often, in properly resolving a dilemma more attention is paid to the minor value than to the major one.

Second, an order of priorities should rest on a deep understanding of the values in conflict and a thorough acquaintance with the circumstances of conflict. Only a deep understanding of the values of perseverance and protection of human life provides an officer with grounds for making decisions with respect to given circumstances as to whether the former value or the latter should be the major one. Only when acting on grounds of a firm conviction that it is justified to give perseverance preference over protection of human life, while making best efforts to minimize casualties, can a commander find in himself and in his subordinates the attitude required for jeopardizing his own and his subordinates' life in an attempt to accomplish a military mission. Understanding is, then, a necessary part of the professional 'toolbox' an officer has to use when facing a dilemma, having to practically resolve it.

Setting

We turn now to a brief discussion of some features of the educational setting of teaching and training military ethics in military colleges.

a) *Role*: Studies in IDF military colleges have often been accompanied by academic studies affiliated with some university. Parts of the academic programmes have even taken place on the campus of the affiliated university. Under such conditions the role of a course in military ethics was ambiguous: since it discusses military ethics, often with respect to classified data, it could be taken to be an element of the pure military programme, but since discussions of military ethics are held with a university professor in a form that is similar to that of a university class, the course could be taken to be part of the academic programme. I would like to suggest that both ways of portraying the role of that course are wrong in their pure form, but some mixture of the two of them is the best way of doing it.

A course in military ethics should be held in a class that is depicted as an extension of a commander's office rather than an extension of a professor's office. Put differently, it should be clear to the officers who study in a military college that by participating in a course on military ethics they are engaged in their own military professional development rather than in some liberal arts programme in which they happen to be interested. Such an attitude towards a course in military ethics seems to us to be a pre-condition for future successful implementation of its contents in the units those officers are going to command.

At the same time, classes in such a course of military ethics should share with good academic classes an atmosphere of tolerating and even encouraging open discussions of each and every point made by the professor or an officer. Such openness should be sanctioned not only for the sake of academic success but mainly in order to facilitate understanding and enhance its pursuit.

b) *Perspective*: A profound difference between the academic atmosphere commonly encountered on a university campus and the required atmosphere of effective military professional development is that of the prevailing point of view to be used in evaluation of states, decisions, procedures and other ingredients of military affairs. Much more often than not, a point of view used in academic discussions of national or international affairs is that of criticism. A person who has adopted such a point of view takes it as his duty to mark deficiencies in whatever is being done. Such a point of view can be used as part of some improvement and advancement project, under which conditions it is helpful and even necessary. However, quite often the academic use of that point of view is not of a constructive nature but rather of a destructive one, which is far from commendable.

The alternative point of view is that of responsibility. Given certain circumstances and a number of possible courses of action, the criticism perspective would confine itself to marking the undesirable effects of each course of action, while the responsibility perspective would justify making a decision on the basis that some courses of action are better than other ones and even that one course of action is the best one, a course that ought to be taken. Professional use of such a point of view is of a responsible and constructive nature, and as such is commendable.

c) *Theory and practice*: Another point where a course in military ethics shares some features with both an academic course and a military professional development is its structure. Having tried different ways of teaching military ethics, our experience shows that the best way is the following combination of elements:

The first element is theoretical background, which presents major parts of the topic, such as the values that constitute the normative identity of the IDF. Understanding of those values is gained by presenting and discussing the 'mini-conception' of each of the values. The conception related to, say, restraint of force will include a presentation of the just war doctrine and its new versions related to fighting terrorism and guerrilla forces.

The second is real case studies presented by military instructors or other high ranking military officers. The presentation and discussion of such cases provide the officers in the class with appropriate examples of professional analysis of the ethical aspects of military affairs.

The third is real case studies presented by each of the officers in class in turn. A presentation starts with a brief description of the circumstances and the problems that emerged in it. The solution opted for under those circumstances is not disclosed at that stage. The presentation is then followed by a general discussion of the ethical issues. Later on, the solution used under the circumstances is presented and generally discussed. Finally, a summary is given by the teacher of military ethics that combines the case and its discussion with elements of the theoretical background.

The real cases are all told from a personal perspective. People talk to the class about their own missions, problems, solutions, errors and successes.

The discussions usually manifest an impressive combination of openness, responsibility, comradeship and professionalism.

Acknowledgments

The present chapter is an extended version of a paper on the same topic delivered at the University of Hull. I am grateful to participants in the discussion of the paper for their illuminating remarks. The paper and chapter express the views of the author and are not official positions of the IDF or the Jerusalem Centre for Ethics.

Bibliography

Axinn, S. (1989), *A Moral Military* (Philadelphia: Temple University Press).

Fotion, N. and Elfstrom, G. (1986), *Military Ethics: Guidelines for Peace and War* (London: Routledge and Kegan Paul).

French, S.E. (2003), The *Code of the Warrior* (Lanham: Rowman and Littlefield).

Kasher, A. (2002), 'Between Obedience and Discipline: Between Law and Ethics', *Professional Ethics* 10:2–4, 97–122.

Kasher, A. (2005), 'Professional Ethics and Collective Professional Autonomy: A Conceptual Analysis', *Ethical Perspectives* 12:1, 67–97.

Kasher, A. (2008), 'Interface Ethics: Military Forces and Private Military Companies', in A. Alexandra, D.-P. Baker, and M. Caparini (eds), *Private Military and Security Companies: Ethics, Policies and Civil-Military Relations* (London and New York: Routledge).

Kasher, A. and Yadlin, A. (2005), 'Military Ethics of Fighting Terror: An Israeli Perspective', *Journal of Military Ethics* 4:1, 3–32 (an abridged version of this paper also appeared in *Philosophia* 34:1, 75–84).

Kasher, A. and Yadlin, A. (2006), 'Assassination and Preventive Killing', *The SAIS Review of International Affairs* XXV:1, 41–57.

Rawls, J. (1971), *Justice as Fairness* (Cambridge, MA: Harvard University Press).

Rawls, J. (2001), *Justice as Fairness, a Restatement*, Erin Kelly (ed.) (Cambridge, MA, and London, England: Belknap Press of Harvard University Press).

Singer, P.W. (2003), *Corporate Warriors* (Ithaca and London: Cornell University Press).

Toner, J.H. (2000), *Morals Under the Gun* (Lexington: University Press of Kentucky).

Walzer, M. (1994), *Thick and Thin: Moral Argument at Home and Abroad* (Notre Dame: University of Notre Dame Press).

Williams, B. (2005), *In the Beginning was the Deed*, G. Hawthorn (ed.) (Princeton and Oxford: Oxford University Press).

Chapter 13

Ethics Training for the Samurai Warrior

Fumio Ota

In his book, *The Soldier and the State*, Samuel P. Huntington stated 'To a larger extent, the officer's code is expressed in custom, tradition, and the continuing spirit of the profession' (Huntington 1972, 16). When looking at the Japanese warrior's ethics, we should go back to the *Kojiki*, written in the sixth century, which is Japan's oldest publication. In the *Kojiki*, we find the ideal warrior, named Itsu-no-ohabari. Amaterasu, the sun goddess, wanted to win over Izumo led by Okuninushi. She dispatched one intelligence god and then another armed intelligence god, but both were convinced by Izumo and made no report back to her. Masao Yaku wrote in his book *The Kojiki in the Life of Japan*:

> Having suffered these two defeats, Amaterasu gave her orders to the god Itsu-no-ohabari, who 'was neither led astray by current opinions nor meddled in politics, but faithfully committed to the essential duty of loyalty.' The god answered with the brief brave words. 'Reverently I will obey and serve.' And his son the god Takemikazuchi went down to Izumo, where after negotiations with Okuninushi, a peaceful settlement of Izumo was agreed upon. The brave loyalty of the warrior symbolized in the words 'Reverently I will obey and serve' was doubtless an ideal at the period of the *Kojiki's* compilation. So too were the men and the spirit called for in a state of national emergency. Also in this same short phrase, for me at that time, lay the authority for the same sort of spirit of utter loyalty as is found in such expressions as 'absolute submission to imperial commands', in the Seventeen Articles of Prince Shotoku, or 'reverence for the majesty of the great lord' of the Manyoshu poet. (Yaku 1969, 48–9)

The Japanese Sankei-News published a book entitled *The Self Defence Force Came from the Country of Bushido: the Iraq Reconstruction Support Group*. This is a story of the Self Defence Forces' operations directed by Colonel Bansho, the first Commander of the Iraqi Reconstruction Support Group. Colonel Bansho said, 'We Japanese should be sincere from the bottom of our hearts, and be dignified with strict discipline, as befits Self Defence Force servicemen from the land of Bushido' (Bansho 2004, 35).

The Japanese philosophical basis for military ethics is derived from Bushido. What is Bushido? Dr Inazo Nitobe, who served as Under-Secretary General of the League of Nations at the beginning of the twentieth century explained:

Bu-shi-do means literally Military-Knight-Ways; the ways which fighting nobles should observe in their daily life as well as in their vocation; in a word, the 'Precepts of Knighthood', the noblesse oblige of the warrior class ... Bushido is the code of moral principles which the knights were required or instructed to observe. It is not a written code; at best it consists of a few maxims handed down from mouth to mouth or coming from the pen of some well-known warrior or savant. More frequently it is a code unuttered and unwritten, possessing all the more the powerful sanction of veritable deed, and of a law written on the fleshly tables of the heart. It was founded not on the creation of one brain, however able, or on the life of a single personage, however renowned. It was an organic growth of decades and centuries of military career. It, perhaps, fills the same position in the history of ethics that the English Constitution does in political history; yet it has nothing to compare with the Magna Carta or the Habeas Corpus Act. (Nitobe 1969 [1900], 33–5)

Dr Nitobe listed Bushido's nine typical virtues. Those are: Rectitude or Justice; Courage, the Spirit of Daring and Bearing; Benevolence, the Feeling of Distress; Politeness; Veracity and Sincerity; Honour; the Duty of Loyalty; the Education and Training of a Samurai; and Self-Control (ibid., contents page). He also wrote:

The venerable professor asked 'Do you mean to say that you have no religious instruction in your schools?' On my replying in the negative, he suddenly halted in astonishment, and in a voice which I shall not easily forget, he repeated 'No religion! How do you impart moral education?' The question stunned me at the time. I could give no ready answer, for the moral Prescripts I learned in my childhood days were not given in schools; and not until I began to analyse the different elements that formed my notions of right and wrong, did I find that it was Bushido that breathed them into my nostrils. (Ibid., 23)

Samuel P. Huntington stated that Josiah Royce's *The Philosophy of Loyalty* was constantly quoted and referred to in military writings on this subject (Huntington 1972, 305). Royce, a professor of the history of philosophy in Harvard University, wrote:

Hereupon we turned for information to our various authorities upon things Japanese, and came to know something of that old moral code BUSHIDO which Nitobe in his little book has called the Soul of Japan. Well, whatever our other views regarding Japanese life and policy, I think that we have now come to see that the ideal of Bushido, the ancient Japanese type of loyalty, despite the barbarous life of feuds and of bloodshed in which it first was born, had very many elements of wonderful spiritual power about it. (Royce 1914, 72)

After the Meiji Restoration, the Minister for the Imperial Army, General Aritomo Yamagata, promulgated the *Soldier's Admonishment* in 1879. This consists of three virtues: fidelity, bravery, and obedience. Then the Emperor Meiji created *The Imperial Precepts to the Solders and Sailors* in 1887. This consists of five articles (set out in full in appendix 1): Loyalty; Propriety; Valour; Faithfulness and Righteousness; and Simplicity. At the end, it stated 'Now for putting them into practice, the most important is sincerity'.

Nowadays, many people criticize *The Imperial Precepts to the Soldiers and Sailors* as obsolete and old fashioned. However, if you extract common aspects of all countries' military codes of ethics, as shown in Table 1.1 (see Chapter 1), then *The Imperial Precepts to the Solders and Sailors'* five codes reflect those common points. Therefore, if we as Western armed forces wish to establish common military codes of ethics for coalition use, I believe that this will be feasible. It is also advisable given that since 2001 the Japanese Self Defence Forces have participated in both Operation Enduring Freedom and Operation Iraqi Freedom with other Western countries such as the Netherlands, Australia, and the UK.

This cooperation has a long heritage. The United Kingdom began to count on Japan militarily after the Boxer Rebellion in 1899. British solders were deeply impressed by the Japanese soldiers' bravery, discipline, and ethical behaviour (Shimada 1990, 23). This was the origin of the Anglo-Japanese Alliance of 1902, which also reflected UK and Japan's common interest of stopping Russian aggression in the Far East; the UK was unable to do that alone because of its commitment to the Boer War.

In January 1941, the *Warrior Code* was promulgated by Army Minister Tojo. This was a reaction to violations against military discipline during the Sino-Japanese conflicts (see Okamura 1986, 29–30). However, the code was not well received because it was written in very difficult Chinese characters, not understood by many soldiers who had not graduated even from elementary school. There are also a couple of wrong theories from a military scientific perspective. For example, the notorious phrase, 'Don't accept with shame being taken alive as a prisoner' is in the *Warrior Code*. Undoubtedly, the Japanese Imperial Army treated prisoners of war brutally during the Second World War. This was a consequence of Japanese arrogance, which came about especially after Japan's victory in the Russo-Japanese War. Many Japanese soldiers and sailors forgot the *Imperial Precepts'* second item, propriety.

Huntington criticized the Japanese soldier's professionalism by citing the *Warrior Code* in his book *The Soldier and the State* (Huntington 1972, 129), but he never mentioned *The Imperial Precepts to the Soldiers and Sailors*, which was much more influential for both soldiers and sailors. In my opinion, *The Imperial Precepts to the Solders and Sailors* is better than not only the *Soldier's Admonishment* but also the Bushido spirit itself. Bushi (or warriors) were a privileged class during the feudal age, set above farmers, artisans, and merchants. Their loyalty was focused only on their lord and not on their country, Japan. Bushido leaves no role for members of classes other than Bushi.

Personally, I have been teaching the *Imperial Precepts* for volunteer cadets at the National Defence Academy since the 1980s. As the British strategist, B.H. Liddell Hart stated in his book *Strategy*, 'Chivalry in war can be a most effective weapon in weakening the opponent's will to resist, as well as augmenting moral strength' (Liddell Hart 1991, 322).

In the Imperial Japanese Navy, 'Five Reflections' were established in 1932 on the occasion of the fiftieth anniversary of the promulgation of the *Imperial Precepts* by Rear Admiral Hajime Matsushita, then the superintendent of the

Japanese Imperial Naval Academy. He was concerned about the views of naval officers involved in the attempted coup d'état by young Imperial Army and Navy officers in 1932. Rear Admiral Matsushita invited a British instructor named Cecil Bullock to be an English teacher, and said to him 'Mr. Bullock, what I want to you do is to teach our midshipmen what the British Gentleman is and how gentlemen behave' (quoted in Yamane 2006, 47–8).

The 'Five Reflections' were: first, 'Hast thou not gone against sincerity?'; second, 'Hast thou not felt ashamed of thy words and deeds?'; third, 'Hast thou not lacked vigour?'; fourth, 'Hast thou exerted all possible efforts?;' and fifth, 'Hast thou not become slothful?' After study and before going to bed, each midshipman was required to read aloud those five reflections and examine himself on that day. The Imperial Naval Academy's infrastructure transferred into the current Maritime Self Defence Forces' Officer Candidate School and the five reflections are still followed by midshipmen today.

In 1961, the Japanese government established the *Ethos of Self Defence Force Personnel*, which consists of five virtues: Awareness of Mission; Individual Development; Fulfilment of Responsibility; Strict Observance of Discipline; and Strengthening of Solidarity (see Defence Agency of Japan 2005, 529). These virtues (set out in full in Appendix 2) are in the Self Defence Force pocketbook and every Self Defence Force member is able to review them at any time. The virtues are often tested by higher officials during inspections. Personally, I believe that *The Imperial Precepts to the Soldiers and Sailors* is much better than the *Ethos of Self Defence Force Personnel* because, first, the *Ethos of Self Defence Force Personnel* does not specify Valour and Simplicity (probably because the *Ethos of Self Defence Force Personnel* was created during a period of pacifism after the Second World War), and second, the *Ethos of Self Defence Force Personnel* has less emotional charge than the *Imperial Precepts*.

Each Self Defence Force has sought to define its own ethos, but they are still not yet firmly established. When the Chief of Japanese Ground Self Defence Forces issues a message, there are always three words at the end, which are Challenge, Dedication, and Sincerity. The Maritime Self Defence Forces tried to create their new ethos, namely Pride, Valour, and Loyalty, but that has not yet been officially authorized. Interestingly, those qualities are very similar to the Imperial Precepts. I believe that servicemen's virtues do not change over time and geography.

The National Defence Academy was established in 1953. The first President, Tomoo Maki, was a graduate of Oxford University. His ethics education derived from the United Kingdom. The class of 1965 cadets created an 'Honourable Conduct' system which consists of three virtues: Honour, Courage and Propriety (National Defence Academy 2005, 1). Those three items are displayed on the floor at the entrance of the main building. Cadets in the National Defence Academy organize an Honour of Conduct Committee, and examine cadets' behaviour. Colonel Bansho also wrote:

> Thinking of Self Defence Force servicemen, I am always reminded of our spirit, Honour, Courage and Propriety to which I became accustomed during my time at the National Defence Academy. Even though names have changed, such as warrior, Samurai, soldier, and Self Defence Force serviceman, I have seen the highest standards

achieved by our people, aiming to complete our mission for the country. (Bansho 2004, 35)

The National Defence Academy has an Honourable Conduct Committee, which monitors how well cadets demonstrate honour in their conduct. When I was a cadet in the late 1960s, I was made Chairman of the Honour of Conduct Committee. I asked all cadets to find out the roots of Honour of Conduct in our history. Then, I reached the conclusion that the primary virtues of the Honourable Conduct system were derived from Tesshu Yamaoka's Bushido in the nineteenth-century which were Propriety, Valour, and Honour (see Katsube 1999, 29).

During their second year, cadets at the National Defence Academy undertake an Iwo-Jima battlefield tour. This helps develop their motivation and provides a good opportunity to consider military ethics. In the Academy and elsewhere, military ethics is also taught in seminars using case studies. Commanders and higher ranking officers occasionally make presentations regarding morals in the service. Additionally, in many Self Defence Force bases there are museums which focus on brilliant soldiers and sailors, from throughout the world and since the beginning of the military history. Self Defence Force personnel look at those examples and are impressed by their achievements. This is the so-called 'Set the Example' method. In conclusion, the current Japanese military training organization has no specific system of ethics training. However, each Self Defence Force member has a philosophical basis of Bushido and then learns ethics through guidance from their superiors and from their seniors' examples displayed at the military museums.

Under the constraints of the current Constitution, the Japanese Self Defence Forces have so far not been used in actual combat missions. They have, however, been conducting peace operations and nation building operations since 1992, including Cambodia (1992 to 1993), East Timor (1999 to 2000), and Iraq (2003 to today). So far, the reputation of the Japanese Self Defence Forces involved in these missions has been good. This indicates that our current military ethics training is effective at the moment.

Bibliography

Bansho, K. (2004), *With People of Samawah* (Obaradai Club Yearly Report vol. 28).
Defence Agency of Japan (2005), *Defence of Japan 2005*.
Huntington, S.P. (1972), *The Soldier and the State* (Harvard: The Belknap Press of Harvard University Press).
Inazo, N. (1900), *Bushido: The Soul of Japan* (Philadelphia: The Leeds and Biddle Co.).
Katsube, M. (ed.) (1999), *Yamaoka Tesshu's Bushido* (Tokyo: Kadokawa Printing).
Liddell Hart, B.H. (1991), *Strategy* (London: Meridien Books).
National Defence Academy of Japan (2005), *National Defence Academy of Japan*.
Nitobe, I. (1969 [1900]), *Bushido: The Soul of Japan* (Rutland, VT: Charles E. Tuttle Co.)
Okamura, T. (1986), *Soshiki-wo-Ikashu* (Tokyo: Keisei-Sha).
Royce, J. (1914), *The Philosophy of Loyalty* (London: Macmillan).

Shimada, K. (1990), 'Saneyuki Akiyama before the Russo-Japanese War', *Asahi*, 23.

Yaku, M. (1969), *The Kojiki in the Life of Japan* (East Asian Cultural Studies Series Vol. 13).

Yamane, T. (2006), 'Etajima and "Five Reflections"', *Hatou*, May.

Appendix 1

The Imperial Precepts to Soldiers and Sailors

The forces of Our Empire are in all ages under the command of the Emperor. It is more than twenty five centuries since the Emperor Jimmu leading in person the soldiers of the Otomo and Mononobe clans subjugated the unruly tribes of the land and ascended the Imperial Throne to rule over the whole country. During this period the military system has undergone frequent changes in accordance with those in the state of society. In ancient times the rule was that the Emperor should take personal command of the force; and although the military authority was sometimes delegated to the Emperor or to the Prince Imperial, it was scarcely ever entrusted to a subject. In the middle ages, when the civil and military institutions were framed after the Chinese model, the Six Guards were founded, the Right and Left Horse Bureaux established, and other organizations, such as that of the Coast Guards, created. The military system was thus completed, but habituated to a prolonged state of peace, the Imperial Court gradually lost its administrative vigour; in course of time solders and farmers became distinct classes, and the early conscription system was replaced by an organization of volunteers, which finally produced the military class. The military power passed over entirely to the leaders of this class; through disturbances in the Empire the political power also fell into their hands; and for about seven centuries the military families held sway. Although these results followed from changes in the state of society and were beyond human control, they were deeply to be deplored, since they were contrary to the fundamental character of Our Empire and to the law of Our Imperial Ancestor. Later on, in the eras of Kokwa and Kaei, the decline of the Tokugawa Shogunate and the new aspect of foreign relations even threatened to impair our national dignity, causing no small anxiety to Our August Grandfather, the Emperor Ninko, and Our August Father, the Emperor Komei, a fact which We recall with awe and gratitude. When in youth We succeeded to the Imperial Throne, the Shogun returned into our hands the administrative power, and all the feudal lords their fiefs: thus, in a few years, Our entire realm was unified and the ancient regime restored. Due as this was to the meritorious services of Our loyal officers and wise councillors, civil and military, and to the abiding influence of Our subjects' true sense of Loyalty and their conviction of the importance of 'Great Righteousness'. In consideration of these things, being desirous of reconstructing Our military system and of enhancing the glory of Our Empire, We have in the course of the last fifteen years established the present system of the Army and Navy. The supreme command of Our forces is in Our hands, and although We may entrust subordinate commands to Our subjects, yet the ultimate authority We Ourself shall hold and never delegate to any subject. It is Our will that this principle be carefully handed down to posterity and that the Emperor always retain the supreme civil and military power, so that the disgrace of the middle and succeeding ages may never be repeated. Soldiers and Sailors, We are your supreme Commander-in-Chief. Our relations with you will be most intimate when We rely upon you as Our limbs and you look up to Us as your head. Whether We are able to guard the Empire, and so prove Ourself worthy of Heaven's blessings and repay the benevolence of Our Ancestors, depends upon the faithful discharge of your duties as soldiers and sailors. If the majesty and power of Our Empire be impaired, do you share with Us the sorrow; if the glory of Our arms shine resplendent, We will share with you the honour. If you all do your duty, and being one with Us in spirit do your utmost for the protection of the state, Our people will long enjoy the blessings of peace, and the might and dignity of our Empire will shine in the world. As We thus expect much of you, Soldiers and Sailors, We give you the following precepts:

1. The soldier and sailor should consider loyalty their essential duty. Who that is born in this land can be wanting in the spirit of grateful service to it? No soldier or sailor, especially, can be considered efficient unless this spirit be strong within him. A soldier or a sailor in whom this spirit is not strong, however skilled in art or proficient in science, is a mere puppet; and a body of soldier or sailors wanting in loyalty, however well ordered and disciplined it may be, is in an emergency no better than a rabble. Remember that, as the protection of the state and the maintenance of its power depend upon the strength of its arms, the growth or decline of this strength must affect the nation's destiny for good or evil: therefore neither be led astray by current opinions nor meddle in politics, but with single heart fulfil your essential duty of loyalty, and bear in mind that duty is weightier than a mountain, while death is lighter than a feather. Never by failing in moral principle fall into disgrace and bring dishonour upon your name.

2. The soldier and the sailor should be strict in observing propriety. Soldiers and sailors are organized in grades, from the Marshal and the Admiral of the Fleet down to the private soldier or ordinary seaman; and even within the same rank and grade there are differences in seniority of service according to which juniors should submit to their seniors. Inferiors should regard the orders of their superiors as issuing directly from Us. Always pay due respect not only to your superiors but also to your seniors, even though not serving under them. On the other hand, superiors should never treat their inferiors with contempt or arrogance. Except when official duty requires them to be strict and severe, superiors should treat their inferiors with consideration, making kindness their chief aim, so that all grades may unite in their service to the Emperor. If you, Soldiers and Sailors, neglect to observe propriety, treating your inferiors with harshness, and thus cause harmonious co-operation to be lost, you will not only be a blight upon the forces but also be unpardonable offenders against the state.

3. The soldier and sailor should esteem valour. Even since the ancient times valour has in our country been held in high esteem, and without it Our subjects would be unworthy of their name. How then may the soldier and the sailor, whose profession it is to confront the enemy in battle, forget even for one instant to be valiant? But there is true valour and false. To be incited by mere impetuosity to violent action cannot be called true valour. The soldier and sailor should have sound discrimination of right and wrong, cultivate self-possession, and

form their plans with deliberation. Never to despise an inferior enemy or fear a superior, but to do one's duty as soldier or sailor, this is true valour. Those who thus appreciate true valour should in their daily intercourse set gentleness first and aim to win the love and esteem of others. If you affect valour and act with violence, the world will in the end detest you and look upon you as wild beasts. Of this you should take heed.

4. The soldier and sailor should highly value faithfulness and righteousness. Faithfulness and righteousness are the ordinary duties of man, but the soldier and the sailor, in particular, cannot be without them and remain in the ranks even for a day. Faithfulness implies the keeping of one's word, and righteousness the fulfillment of one's duty. If then you wish to be faithful and righteous in any thing, you must carefully consider at the outset whether you can accomplish it or not. If you thoughtlessly agree to do something that is vague in its nature and bind yourself to unwise obligations, and then try to prove yourself faithful and righteous, you may find yourself in great straits from which there is no escape. In such cases your regrets will be of no avail. Hence you must first make sure whether the thing is righteous and reasonable or not. If you are convinced that you cannot possibly keep your word and maintain righteousness, you had better abandon your engagement at once. Ever since the ancient times there have been repeated instances of great men and heroes who, overwhelmed by misfortune, have perished and left a tarnished name to posterity, simply because in their effort to be faithful in small matters they failed to discern right and wrong with reference to fundamental principles, or because, losing sight of the true path of public duty, they kept faith in private relations. You should, then, take serious warning by these examples.

5) The soldier and the sailor should make simplicity their aim. If you do not make simplicity your aim, you will become effeminate and frivolous and acquire fondness for luxurious and extravagant ways; you will finally grow selfish and sordid and sink to the last degree of baseness, so to save you from the contempt of the world. It is not too much to say that you will thus fall into a life-long misfortune. If such an evil once makes its appearance among soldiers and sailors, it will certainly spread like an epidemic, and martial spirit and moral will instantly decline. Although, being greatly concerned on this point, We lately issued the Disciplinary Regulations and warned you against this evil, nevertheless, being harassed with anxiety lest it should break out, We hereby reiterate Our warning. Never do you, Soldiers and Sailors, make light of this injection.

Those five articles should not be disregarded even for a moment by soldiers and sailors. Now for putting them into practice, the all important is sincerity. These five articles are the soul of Our soldiers and sailors, and sincerity is the soul of these articles. If the heart be not sincere, words and deeds, however good, are all mere outward show and can avail nothing. If only the heart be sincere, anything can be accomplished. Moreover these five articles are the 'Grand Way' of Heaven and Earth and the universal law of humanity, easy to observe and to practice. If you, Soldiers and Sailors, in obedience to Our instruction, will observe and practice these principles and fulfil your duty of grateful service to the country, it will be a source of joy, not to ourself alone, but to all the people of Japan.

The 4th day of the 1st month of the 15th Year of Meiji.
   (Imperial Sign Manual.)

Appendix 2

The Ethos of Self Defence Force Personnel (Adopted on 28 June 1961)

Ours is a country with a long history and splendid tradition that has emerged from the many trials it has faced, and is now in the process of developing as a nation based on the principles of democracy.

Its ideals are to cherish freedom and peace, encourage social welfare and contribute to a global peace that is founded on justice and order. In order to bring about these ideals, it is essential that we ensure the continued existence and security of a Japan that stands on the premise of democracy by protecting its peace and its independence.

In observing the realities of the world, we find that countries are making ever greater efforts to prevent war through international cooperation. At the same time, the development of weapons of mass destruction means that the outbreak of large-scale war would be disastrous, and thus efforts to keep such weapons under control are growing stronger. International disputes, however, continue unabated, with countries seeking to protect their own peace and independence by putting in place the defence arrangements they need to serve their continued existence and security.

While retaining the sincere hope that the wisdom of mankind and the cooperation of people of all countries will lead to a lasting world peace, the Japanese people have created the present-day Self Defence Forces to protect their own country.

The mission of the Self Defence Forces is to protect the peace and independence of the country and preserve its security.

The principal task of the Self Defence Forces is to prevent the occurrence of direct and indirect aggression against Japan, and to repel any such aggression should it take place.

The Self Defence Forces exist as part of the nation. In accordance with the principles of democratic government, the Commander-in-Chief of the Self Defence Forces is, as such, the Prime Minister, who represents the Cabinet, and the basic administration of the Self Defence Forces is subject to control by the National Diet.

Whether in peacetime or in the event of an emergency, Self Defence Forces personnel must, at all times, be prepared to identify themselves with the people and take pride in serving the public without regard to themselves.

The spirit of Self Defence Forces personnel is founded on the healthy spirit of the nation itself. Cultivation of the self, love of others and concern for the motherland and its people, these particular attributes provide the Self Defence Forces with the proper sense of patriotism and identification with their own people that lie at their spiritual heart.

We must remember the true nature of us as members of the Self Defence Forces, and refrain from taking part in political activities, reflect deeply on the distinguished mission bestowed on us as members of the Self Defence Force and take great pride in our work. By the same token, we must devote ourselves unstintingly to training and self-discipline and, in the face of events, be prepared to discharge our duties at risk to ourselves, acting on the basis of the following criteria.

1. Awareness of Mission
   (1) We will protect from external aggression the nation of Japan, its land and people, which we have inherited from our forefathers and which we will bequeath to next generation enriched and developed.
   (2) We will safeguard the peace and order of our national life, which is founded on freedom and responsibility.
2. Individual Development
   (1) We will strive to make ourselves into positive and upstanding members of society who are free from prejudice, and cultivate sound judgment.
   (2) We will develop into well-balanced individuals with regard to qualities such as intellect, initiative, trustworthiness and physical fitness.
3. Fulfilment of Responsibility
   (1) We will go about our duties with courage and perseverance at the risk of our lives as dictated by our responsibilities.
   (2) We will be bound to our comrades by love and protect our posts steadfastly in the spirit of public service.
4. Strict Observance of Discipline
   (1) We will be true and impartial in our observance of the law and submission to orders, in the belief that discipline is the lifeblood of a unit.
   (2) We will make sure that the orders we give are appropriate, and cultivate the habit of positive, considered obedience.
5. Strengthening of Solidarity
   (1) Outstanding leadership and warm comradeship will allow us to develop the confidence to endure hardship and suffering collectively.
   (2) We, the Ground, Maritime and Air Self-Defence Forces, will do all we can to respond to the responsibilities with which we are entrusted by devoting ourselves as one to ensuring the continued existence of our country and its people.

PART II
RESPONSES

Chapter 14

What is the Point of Teaching Ethics in the Military?

Jessica Wolfendale

Introduction

The chapters in this volume describe military ethics programmes from countries with different and unique military traditions. The authors discuss the ethics programmes in their respective institutions with clarity and insight, and offer important suggestions for how military ethics education and training can be improved. Yet it is striking how many commonalities exist between the programmes discussed in this book, despite differences in military traditions, in the structure and content of military ethics programmes, and in how the military's role is perceived. It is, for example, abundantly clear that military forces around the world recognize a commitment to maintaining high ethical standards and upholding the laws of war, and a commitment to training military personnel to be both ethical and effective. The military forces described in this volume see themselves as far more than unthinking tools of their respective governments; they see themselves as part of a morally worthy Profession of Arms serving morally important ends such as the protection of national security and human rights.

Yet *how* this commitment to high moral standards is maintained varies greatly from country to country. There are significant differences in who teaches ethics, who is taught ethics, and in the content and duration of ethics programmes. In this chapter I do not dwell on these differences, and I do not discuss the problems associated with the implementation of ethics programmes, as these are addressed by several of the authors in this book. Instead, I consider the question that any military force must answer before a suitable military ethics programme can be developed: why teach military ethics at all? Is the point of military ethics education primarily *functional* – does it aim to produce military personnel who will carry out their duties efficiently and within the bounds of law? Or is it primarily *aspirational* – does is aim to produce military personnel who are virtuous people as well as effective fighters? It is only once these questions are answered that we can begin to address the practical questions of how, to whom, and by whom military ethics should be taught.

The ethics programmes discussed in this book do not always explicitly address the purpose of military ethics education and its place in doctrine and military organization. With some notable exceptions, many of the programmes are not based on a careful analysis of the purpose of military ethics education – a problem noted by several authors. As I will show, the structure and stated purpose of these programmes reveal different and sometimes incompatible conceptions of the proper aim of military ethics education and training, which can result in a mixed-bag approach to ethics teaching. Without a clear and thorough analysis of the purpose of military ethics education and training, military ethics programmes are likely to continue to be a mixture of approaches and styles, lacking internal consistency and coherent theoretical underpinnings, and taught by people with various credentials and from different academic, military, and religious backgrounds.

Clarifying and articulating the functional and aspirational views of the purpose of military ethics education and training, and the differences between them, will significantly aid the development of a well thought-out and coherent military ethics programme. Knowing the purpose of ethics education and training will determine how and by whom ethics is taught, which ethical theories are taught, and how military personnel should be encouraged to think about military ethics and their roles as members of the Profession of Arms, a profession which must maintain the support and trust of the civilian population if it is to be morally different from mercenary forces. In this paper, I discuss the differences between the functional view and the aspirational view, and explain the implications that each view has for the structure, audience, and content of military ethics programmes – implications that are far more wide-ranging and demanding than has been recognized. This will allow us to assess which approach best fits with the military's conception of itself as a profession serving an important moral good.

Two Views of Military Ethics Training

It might seem obvious that the primary aim of military ethics education and training is to produce military personnel who will strive not to give or obey illegal or manifestly immoral orders, and to follow the rules and regulations governing the conduct of war as well as those governing the organizational aspects of military life. (These two areas of ethical regulation track Patrick Mileham's helpful distinction (see Chapter 4) between operational ethics (ethical guidelines and issues associated with military operations) and institutional ethics (ethical practice governing good institutional functioning).) Whatever else we might hope from military ethics education and training, at the very least we want military personnel to obey the guidelines governing their roles as members of a military organization and as combatants in many different and challenging military operations. Exactly how this should be achieved is up for debate, but there is absolutely no question that getting military personnel to behave correctly has to be one of the central aims of military ethics programmes. The functional view holds that this should be the *most* important aim of military ethics education.

In the ethics programmes discussed in this book, perhaps the clearest example of a functional account is offered by Asa Kasher in his discussion of the ethics programme of the Israeli Defence Force. The goal of the current ethics programme is, according to Kasher, to educate Israeli military personnel 'to follow the principles of military ethics necessary for the effective functioning of the military force, but to avoid any attempt to change their character in a deep way' (see Chapter 12). Military ethics is construed as a 'conception of the proper behaviour of people as members of a military force in general and combatants in particular'. This conception of the aim of military ethics education has led to the development of an ethics programme that is incorporated into officers' professional development training, and that is conceived of as an essential part of that development. This involves a carefully thought-out ethics programme incorporating case studies, ethics lectures, and discussion groups in which officers are encouraged to see ethics training as a necessary part of their professional development rather than an academic subject that, while interesting, has little direct bearing on their own roles and duties.

Peter Olsthoorn argues for a similar perspective on military ethics education and training in his discussion of the ethics programme at the Netherlands Defence Academy. This is not in fact functionally-driven. Instead, it is largely aspirational; heavily influenced by virtue ethics, and aiming to develop right intention, 'moral competence' and morally good character (see Chapter 11). However Olsthoorn is critical of this emphasis on developing right intention and virtuous character. He argues that most military personnel are too young to be taught high-level moral reasoning skills, and that relying on good character to motivate correct behaviour is unrealistic. Instead, the current approach should be replaced by a greater emphasis on encouraging military personnel to follow moral rules because 'not doing so brings disesteem'. Placing greater emphasis on seeking peer esteem, praise and reward, and avoiding blame and peer disrespect would, he argues, provide a far more effective motivation for good behaviour than the current attempts to cultivate virtuous character or train military personnel to reach Kohlberg's highest level of moral reasoning (Olsthoorn raises a similar argument in Olsthoorn 2005).

While Olsthoorn and Kasher offer different solutions to the problem of promoting ethical behaviour (one through promoting the motivational powers of praise and blame, and the other through incorporating ethics into officers' conception of themselves as professionals), they both share a belief that the purpose of teaching military ethics is not to improve the moral character of military personnel *per se*, but to teach them how to behave correctly when carrying out their professional duties. What matters most under this view is correct behaviour. The intentions, motivations and moral character of military personnel are important only instrumentally, only so far as they are effective in producing the desired behaviour. This instrumental view of character, motive, and intention means that the functional view is largely agnostic as to what kind of moral character or motivation is preferable – the sole criterion for preferring one kind of character, motivation, or intention over another is simply whether or not it effectively promotes the desired forms of behaviour. As a result, under this view there is no *prima facie* reason – and certainly no moral reason – to prefer an Aristotelian style of character development over, say, reward-and-punishment inducements to model good behaviour, if both proved equally effective in promoting desired forms of behaviour.

Indeed, the functional view is not clearly an ethical view at all. This does not imply that it is an unethical view. Rather, it means that the functional view is not directed *solely* towards promoting ethically right action. Under the functional view, the end of teaching military ethics is the promotion or enhancement of military efficiency. This term is not defined by Kasher and Olsthoorn, but a plausible definition might be effective military functioning within the bounds of legality, and this is a non-moral concept. As noted earlier, Kasher defined military ethics as the 'conception of the proper behaviour of people as members of a military force in general and combatants in particular'. This conception of proper behaviour is defined in relation to the overall functioning of the military; it is not just a conception of proper *ethical* behaviour but of proper *occupational* behaviour. If the sole aim of the functional approach was to make sure that military personnel did the *morally* right thing, then the functional view would be a moral approach. But the aim of promoting effective military functioning is not equivalent to or reducible to the aim of getting military personnel to do the morally right thing, and for this reason it is incorrect to think of the functional view as an ethical view. Instead, in the functional view, ethics teaching is an instrumentally valuable tool that can be used to promote the behaviour that is considered to be essential for effective military functioning.

Yet it is not so obvious that enhancing military functioning should be the primary aim of military ethics education and training. Many of the military ethics programmes described in this book aim for more than rule-following and increased efficiency. Their aim is aspirational, aimed at improving the moral character of military personnel not just because this will lead to more reliable behaviour, but also as an end in itself. The aspirational view does not ignore behaviour – an approach to ethics education and training that had no interest in whether individuals behaved well would be useless. Instead, the aim is (partly) to cultivate good behaviour through the cultivation of good moral character. But the justification for cultivating good moral character is not purely instrumental; it is taken to be a morally desirable end in and of itself. So this perspective is aspirational because it seeks to do more than achieve the minimum requirements of ethical behaviour (i.e. personnel who do not break the rules); it aims to improve the moral character or moral capacities of military personnel – to make them good people, not just well-behaved people.

A version of the aspirational view is expressed by Tor Arne Berntsen and Raag Rolfsen in their discussion of the ethics programme of the Norwegian Defence Forces in Chapter 8. They claim that 'the *primary fundamental* motive for teaching ethics in the military is neither to clean up the act of military operations under the gaze of the media, nor to make military operations more efficient. We teach ethics in the military because we want to *promote good and prevent evil*'. In this view, improving military efficiency should not be the explicit aim of military ethics education and training. Instead, military ethics programmes should also aim to improve the moral character of military personnel. Such a view of military ethics is shared by the Netherlands Defence Academy, whose stated aim is 'Contributing to future officer's moral competence ... at the cognitive, affective, and volitional level ... moral questions should be recognized as such, and not merely as practical problems' (see Chapter 11). This implies a belief that moral issues should not be treated simply as operational effectiveness issues, and that moral competence is not simply a form of professional competence.

However, in most of the programmes discussed in this volume, the primary purpose of the ethics education and training is not so clearly stated. Many of the programmes exhibit an uneasy and largely unarticulated tension between the functional and the aspirational approaches.

Mixed Aims in Current Military Ethics Programmes

In many cases, the different methods used to teach ethics revealed an unresolved tension between the twin aims of simply getting military personnel to behave correctly, and trying to also make them more sophisticated moral thinkers and people of good moral character. Martin Cook, for example, explains how the strict enforcement of discipline at the US Air Force Academy through rewards and punishments is intended to train cadets into the right habits, which are 'justified functionally: the resultant consistent and reliable patterns of behaviour are believed to be essential for a well-disciplined and reliable officer corps' (see Chapter 5). Yet cadets also take Character Development Courses and are given lectures by presenters such as retired service personnel, with the intention of educating the students using models of behaviour that they should aspire to. Students also take lessons in theoretical ethics in the third or fourth year of their training. This combination of, on the one hand, strictly-enforced rules and regulations, an emphasis on correct behaviour and good military functioning and, on the other hand, exposure to aspirational role models and academic training in ethical theory is found in many of the other military training establishments described in this book.

The tension between the aspirational and the functional views also appears in less obvious ways. It is evident in the language that is used to describe the content and aim of military ethics training, and it is evident in the lack of ethics training given to enlisted personnel as opposed to that given to officer cadets. In relation to the use of language, it is clear that developing the moral character of military personnel is considered *one* of the aims of military ethics programmes (even if it is not explicitly stated as such) in the institutions that use the concepts and language of virtues and values. The US Air Force Academy, for example, constantly uses phrases such as 'integrity' and 'core values' and runs teaching programmes involving the use of exemplary moral role models and inspirational speakers (see Chapter 5). Students at the Japanese National Defence Academy have an Honour of Conduct System based on the virtues of Honour, Courage, and Propriety (see Chapter 13), and are given presentations by high-ranking officers regarding 'morals in the Service'. These students, and cadets from other military bases, are encouraged to visit military museums to see examples of honourable military personnel whom they should emulate.

The emphasis on aspirational role models and the use of aspirational language – the language of virtues and values – is shared by the majority of the programmes described in this volume. Most of these publish lists of values, precepts, and virtues. For example, the core values of the Norwegian Defence Force are Respect, Responsibility, and Courage; the core principles of the Canadian Defence Ethics Programme are: respect the dignity of all persons, serve Canada before self, and obey and support lawful authority; the values of the Australian Defence Force include Loyalty, Courage, Innovation, and Integrity; the Japanese Imperial Precepts for Soldiers include Loyalty, Propriety, Valour, Faithfulness, Righteousness, and Simplicity; the values of the British Army include Integrity, Loyalty, and Courage; and so on. The exact content of these lists of values and principles varies from country to country (although there is also significant overlap), but the almost universal use of such lists indicates a widespread belief that military personnel should cultivate character traits or dispositions that are morally admirable, not simply expedient. This frequent use of the language and concepts of virtue gives rise to a highly moralized picture of the good fighter. The good fighter not only aims to carry out her duties efficiently and within the bounds of legality; she aims to cultivate a set of morally admirable character traits such as loyalty, courage, integrity, and trustworthiness.

Now a supporter of a purely functional approach might argue that the reason for the widespread use of the aspirational approach is simply that it is the most effective way of encouraging correct behaviour. Military personnel are more likely to do the right thing, such a supporter might argue, if they believe that they are fulfilling a morally honourable role requiring high moral character rather than seeing themselves as mere cogs in a war machine. A version of this argument is put forward by Hilliard Aronovitch (2001). Aronovitch argues that virtue ethics is the most appropriate ethical theory for military ethics teaching not because it enables military personnel to develop virtuous characters but because, he claims, the virtues of the ethical soldier are also those of the effective soldier. By carefully cultivating the virtues of truthfulness, courage, good judgment and temperance (self-control), military education can produce personnel who will not obey or give unethical orders (ibid., 19–20). So teaching virtue ethics will be the best way to ensure that soldiers abide by the deontological constraints imposed by the laws of war and broad-based morality (ibid., 16). Should this be the case, and the use of the language and concepts of virtue is simply the most effective way of producing correct behaviour, then the apparent difference between the aspirational view and the functional view disappears. The aspirational approach is simply one way of getting military personnel to do the right thing.

It might well be the case that using the language of moral virtue and teaching virtue ethics are effective tools for motivating good behaviour. (Although some authors in this volume question this belief. Peter Olsthoorn, for example, is very critical of the use of virtue ethics in military training and Martin Cook also discusses problems with the emphasis on memorizing lists of virtues and values.) But the crucial difference between the views I have described is that under the aspirational view, this would not be the main reason for adopting the language and concepts of moral virtue. Under Aronovitch's approach (and under the functional view more generally) the value of virtue ethics (and any other ethical theory) is purely instrumental – it is judged by whether or not it promotes military efficiency. However, believers in the aspirational view would argue that there are *moral* reasons for preferring virtue ethics to another, perhaps more effective, approach. The preference for the language and concepts of virtue does not arise from a belief that such language is the most effective way of producing ethical behaviour or good military functioning (although such a belief may also be present). Instead, it arises from the belief that the language and concepts of virtue best capture the moral dimension of military service – the 'moral component of fighting force', in the words of the British General Sir Michael Rose (quoted in Torrance and Roberts 1998). Martin Cook, for example, describes how 'many in the US military openly state that the military and its culture is in many ways morally superior to the civilian population' (see Chapter 5). The belief that the military is essentially a moral profession requiring high moral character is shared by many others in the military profession. This is evident from the number of publications and statements that refer to the military as an honourable profession, and that present a moralized conception of the character of ideal military personnel. For example, in websites such as those of the Royal Military College Duntroon in Australia and the Australian Defence Force Academy, also in Canberra, there are references to developing 'professionalism'; to creating 'professional officers'; and to the military as a profession. Most writers in military ethics also refer to the military as a profession, and present a moralized conception of the ideal fighter.

The range of military ethics programmes also reveals a tension between the functional and the aspirational approaches. In all the programmes described in this book it is officers who are, without exception, given the bulk of military ethics education and training. The duration and content of these programmes varies greatly, from no formal academic training in ethics to one-and-a-half or two-day workshops to semester-length courses.

On the other hand, the ethics programmes offered to non-commissioned officers (NCOs) and enlisted personnel, when they do occur, are usually of short duration or non-existent. In Norway, NCOs and conscripts are given six double lessons in ethics, but this amount of ethics education is the exception rather than the rule. NCOs in Canada, for example, are given a brief introduction to the Defence Ethics Programme, and then take a two-hour workshop on ethics (see Chapter 6). What is far more commonplace is for enlisted personnel to be given detailed instructions on the rules of engagement prior to their deployments, and (more rarely) one-day or shorter character development or ethics workshops.

This emphasis on teaching officers could be explained simply by reference to the amount to time and resources available for officer training compared to that available for the training of enlisted personnel. However, I suspect this explanation is too simplistic. If it were felt necessary, I am sure ethics education of the sort provided to officers (although probably not semester-length courses) could be provided to all ranks. Instead, the focus on officers reveals a tension between the functional and the aspirational views. As mentioned earlier, highly moralized language is used in the descriptions of the good officer and in the ethics programmes available to officers, which is consistent with the aspirational view of the purpose of ethics education and training. Officers, in most cases, are supposed to develop good moral character, moral sensitivity and moral judgment through their training. However, while enlisted personnel are also exposed to highly moralized language about their role and the values of their services, in practice and in their present limited training, it appears that they are generally only expected to memorize their service's lists of values, the laws of war, the institutional regulations relevant to their roles, and the different rules of engagement relevant to their particular deployments. The emphasis in their training is on rule-following, not on developing good moral character or high-level reasoning skills, an approach that is consistent with the functional view.

What seems to be operating as a largely unspoken reason for this practice is the assumption that officers will 'pass on' their ethical behaviour and character to their subordinates, who will be encouraged to follow the example set by their officers. If this is true, then educating officers to be of good moral character means that they will become ethical role models that can guide and inspire military personnel of lower ranks. This view is most clearly expressed in Stephen Deakin's discussion of the Royal Military Academy Sandhurst in Chapter 2. Deakin notes that the British military's traditional view of ethics teaching held that officers would embody the ideal of the Christian gentleman, and would then set an example to their subordinates through their character and behaviour. Enlisted personnel should be trained to obey the military's institutional rules and the legitimate orders of their superiors (on the assumption that their superiors would not give immoral or illegal orders); yet, it seems, it is neither necessary nor time-efficient to attempt to teach all military personnel to develop virtuous characters.

Is there any problem with this division between the attitude towards officers and the attitude toward enlisted personnel? In a hierarchical institution such as the military, it might appear more important to ensure that those giving the orders are of good moral character than it is to make sure enlisted personnel are morally upright people. As Ian Huntley points out (2003, 2), 'In a strictly hierarchical organization, such as the armed forces, it is reasonable for soldiers to expect their leaders to provide them with guidance'. So long as lower ranks are taught to obey all legitimate orders, there should be minimal violations of the laws of war and institutional regulations.

There are two reasons to be concerned about the difference in the aim and content of ethics education and training given to officers and that provided to enlisted personnel. First, in a combat situation it is often the military personnel on the front line – the 'strategic privates' – who are faced with the most immediate and pressing ethical issues, and yet it is frequently these personnel who have, at best, a scant level of ethics education. If moral sensitivity and moral judgment are considered necessary and morally admirable traits for officers because they enable them to maintain moral courage in the face of extreme situational pressures, then it is even more important for enlisted personnel to develop these traits as well. They are the ones at the front line, and they are the ones who will have to find the courage to uphold the laws of war when external pressures of time and threat (as well as, sometimes, pressure from their superior officers) might tempt them to break them. It is patronizing to treat enlisted personnel as less capable of moral development than officers, particularly since they are required to carry out acts of extreme violence that require a substantive moral justification. As Patrick Mileham points out in Chapter 4: 'Gone are the days when the *jus ad bellum* tradition meant that politicians alone took responsibility for justifying the use of force and soldiers, with relatively clear consciences, attended to the technical details, including lethal means, and widespread destruction.' Military personnel in today's military forces are all too aware that they cannot escape moral responsibility for what they do in combat (see Crossley 2006).

Furthermore, when war crimes occur, such as those at Abu Ghraib in Iraq and My Lai in Vietnam, it is usually not the senior officers but the lower ranks who commit the atrocities (sometimes when ordered to do so by their junior-ranked officers). Since the post-Second World War trials at Nuremberg, the 'just following orders' excuse is no longer considered tenable; military personnel of all ranks are morally and legally responsible for their actions in warfare. It is therefore even more important to enable *all* military personnel to develop the skills that will enable them to disobey illegal orders and take responsibility for their actions. The assumption that enlisted personnel may simply follow the example of their leaders threatens to treat enlisted personnel as little more than automatons who must be guided properly by their leaders, rather than treating then as autonomous moral agents who will have to take responsibility for their actions and decision-making under high-stress situations.

For these reasons it is extremely important to develop a *consistent* approach to military ethics education and training. Using one approach for enlisted personnel and another for officers reveals a lack of clarity about the aims of military ethics education. Either the aspirational view should govern ethics education for *both* officers and enlisted personnel, or the functional view should dominate. What can be said in favour of each view? What we want is a perspective on the purpose of ethics education and training that is consistent with the military's ethical commitments, and that is consistent with respect for the moral autonomy of all military personnel – their status as rational agents who have the capacity to reflect upon and understand moral reasons. As will become evident, both these views, if applied consistently, are far more demanding than has been recognized.

The Functional View versus the Aspirational View

Adopting the functional approach to military ethics education and training would mean that decisions about which ethical theories to use, how to teach ethics, and who should be taught ethics will be driven by considerations of how to achieve an efficient military force that carries out its duties within the bounds of law. Competing approaches to ethics teaching will be judged purely on their success in promoting good military functioning. Adopting the aspirational view, on the other hand, would mean that decisions about the structure and focus of ethics teaching would be governed by a conception of good moral character. While both views may appear straightforward, in practice they are both extremely demanding.

If the functional view is taken seriously, implementing it would require a comparative study of the effectiveness of different ethical theories (e.g. virtue ethics, deontological ethics, rule-based ethics, reward-and-punishment theories) and the effectiveness of different pedagogical methods (e.g. case studies, role-playing, lectures) in promoting the desired forms of behaviour. It would also require the extension of ethics training to *all* military personnel – not just officers – and a thorough analysis of the impact of other areas of military education and training on the behaviour of military personnel.

Analyzing other areas of military education and training is essential because the behaviour of military personnel is influenced not only by the lessons they receive in ethics or character development, but also by their immersion in the all-encompassing group-oriented military environment and by their training in acts of violence. A serious commitment to promoting good behaviour in the military would have to take into account research into the effects of group-think and peer pressure on the behaviour of military personnel (Bordin 2002), the psychological effects of learning to kill (Grossman 1999; Bourke 1999), the processes that can lead to institutional wrongdoing (Hamilton and Sanders 1999), how crimes of obedience occur (Milgram 1974; Kelman and Hamilton 1989; Osiel 2002), and the moral psychology of war crimes (Muñoz-Rojas and Frésard 2004). Of the ethics programmes described in this volume, the only one that explicitly addressed some of these issues was that of the Netherlands Defence Academy, which includes classes on moral disengagement and the psychology of obedience to authority (see Chapter 11), although these classes are only available to officer cadets who major in management studies.

The functional view must also address the problem of situational factors overriding pre-existing dispositions to behave correctly. Whether or not one believes that character traits exist as stable action-guiding dispositions, several experiments have shown that the situations we find ourselves in can, at times, exert an influence on our behaviour that is far greater than we would have expected or predicted (Sabini and Silver 2005). For example, in Stanley Milgram's famous experiments on obedience to authority ordinary people administered what they believed were severe electric shocks to a person who was begging to be released from the experiment (Milgram 1974), and in Phillip Zimbardo's infamous Stanford Prison Experiment seemingly normal young men became sadistic guards within two days when placed in a mock-prison and given the job of guarding prisoners (Zimbardo 2007). Clearly, an effective ethics programme that is aimed specifically at promoting correct behaviour should look at ways of combating the negative impact of situational factors on the behaviour of military personnel. Again, this would be vitally important not only for officers but for military personnel of all ranks.

The aspirational view would require an in-depth analysis of theories of moral character and moral education. Incorporating the aspirational approach would require far more than creating lists of desired virtues and values; it would also require a strong consistent theoretical understanding of the basis and nature of moral character. As is the case with the functional view, a commitment to the aspirational view would require an analysis of the influence of situational forces. But, unlike the functional view, this analysis would consider the influence of situational forces on the character and not just the behaviour of military personnel. It may be the case that there are aspects of military culture, education, and training that encourage negative character traits that, while they may aid or at least not undermine effective military functioning, may be morally objectionable on other grounds. For example, a desensitized attitude towards killing might enable military personnel to kill when required to do so without suffering severe guilt, but such an attitude might develop a failure to appreciate the moral impact of one's actions in warfare.

Unlike the functional view, the aspirational view is committed to a view of individual military personnel as autonomous moral agents who are responsible for their behaviour and capable of rational deliberation, moral reflection and moral change. Henri Hude makes the point in Chapter 10 that it is crucial to treat officers 'not as nobodies but as responsible individuals and citizens who need to really know what their country stands for and what they are really training themselves to fight against'. This means that proponents of this view must make sure that military education, training and culture does not undermine or corrupt the capacities for moral autonomy, either through coercive practices that restrict the ability of military personnel to act autonomously, or through the use of training methods that undermine or strongly discourage moral reflection and an awareness of the moral aspects of military actions. For example, using morally neutral language such as 'mopping-up operations', 'surgical strikes', and 'dealing with a target', to describe acts of violence can encourage military personnel to ignore or neglect the fact that they are committing acts of violence against other human beings (see Muñoz-Rojas and Frésard 2004, 9). Captain Pete Kilner (2000, 1) has argued that modern combat training 'maximizes soldiers' lethality, but it does so by bypassing their moral autonomy'. Such practices would be problematic for proponents of the aspirational view but not, it should be noted, for the functional view, which involves no such commitment to maintaining the moral autonomy of military personnel, and it is here that the central difference between the two approaches is apparent.

As I noted earlier, the functional view is agnostic as to which ethical theory is preferable. Ethical theories and theories of moral education would be assessed entirely on instrumental grounds. So a system of behavioural conditioning and post-hypnotic suggestion that produced the desired forms of behaviour would be equally as good as a system of training in moral judgment that produced the same result. If it turned out that military personnel could be given an implant or drug that increased the likelihood of correct behaviour, there would be no grounds under the functional view to object to such methods. This is problematic as it threatens to treat military personnel as objects to be manipulated rather than rational moral agents whose moral autonomy restricts how they may legitimately be treated. Such an approach is also inconsistent with the conception of military personnel as professionals serving in a morally honourable profession – a conception that requires military personnel to develop their capacities for moral judgment and moral reflection.

The aspirational view, on the other hand, because of its commitment to a conception of military personnel as autonomous moral agents who are capable of developing virtuous characters, would rule out the use of implants, drugs, and methods such as behavioural conditioning or hypnosis as ways of promoting ethical behaviour. This view is more consistent with the commonly held view that military personnel are professionals, and it treats all military personnel as responsible moral agents who must live with the moral implications of their participation in combat.

However, if taken seriously, the aspirational view could require far more radical changes to military training and educational practices that the functional view. There may be elements of military training, education, and culture that would have to be revised under the aspirational view that could remain intact under the functional view (assuming they did not encourage unethical behaviour). This could mean that some current training methods (such as those discussed by Kilner above) that enhance the efficiency of military personnel but undermine their moral autonomy would have to be revised, so it is possible in theory at least that a serious commitment to the aspirational view would mean a trade-off with some aspects of military efficiency.

The aspirational view also demands more from military personnel themselves. It requires a strong theoretical understanding of virtue and character development. This requires teachers who are experts in such topics and who are also experts in moral education (which should not be beyond the resources of military forces to provide), and it also requires military personnel to be willing and able to take seriously a commitment to developing good moral character, which may be difficult given the different ages and educational backgrounds of military recruits (see the comments of Peter Olsthoorn in Chapter 11). Furthermore, several of the authors in this volume have noted that military personnel are often resistant to the academic study of ethics. Patrick Mileham, for example, notes in Chapter 4 that many officers 'would prefer ethical judgment to be prescribed and rendered as orders, drills, procedures and instructions, not a matter of personal interpretation of observed events against hard to understand, abstract principles'. Because the aspirational approach requires military personnel to engage seriously with training in moral judgment, decision-making, and moral reflection, this might require a widespread change of attitude toward the value of ethics training, as well as a significant increase in the level of ethics education available to enlisted personnel.

How then, do we decide between the two views? The functional view is a non-moral approach that places the maintenance of military efficiency as the primary value and views the value of ethics training instrumentally, whereas the aspirational view puts the importance of the moral character of military personnel on a par with military efficiency. The aspirational view puts constraints on what may be done to military personnel to get them to behave correctly but respects their status as responsible moral agents, whereas the functional view provides more options for producing desired forms of behaviour but runs the risk of failing to respect or even undermining the moral autonomy of military personnel.

Conclusion

Deciding between these two approaches requires careful consideration of what is entailed by the military's commitment to the laws of war and high professional standards. If the military is genuinely a profession serving an important moral good, then military personnel are professionals fulfilling important and necessary roles and they should be treated as such. The military's professional status, and its commitment to the laws of war, imposes constraints on what may be done in the name of improving military efficiency, including constraints on how military personnel may be trained and educated to make them effective fighters.

If the military's commitment to maintaining high ethics standards is genuine, and I believe it is, then a purely functional approach to military ethics training is inconsistent with the claim that military personnel are morally responsible professionals serving an important moral good. Because a commitment to value of the moral autonomy of military personnel is only instrumental under the functional view, this approach fails to respect military personnel as moral agents who must live with the consequences of their actions, and it fails to adequately reflect the military's ethical commitments.

Furthermore, if a purely functional view is adopted, then the language of military ideals and virtue and the moralized conception of the good fighter that is evident in nearly all the military ethics programmes discussed in this book is simply rhetoric. The reasons for adopting such language and the moralized picture of the good fighter are purely instrumental. Yet this view of the purpose of military rhetoric is both deeply cynical and, I believe, untrue. As is well-demonstrated by the authors in this volume, military forces world-wide take very seriously the professional and moral ideals that govern their profession and that form the moralized conception of the good fighter. To give up a genuine belief in these ideals would lead to a justifiable scepticism about the military's claim to be an honourable profession, a scepticism that would seriously undermine the public's trust in it. Adopting an aspirational approach to military ethics education and training, while it may require significant changes to military educational and training practices, would maintain the military's public image as an honourable profession, as well as demonstrating a sincere commitment to the ethical constraints on the use of military force.

Acknowledgments

I would like to thank Daniel Star and Lieutenant Colonel (Retd) Alan Howes for their helpful comments on this chapter.

Bibliography

Aronovitch, H. (2001), 'Good Soldiers, A Traditional Approach', *Journal of Applied Philosophy* 18:1, 13–23.

Bordin, J. (2002), 'On the Psychology of Moral Cognition and Resistance to Authoritative and Groupthink Demands during a Military Intelligence Analysis Gaming Exercise', paper presented at the *Joint Services Conference on Professional Ethics*, Springfield, Virginia, <http://www.usafa.af.mil/jscope/JSCOPE02/Bordin02.html>.

Bourke, J. (1999), *An Intimate History of Killing: Face-to-Face Killing in Twentieth-Century Warfare* (London: Granta Books).

Cook, M. (2004), *The Moral Warrior: Ethics and Service in the US Military* (New York: Suny Series, Ethics and the Military Profession).

Crossley, N. (2006), 'To What Extent is the Modern Operational Soldier Responsible for his Moral Decisions?', Farmington Trust Fellows Report ME 19, <http://www.farmington.ac.uk/documents/reports/framed/moral_ethical.html>.

French, S.E. (2007), *The Code of the Warrior: Exploring Warrior Values Past and Present* (Lanham, MD: Rowman and Littlefield).

Grossman, D. (1995), *On Killing: The Psychological Cost of Learning to Kill in War and Society* (Boston: Little, Brown and Co.).

Hackett, J. (1983), *The Profession of Arms* (New York: Macmillan).

Hamilton, V.L. and Sanders, J. (1999), 'The Second Face of Evil: Wrongdoing in and by the Corporation', *Personality and Social Psychology Review* 3:2, 222–33.

Hartle, A (2004), *Moral Issues in Military Decision-Making*, 2nd edition (revised) (Lawrence, KS: University Press of Kansas).

Huntley, I. (2003), 'Ethical Military Leadership', Farmington Trust Fellows Report ME 10, <http://www.farmington.ac.uk/documents/reports/framed/moral_ethical.html>.

Kelman, H.C. and Hamilton, V.L. (1989), *Crimes of Obedience: Toward a Social Psychology of Authority and Responsibility* (London: Yale University Press).

Kilner, P. (2000), 'Military Leaders to Justify Killing in Warfare', paper presented at the *Joint Services Conference on Professional Ethics*, Washington, DC, <http://www.usafa.af.mil/jscope/JSCOPE00>.

Martinelle-Fernandez, S. (2006), 'Educating Honourable Warriors', *Journal of Military Ethics* 5:1, 55–66.

Milgram, S. (1974), *Obedience to Authority: An Experimental View* (London: Tavistock).

Muñoz-Rojas, D. and Frésard, J. (2004), *The Roots of Behaviour in War: Understanding and Preventing IHL Violations* (Geneva: International Committee of the Red Cross).

Olsthoorn, P. (2005), 'Honor as a Motive for Making Sacrifices', *Journal of Military Ethics* 4:3, 183–97.

Osiel, M.J. (2002), *Obeying Orders: Atrocity, Military Discipline and the Law of War* (New Jersey: Transaction Publishers).

Sabini, J. and Silver, M. (2005), 'Lack of Character? Situationism Critiqued', *Ethics* 115, 535–62.

Torrance, I. and Roberts, S.J.L. (1998), *Ethics and the Military Community* (Camberley: Strategic and Combat Studies Institute).

Wakin, M. (1986), *War, Morality, and the Military Profession*, 2nd edition (Boulder, CO: Westview Press).

Zimbardo, P.G. (2007), *Stanford Prison Experiment: A Simulation Study of the Psychology of Imprisonment 1999-2007*, <http://www.prisonexp.org/>.

Chapter 15

The Ethical Warrior:
A Classical Liberal Approach

Alexander Moseley

From the recent revival of just war theory (in the wake of the apparent total war against terrorism as waged by some of the Western powers) emerges a resurrected discussion on military ethics – on what it means to be a good warrior – and how training colleges may best teach ethical behaviour. The wisdom sought is authentic, the desire to produce ethically minded soldiers similarly sincere, and the discussions are intellectually invigorating, but one has to be mindful of the assumptions upon which ethics is to be taught. Which raises the question: is there a basis upon which a military ethic ought be formed? And given a decent answer to that, what changes may follow to the reflections and arguments generally put forward in this volume?

The position proposed here derives from the political philosophy of classical liberalism: the belief in human nature and universal moral codes; minimal, representative and accountable government; and rights to life and property. (The writers in this tradition, which comes from the natural law tradition, include John Locke, David Hume, Adam Smith, David Ricardo, Jeremy Bentham, Richard Cobden, Wilhelm Humboldt and Ludwig Mises: cf. Mises 1985). Classical liberalism implies that soldiers ought to be ethically minded, but so too should the institutions that employ them, and while the traditions that have been passed down are thoroughly useful and practical, and while the need to teach ethics is paramount in an enterprise that may wrench people far from the norms of everyday morality, the teachers and supporters of ethical education should not baulk at encouraging critical and reflective thought beyond immediate and apparent military requirements.

Rejecting Relativism

Classical liberalism supports the proposition that there is such a thing as human nature and that we can discern what is conducive to life and peace (Rothbard 2002). It consequently upholds the right to life, liberty, and the pursuit of happiness; society is deemed predominantly (and even absolutely) self-regulating and hence favours minimal government and the employment of state sponsored force limited to defence against foreign aggression. It upholds the right of individuals to contract freely with other individuals and the concomitant right to break contracts subject to commonly agreed legal practices.

Accordingly, providing a classical liberal foundation to military ethics leads to a rejection of any attempt to found military ethics on realist or statist principles as being morally relativistic and thereby imbued with inconsistency and contradiction – states and their interests typically being peculiarly relativistic. One of the tenets of relativism is a rejection of human nature, for relativism upholds that what is good for one person is not necessarily good for another, and while that may hold an attraction to superficial thinking (I like spinach, you can't stand it, how can there be a common morality?), it dissolves quickly under a deeper search for commonalties (we both need to eat) (Rachels 1986).

In contrast to relativism, liberalism asserts that human nature not only exists but also guides the codes of social interaction. These codes tend to reflect that which is good for the people and the societies that they form, adjusting subtly to particular environmental conditions or inter-social arrangements, but generally speaking following the same themes of protecting and securing life and property through all societies. They are filtered through to military teaching and can be recognised by the similar aims and concepts used to teach recruits, as Fumio Ota comments in his chapter in this volume (see Chapter 13). In peace, it quickly becomes apparent what forms of action and interaction are conducive to maintaining social cohesion and the benefits that flow from mutually reciprocal arrangements. For the voluntaristic society of peaceful interaction tends to converge onto beneficial values and forms of behaviour and to reject those which are inimical.

Similarly in war, codes of conduct tend to emerge that act to bind a troop together, to maintain channels of peace with the enemy and to diminish the chances of total or prolonged war (Moseley 2003, 167). The latter are summarized in the just war conventions and the military academy moral codes, which, although having been codified to some extent, evolve from interaction and from conflict between peoples at war. They may thus be said to reflect the driving human aim to reject total, whimsical or wanton warfare as thoroughly inimical to life.

The guiding ethic of these codes, which stems consistently and logically from our understanding of human nature, and which thus ought to underpin any military's ethics, is the protection of life and property. Indeed it is for these two cardinal values for which the armed forces are theoretically (but not always historically) established. Although philosophically justifying this position lies beyond the remit of this chapter, suffice it to say that the classical liberal doctrine demands that the military be an instrument for the political representatives of the people and should only act in defending their lives and property from external aggression. Any reneging on that contract is to dissolve the military covenant with the people, even if the blame may be said to lie with political authorities who exploit their position for personal gain: when the military acts like the criminals that it is meant to protect the people from, then the people become justified in removing their sponsoring sanction and in refusing to obey its edicts.

Each army possesses its own catalogue of misdemeanours and crimes. These rightly become reminders for the next generations of recruits to maintain proper codes of conduct due our human nature. The similarity of such codes across nations again testifies to the core values that the military is set up to protect, which classical liberals emphasize as reflecting the right to life and dignity and the right to property and corresponding safety; the military virtues seek to ensure that soldiers retain an ethical understanding of their purpose and of their potential effects on life and civilians, and so they tend to reflect the broad ethical visions that are naturally part of peaceful and voluntaristic life, adjusted indubitably for the extraordinary moral realm in which soldiers act.

Relativism, we have noted, presents an unedifying plasticity that can be warped for ends far removed from core human values. It cannot therefore form the basis of ethical education. Similarly, teaching recruits 'the ethics of serving the state' (as is the practice in the French Military Academy; see Chapter 10) is highly questionable. The title presumes that serving the state is a good thing, which of course has to be established: after all, an Iraqi serving the state of Saddam Hussein would thus be accordingly judged on an equal footing to a French soldier serving the government of Sarkozy. To reply that such equality is not inconsistent with ethics is to commit a serious fallacy: the good does not emanate from serving government *per se*, for governments' policies may differ enormously, and the argument would permit the serving of opposing moral positions – notably, serving the right to aggress against another country compared to serving the right to defend a country. Such contradictions cannot be entertained for long, except at the cost of much confusion and resulting intellectual fogginess, which, if we are serious about military personnel learning to think ethically, cannot be of any assistance whatsoever to the soldier on the field faced with apparent dilemmas. (Classical liberal thinking tends to reject the existence of such dilemmas.) Naturally, such a course as 'the ethics of serving the state' should stretch into discussions concerning the merits of various state policies, but they should also leap into anarchic discussions of whether the state can ever be deemed good as well as establishing the criteria of judging good state conduct from bad – e.g., securing the rule of law, minimizing intervention with human liberties, establishing impartial political procedures and democratic representation, and so on.

The military is not too prone to the revolutionary or intellectual zealousness that can fire the pamphlets and books of intellectuals; its generally conservative momentum is reflected in values which may appear atavistic to some, but which tend to reflect the military context and experience. Arguably, the military context and experience that forms the traditional codes reflect a deeper, often tacit, commitment to human life and its moral worth. Time and the vivid expediency of action (and reflection thereon) will act to weed out the useless precepts and those that fall far from the civilian expectations of moral conduct, but we must be aware of the potential military and therefore human cost of tying soldiers to irrational or whimsical fashions that capture media and political attention.

Only the so-called virtues of obedience and self-sacrifice would the classical liberal question as being the military's weakness for ascribing to political ambitions, for these play well into the hands of relativist and fashionable thinking and act to denigrate the innate dignity and will of the individual soldier. It hardly needs to be said that obedience (rather than cooperation) lends itself to uncritical thinking and thereby the implied demand that the self is sacrificial to those who demand obedience. (It is absurd to claim that man 'sacrifices' himself for a value that he thoroughly believes in, e.g., defence of his homeland or family, for the term sacrifice implies giving up higher values in favour of lower values (Rand 1964).)

A Critical Overview of Military Ethics Based on Classical Liberal Principles

Some authors within the classical liberal camp proclaim the precedence of utilitarian (Mill 1884) or Kantian ethics (Kant 1949), but neither reflects consistently well the requirements of human nature and interaction; instead, drawing on the robust tradition of virtue ethics, I will argue that ethical and conscientiously authentic action stems from the prime virtues of being focused and rational, and that a broader and deeper examination appropriate to the level of training should be included in officer or recruit education, which in turn demands an invigorating (or brutal if you will!) examination of all that is held dear as well as a thorough assessment of context, conditions, and criteria for action.

Above all, soldiers ought to be taught to think. The capacity to think is not only that which distinguishes us as human but also provides our means of survival. Of course, thinking promotes critical examination, but that must be allowed to run its conscientious course in each soldier, even if those thoughts lead to a rejection of the military covenant. To demand a rejection of thought is in effect a demand to reject a person's faculty of survival – it is to demote them below humanity, just as we say that a thoughtless brute acts *inhumanely*. Second, with regards to specific ethics teaching, this means that the values that have emerged from military experience, while possessing an excellent grounding for initial training, must also be subject to soldiers' thorough examination. And while a soldier may learn to pull apart a regiment's or college's cherished moral banners (and should learn in dialectical exercises), I would imagine that through critical and persistent examination, recruits who sincerely wish to stay the course and to become good soldiers will usually come to understand – through experience and maturity as much as through reflection and discussion with veterans – that the guiding epithets often retain a usefulness beyond their apparent ethical shallowness and that they do not have to be read as the mere advertising slogans of political expediency. But such an education will also act to raise soldiers' sensitivity to political and moral inauthenticity around them, and should their conscience so lead them, they may reject the military covenant. This is their human right. (I shall be addressing this issue in more detail in a future paper.)

The Nature of Military Ethics

A tenuous moral cord connects the civilian realm to the military realm, which may be severed or strengthened for a variety of reasons. Properly speaking for the purposes of civilization, as the classical liberal upholds, the military exists as an instrument to defend the values of life, property, and peaceful social interaction of the people who sponsor it. The moral cord extends provisionally to the military to uphold a set of core values which reflect the sponsoring people's requirement to have their lives and property protected from external threats (the police possessing the same provision for the protection of life and property from internal threats). In reacting to an external threat, the military must abide by the same rules for which it upholds domestic peace and it should not engage in wanton destruction of enemy life or property. When that relationship is strained by unethical and compromising behaviour, that moral provision presented to the military falters. A military designed and used to invade, pillage or interfere with the political, cultural, or religious processes of another nation differs not from a gang of robbers or extortionists, who use their weaponry to exact property or changes: such a military organization is not civil. So should the moral cord be severed, the military realm falls below the levels of acceptable morality and sinks into the immoral chasm of murder, plunder, rape, and pillage and thereby cannot be distinguished from pure brigandry and the evils that it ought to be instrumental in protecting people from.

The cry for the military to become (more) ethical – that is, to uphold a decent set of values and codes appropriate to their status both as soldiers and as instruments of the civilian realm – is often raised when the military is employed in dubious endeavours that stretch the moral codes commensurate with humanity. A great part of the ethical framework of the God-fearing chivalric Christian warrior originated from civilian and clerical condemnation and rebellion against predatory soldiers and bandits a thousand years ago: the tenth and early eleventh centuries witnessed the Peace of God movement that sought to reorient the soldier's ethic from predation to what amounts to an ethical protection of the poor and clergy (Morris 1991). Knighthood (ethical soldiery) was slowly Christianized by this effective popular movement that came from the South of France. Knights were to avoid fighting on certain Christian days and any fighting had to reflect codes of conduct: as part of the new ethical order imposed on them by the civilian authorities, knights were to remain true and loyal to domestic, feudal, and political orders. They were to be harnessed by the civilian powers from which they ultimately drew their economic sustenance. No longer was it the knight's singular purpose to kill but to show off his skills – his prowess (*prouesse*) – in a fight or joust. Self-interest and adherence to a strong family (regiment) and class code of conduct bound the medieval knight to an international code with high expectations of just and proper conduct.

The modern code of chivalry was thus born and still guides the precepts of the ethical soldier today insofar as it continues to reflect the underlying needs of human morality. We could say that we still have echoes of the 'Peace of God' movement whenever the military is felt or observed by civilians to have stretched or broken its fragile contractual cord: the call is made to rein it in and to teach soldiers the moral limits to their realm, and gradually that realm was limited by classical liberal thinkers reflecting on the proper and moral role of government in general to involvement in protecting life and property, not predation upon it. In theory that is; but assuredly with present Western armed forces involved in distant actions motivated by vague political goals or interfering with political and cultural processes outside of their jurisdiction and soldiers compromising the values of civilization which they are employed to defend, it is unsurprising to hear calls for explicit ethics teaching in the military academies.

Historians can chart the relationship between popular outcries at military atrocities and the reactions produced (cf. Glover 1999); military ethics can respond to those demands to help produce a more effective teaching programme to help recruits work through ethical issues and dilemmas; but the job of the philosopher is to justify and explore that relationship and to examine the justifications and subtleties of that relationship.

Even though the great moral purpose of the soldier is to protect life and property, the armed man stands in an awkward moral realm – ideally (or we may say, traditionally) presented as ready to kill or be killed, defend property as well as fire upon it when necessary, and ready to obey orders from above. If we ignore the ultimate purveyors of orders, whether the politico-military leaders of a junta or representatively elected politicians, we can see that the soldier exists in what truly is a strange moral limbo in which the assumptions of peace that drive the mores of the civil realm are laid aside. The soldier's realm apparently would barely justify any thought; it is ostensibly characterized as a game of predator and prey in numbers ranging from two to thousands in which highly tuned skills are deployed and physical and mental abilities to cope with extraordinary conditions stretched. It follows that if we describe the warrior as one resigned or trained into a habit of low level thinking or mimicry, then there is no purpose to teaching soldiers ethics as such, except insofar as new commands governing particular situations are driven into soldiers' training: don't fire upon surrendering troops, avoid killing non-combatants who stray into range, etc., with various behaviourist models set up to attract low thinking recruits into doing the desired actions. The onus for acting properly would seemingly thus rest with superiors. But they may excuse themselves as acting merely as technical and strategic advisors to the political representatives who command and justify their deployment.

Such is the Clausewitzian ideal of course, that war is the continuation of politics by other means (Clausewitz 1968), with its implication that the military is subservient to the political authorities. But for the classical liberal, political activity is to be restricted to ensuring the smooth running of the civil order and its protection from external and internal aggression. Leaders may go astray, as patently they often have done and do, but that does not alter the moral judgment that may be laid at their feet, and neither should it weaken the ability and right of inferiors in the institutional ranks to question the morality of orders and policies.

While the traditional reading of Clausewitz would apparently imply that recruits need not worry their minds about the purposes of the political masters, the classical liberal reading presents a radical departure from what is normally understood as political processes. It has been around for centuries, but in the cacophony of nationalist policies and interventionist 'liberalism', the fundamental moral connections that should exist between the armed forces and their political controllers and between the institutional arrangements of the armed forces and their recruits have been muted – thus the humanist vision is silenced. Alternatively, the classical liberal proclaims that the ethical warrior cannot afford to assume that his or her superiors possess the moral right to do anything, for to do otherwise would be to uphold a slave mentality which is not appropriate for civilization. Ethics demands reflection and the seeking of understanding, and when that is delegated to others (even superiors), then the potential for true and authentic ethical action becoming a human is negated.

It follows that any explicit teaching of ethics which is designed to acknowledge its existence but without any provision for authenticity of choice and the possible rejection of orders is mere cant.

Indubitably, the historical inheritance of many martial values stem from older hierarchical societies (notably feudal in the west) that presume the relegation of thought in the lower orders of the ranks. And the extent to which such values demand an oppression of thought and moral evaluation, so they render ethics redundant. Those values, which find expression in the particular academies' and regiments' banners, understandably seek to promote professionalism and an upholding of collective disciple and virtue, the cooperative nature of military action, the need for unified values and action. Such values are there to be learned and understood, but never at the cost of extinguishing the individual soldier's conscientious and inalienable human right of exit: what ethic would demand that it be trammelled upon, or the soldier imprisoned or shot? Not one that can sit well with classical liberal principles of individual freedom of life and property and not one that can sit well with any humanist, who believes that certain codes and forms of behaviour are thoroughly and rightfully human and universal. To demand unconditional acceptance of orders or service is to demand recruits become obedient robots – a painful vision for any humanist.

Nonetheless, it is undeniable that the obedient robotic soldier ideal has been very influential in the military history of institutionally founded and sponsored armies: the allegedly ethical institutionally organized recruit was to be an obedient killing machine, ready to lay down his life for political or ideological ends that could rarely be said to be of his choosing: 'theirs was not to reason why, theirs but to do and die'. Such was, indeed is, the archetypal soldier of institutionally organized warfare, a single expendable element drowned in a collective entity to be wielded by superiors. Obedience (rather than agreement and cooperation) is the supposed ethical norm of such armies, but obedience cannot be ethical, for it implies the negation of one's own conscience in favour of another's and thereby the renunciation of much that makes us human.

Compare the obedient institutional soldier with the archetypal individualistic warrior – Achilles – who sets his own ends or fights on his own terms, whose glorious achievements famed in history and legend fire the minds and intentions of the more individualistic warriors within and without institutions. The heroic warrior, who we may characterize as the great individualist warrior of battles of yore swinging his sword against the onrush of the enemy, or his modern counterpart in the guise of the quirky general outwitting both friendly and enemy institutions through tenacious genius and dogged determination. The heroic individualist presents an unedifying role model for the military colleges, for their purpose charges them to produce soldiers capable of being part of a smoothly running fighting organisation: the Spartan 300 who defended Thermopylae presenting an eternal example of the best that a team can present (Herodotus 1996). Naturally, there is much irony in the uncritical soldier obeying the orders of superiors while believing himself to be an individualist hero incarnate, for the archetypal hero tends to possess a more finely tuned critical apparatus particularly with respect to institutional commands!

On the modern battlefield or in other forms of military operation, the opportunity for individualist feats of great soldiering still present themselves, but most action will be tied to closely interacting group work with varying intricacies and nuances between groups of the same regiment, other regiments, other elements of the armed forces, and of course, political and civilian colleagues. A group dynamic – sociological and ethical – is thereby going to present an important aspect of the formation of the ethical and philosophical modern warrior, and this is typically reflected in colleges' aims. But do they go far enough? If, as I mentioned above, the ethical soldier ought to be focused, to be consciously awake to all that he is and all that is around him, then the colleges are justified in seeking to raise the philosophical focus of its students. Once criticality is raised, how far ought it to proceed? Arguably, there should be no bounds – authenticity cannot come from holding inquiry back, and this is as true in military life as it is in civilian, despite the rising chorus of worried superiors and mandarins that such a claim may provoke: nothing should be off limits to the human mind.

Arguably, the less critically thinking and more obedient a soldier is either to his or her superiors or to culturally or religiously imbibed habits, the less philosophical and the less ethical a soldier can be both in being and action. Ethical choice demands an authenticity from conviction of right intention and application concerning means and ends; in contrast, the uncritically obedient soldier relegates his or her very being below the threshold of what it is to be human, never mind that of an ethical warrior. The better path encourages reflection and understanding and opens the way for an authentically ethical individualism underpinned philosophically by a *hyper criticality* – a thorough going and continuous focus and thinking, consistently checking philosophical bases as it were. Only then, when the soldier has thought through – and persists in thinking through – his or her reasons for acting, working separately or working effectively with a team, being part of the armed forces or resigning from them, only then can it be said that the soldier is truly and authentically ethical.

Authenticity implies that the soldier is focused and by that is meant that he or she brings to work and tasks an appropriate level of thought and examination of context, conditions, and criteria of action. To parry a rising retort, it would of course be inappropriate to muse philosophically in the middle of an engagement that requires all of a soldier's professional training and skills. To be focused means to be focused on the job at hand and thereby to act appropriately (Branden 1997), and while I would strongly argue that that demand may lead to a rejection of a soldier's contract (and that a soldier possesses an inalienable right to break that contract at any time), it mainly implies that when on exercise or on duty, a soldier should bring his or her context into focus: that is, he or she lives consciously and *is* there, rather than acts 'automatically' (i.e., with a lowered level of focus) or is 'somewhere else' – typically in the foggy realm of unfocused thought.

Focusing on the job stems from the training and education that the soldier learns through the academies and military colleges. It would seem to be an increasing requisite of the modern armed forces, especially, as has been noted many times, because of the increased use of more intricate technology on the field which necessitates a higher intelligence and awareness level; but while the professional focus of tactics and use of weaponry are thoroughly learned through practice, the call to focus demands a more thorough philosophical and hence ethical training.

Naturally, a great deal of this can be gleaned from practice as well as from the experiences and lectures of veterans, which is why the colleges' educational programmes are apparently successful in raising complex issues, but intellectual discussion and provocation must also play a vivid role in training the recruit's mind to think clearly above and beyond the physical reactions and habits that drill can instil. Initial physical training is necessarily tough to promote endurance and discipline; it also acts to wake up the body with respect to what it is capable of. So why should colleges not also seek to put recruits' minds through the same mental training? The soldier's body must be prepared for the eventualities that it may be subject to, so why not the mind? Some commentators (for instance Martin Cook in Chapter 5) note the slovenliness of recruits' thinking: not knowing, for example, what the true purpose of the armed forces is or why they joined; or they may be immersed in the catch-all and popular epithets of relativism and quasi-nihilist quips. The lack of mental focus and poor or nonexistent application of mind to ethics or to wider visions is equivalent to physical slovenliness that physical training aims to overcome. A physically fit man or woman can be said to be physically focused on and in the environment, but a dividing duality of permitting a slovenly or indolent mind within a fit body cannot be justified.

In many respects, the demand that soldiers should raise their focus beyond the mere technical aspects of soldiering to persistent reflection and criticality is not a path that may gain institutional applause. Institutions, especially those far removed from the ever adapting interplay of market and voluntaristic social forces, tend to foster ideals of artificial corporate identity which act to subjugate individuality, reduce members' rationality, and hence demote their critical and authentic ethical being. But if military authorities and academics are going to be serious about teaching ethics to soldiers, they must accept that it implies encouraging unlimited criticality; after all, it would be ironic that unlimited liability is assumed for a soldier's life but not permitted for his or her thinking. Here, for example, the right to dissolve a contract or a promise, so cherished in the voluntary order of the open society, must reach out into the armed forces to allow the recruit or professional soldier to withdraw his services at any time (for a financial penalty). If that right is evaded or rejected by those who would prefer quietly obeying troops who merely react to orders, then ethics cannot be taught in any meaningful manner except that of hypocrisy.

Basic training sharpens the body's abilities and responses, and implicitly it acts to instil a set of values and codes appropriate to the collective. In turn, it may be trite to add that the donning of a uniform acts to *negate* individuality by reminding its wearer of his or her institutional affiliation and his or her acceptance of what the collective stands for and aims to achieve; but it is also symbolic of the contract that the individual has committed to, and that demands an awareness of both the particular regimental and general military ethos and of his or her commitment to serve. The former may be generally instilled through team exercise and the gentle education or turning of the mind to the traditional morals of the armed forces and academy or regiment, but the latter, the awareness of the commitment to serve, demands the thorough-going focus that many a military mind may baulk at. But why? To reject the right of an individual soldier to question the nature and breadth of service is itself a renunciation of focus, a focus that is not rejected when it comes to filtering out those who are not physically (or concomitantly psychologically) appropriate for the armed forces. The wearing of a uniform need not be a rejection of mind – indeed, it should act to sharpen the wearer's mind to the conditions and criteria of the military contract, a refocusing of individual action as it takes place with and through co-operative team work. Here the Federal German conception (see Chapter 9) that the soldier is a citizen, or even a 'social worker' (see for instance Rosenberg 2006) in uniform presents a useful, albeit a little strange, reminder to wearers that they owe their allegiance to the overarching civilian code that sponsors them morally and financially. However, I would be concerned that the concept of 'citizen in uniform' is too reminiscent of total war thinking – that the soldier bearing uniform is a legitimate target in war is agreed upon, but a small logical step can demand that the civilian is merely a soldier without a uniform, and hence a legitimate target.

To become ethical, a soldier must be focused and consciously aware, and as mentioned above he or she must be focused appropriately on the task at hand, whether the task is interrogating a prisoner, patrolling a dangerous street, presenting commands, obeying commands, organizing supplies, killing a close target, firing upon a distant target, or anything else. Focusing appropriately on the situation gives the soldier the means by which to act ethically and the means by which his or her actions can also be judged.

Focus and conscious awareness are governed by surroundings and particular context, but it is also governed by *how* to think rationally, logically and consistently, and thus critically (Branden 1997). Ethics training in the military academies aims to expand the vision of awareness for recruits, to encourage them to think beyond the immediate situation and, as has traditionally been effective, to think about the repercussions for the corporate reputation of the regiment or armed forces generally, but also, especially these days, to consider the impact on the wider non-military world of civilian morals and legal norms. To foster that, recruits ought to be taught how to think by exploring logical arguments and fallacies, which would help sharpen their minds to contradictions in orders or policies, but also sharpen their thinking for dealing with awkward and ethically challenging scenarios.

However, again it must be noted that the very nature of state sponsored armed forces does not present many incentives to raise the individual soldier up from an uncritical level to the philosophical realm, which, if we are honest, demands that hyper criticality that can lead to a rejection, at any time, of the armed forces' demands, commands, and even contract. But the philosophical path that rekindles or inspires focused mental individualism nonetheless lies there to be discovered and should not be ignored. The classical liberal strongly believes that it is a path that cadets and recruits need to be shown as a valid and morally appropriate one, even though it may ostensibly compromise military effectiveness (which I doubt) should serving soldiers prefer to lay down arms rather than serve in a particular campaign or war.

Consider as a final point instead, the moral consistency of soldiers who consciously agree to work and fight together and the bonds they may create – it is a more helpful image than that presented by conscripts forced to give up months or years of their life or by soldiers suddenly thrown into a war not consistent with their ethics. This is apparently what the Federal German programme is seeking to instil, and although it may be noted with irony that the German army, which is not in active service, is enjoying pax's luxury of educating its troops to think deeper, it should also be remembered that, indeed, the German army is *not* engaged in controversial campaigns. However, it is morally thwarted instead by conscription, which the classical liberal cannot condone (cf. Locke 1997).

When an army is at war, ethical considerations appear luxurious, but in the aftermath of war they are soon be seen as imperative. The intentions behind the programmes described in this volume are certainly sincere and each acknowledges the need to reflect local and particular histories and issues as they have arisen – the theoretical programmes cannot be faulted, although I would strongly err in favour of those that imbibe traditional virtues through example as being more conducive to moral authenticity than through rote learning of ethical positions. However, the blast of war does strain the ability of an army to contain belligerent excesses, which have a tendency to rise to notable infamy because of the swiftness of modern media. The disparity between what is learned in the classroom by tired cadets and what is learned on the field can hardly be removed, but if active soldiers knew in advance that they would have to return regularly to the classroom as part of their training to discuss their actions (having seen veterans return), they might raise their immediate awareness and focus to consider longer term repercussions and accountability both on the self and regiment, thereby satisfying both classical liberal and military concerns.

Bibliography

Branden, N. (1997), *Art of Living Consciously* (New York: Simon and Schuster).

Glover, J. (1999), *Humanity: A Moral History of the Twentieth Century* (London: Jonathan Cape).

Herodotus (1996), *Histories* (London: Penguin).

Kant, I. (1949), *Fundamental Principles of the Metaphysics of Morals* (New York: Liberal Arts Press).

Mill, J.S. (1884), *On Liberty* (London: Longmans, Green and Co.).

Mises, L. (1985), *Liberalism* (Irvington, NY: Foundation for Economic Education: Irvington).

Morris, C. (1991), *The Papal Monarchy: The Western Church from 1050 to 1250* (Oxford: Clarendon Press).

Moseley, A. (2003), 'The Rules of War in Sub-Saharan Africa', in P. Robinson (ed.), *Just War in Comparative Perspective*, pp. 167–84.

Rachels, J. (1986), *Elements of Moral Philosophy* (New York: Random House).

Rand, A. (1964), *The Virtue of Selfishness* (New York: Random House).

Robinson, P. (ed.) (2003), *Just War in Comparative Perspective* (Aldershot: Ashgate).

Rosenberg, S. (2006), 'German Army on Afghan Charm Offensive', BBC News, 15 December, <http://news.bbc.co.uk/1/hi/world/south_asia/6182845.stm>.

Rothbard, M. (2002), *Ethics of Liberty* (New York: New York Press).

von Clausewitz, C. (1968), *On War*, Vol. I, trans. Colonel J.J. Graham)(London: Routledge and Kegan Paul).

Chapter 16

The Future of Ethics Education in the Military: A Comparative Analysis

Don Carrick

Introduction

One of the stated objectives of this volume is 'to consider the appropriate roles of military personnel, chaplains, philosophers and others within the structure of a military ethics training and development programme'. Martin Cook suggests that the role of philosophers is the inculcation of thinking skills: 'the Core philosophy class [at the US Air Force Academy] accomplishes two central development purposes: 1) it is the one place where [the cadets] engage in sustained normative reflections and learn some skills for doing so; and 2) it is one of the few points in their Academy education where they engage in sustained critical thinking about complex problems' (see Chapter 5). This seems right. Philosophers, by definition, think, and professional philosophers think for a living; they teach others to do so and get paid for it. This pedagogic function identified by Cook is an illuminating example of how history has a tendency to repeat itself. The picture of philosophers as practitioners in, and teachers of, *practical* philosophy (now more commonly called applied ethics) portrayed by him would have been entirely recognizable to Plato and Aristotle (particularly the latter). Indeed, I suspect that they would have been somewhat puzzled by the (relatively) modern view of philosophers which prevailed until at least the late 1960s, namely as academics detached from 'real life' who spend all their time theorizing (an image which still lingers in some circles; see for instance Chapter 4 of this volume). However, the truth is that the well-rounded philosopher-teacher has to be able to operate in both areas. And when circumstances bring about a situation in which those in a particular role can no longer function in that role simply by (unthinkingly) 'doing their job' and 'playing it by the rules', then the need to call in the philosophers in order to critically examine the foundational assumptions, theories, norms and principles (which at some deep level provide the *justification* for the role-defined actions) becomes acute. Such is now the situation with the military, where something like a paradigm shift is taking place in the area of ethics education. The time seems ripe for calling in the philosophers, possibly as part of team of advisers from various disciplines. Let us therefore now set the scene in a little more detail, to see how philosophers in particular might be of assistance in the present context.

Background

A study of the papers presented here reveals that the *general* training and education programmes of the military in the many and varied cultural and geographical contexts represented still have a great deal in common, as least as far as pedagogical methodology is concerned, and that their teaching programmes have changed very little over the years, any differences being more of form rather than substance. This is hardly surprising given that, in the past, the primary aim of the programmes was the production of good (i.e. efficiently functioning) soldiers [a term which, for the sake of brevity, I shall use to encompass members of all branches of the military services, male and female]. This aim has remained constant since the inception of the programmes. The objective of the training establishments has been to turn out soldiers who can be relied upon to carry out their role-defined task – traditionally reducible to killing people and breaking things – *well*.

But what we have witnessed latterly is the coming into prominence of a second aim of the programmes, namely the production, through 'ethics education', of good soldiers who are also good *people*. Most (but not all) of the authors on view appear to have little doubt that *character education*, in one form or another, has to be an integral part of soldiers' education and training: Martin Cook in Chapter 5 and Stefan Werdelis in Chapter 9 incorporate 'character development' into the very titles of their papers. This was by no means the case in the past. It was assumed in most of the nations on show here that the character of would-be soldiers, and especially officers, was something of a 'given', by reason of the social circumstances or religious faith of the cadets involved (very obviously so in the case of the British Army, at least until very recently; see Stephen Deakin's masterly portrait of the 'English Christian Gentleman' in Chapter 2). 'Morality' was something that was caught rather than taught (see Chapman 2002 for an overview of a similar history of ethics education in the legal profession). Now, it seems, ethics has made it onto the teaching syllabus, permanently, as a discrete subject.

This shift of emphasis in the pedagogical aspects of soldiers' training has been tracked by a growing awareness of the need to provide a sound psychological and philosophical underpinning for the new teaching programmes; (very) broadly speaking, since the late 1950s the philosophy of choice has come from Plato via Immanuel Kant and the psychology of choice from Jean Piaget via Lawrence Kohlberg. Now, it seems, the time has come for a change of philosophical scenery, at least; one philosophical giant of the past, Aristotle, figures strongly in the present papers. There is no doubt about the intuitive appeal of his particular combination of sophisticated philosophical reasoning, acute psychological insight into human nature, and down-to-earth common sense. Yet it is also easy to see why the approach of the other great founding father of Western philosophy, Plato, is so appealing, especially in the military context; the education of the 'Guardians' (*Republic*, Book II) provides a virtually 'off-the-shelf' model for old-style military training. Plato has been the preferred model in military ethics education for some time (as Jeffrey Wilson eloquently demonstrates in Chapter 3). So why the change? To discover the reasons, I now offer a brief overview of the history of ethics education in general, starting with a little more about Aristotle and his project.

Ethics Education in History

Aristotle was himself a teacher; the *Nicomachean Ethics* is a collection of his lecture notes, not a work of philosophical theory. But Aristotle was not a philosophical theorist in our sense of the term; he was essentially a practical philosopher wanting to equip help his students in a practical way. He was not concerned with equipping his students to answer questions like 'What should I do?', but rather with trying to help his students answer, for themselves, Socrates' old question 'How should we live?' Note immediately that this is a very *general* question. It encompasses the whole of our lives. It was also posed with teleological intent; Aristotle, comparing human life with plant and animal life, suggested that we should aim at achieving a state of *flourishing* (the nearest we can get to an accurate translation of *eudaimonia*, although it is important to note that *eudaimonia* is not a *state*, it is rather an *activity*). To flourish, according to Aristotle, we need to acquire a *virtuous disposition*, that is, we need to be in possession of all the virtues. Once we have taken on a virtuous character, and acquired practical wisdom (*phronesis*), we shall be disposed to act virtuously from then on.

Coming right up to date, it is therefore relatively easy to see why 'virtue ethics' currently has centre stage in terms of being the moral theory most in favour: there is a lot of truth in the observation (made by Martin Cook in Chapter 5) that Aristotle is the 'intellectual father' of virtue ethics. However, we should also remember that we may not be comparing like with like here. Our notion of the nature and scope of *morality* itself is very different to Aristotle's. For him, what we would call 'the moral virtues' were but one part of a much larger class of virtues which we still split between 'intellectual' and 'moral', as he did, but without our emphasis on the supposed *primacy* of the moral virtues. (Bernard Williams makes a similar point in his argument that 'morality' is only a relatively minor part of 'ethics'; see Williams 1985 passim.) Further, Aristotle would have been more than a little puzzled by our notions of *moral* obligation and *moral* duty. That these notions came to dominate the ethical scene is almost certainly due to the intervening influence of Judaeo-Christian teaching. What such teaching has produced is a *law-like* conception of morality; morality, according to the teaching, derives from a *law-giver*, namely God. And this is where we can identify the beginnings of a sea-change in our Western perceptions of the *authority* of morality and its place in our lives, a change observed and perceptively (and presciently) commented on 50 years ago by Elizabeth Anscombe in her seminal paper 'Modern Moral Philosophy' (Anscombe 1958). She argued that for so long as morality had the backing of divine command and the threat of divine sanction to enforce any breaches of the code, all was well, but in a *secular* society, which did not have a moral law-giver in place, a law-like morality, consisting of rules to be followed and duties to be obeyed, simply lost its guiding force.

But the problem for educators in the military is that the military ethos – best encapsulated at its most succinct in the West Point motto 'Honor, Duty, Country' – surely derives from the very same law-like, religion-backed conception of morality that we operated with for so long. It is surely correct to say that this ethos has survived longer in the military than in any other section of society (as suggested in Berntsen and Rolfsen's observations on the decline of hierarchical and command-based social structures; see Chapter 8). So is it time for the education establishments in the military to catch up with the high fashion in moral theory? I do not believe so. I believe that a Kantian law-like morality and a neo-Aristotelean theory of ethics *both* have a part to play in underpinning a soldier's ethical education. To understand why this should be particularly important at the present time, we have to take into account some more historical background, this time by way of an exposition of the changing nature of war and of its supposed justifications.

Warfare Old and New

We are living at a time when, for many of us, 'old-fashioned' wars have become the exception rather than the rule (but not for all; Asa Kasher notes that Israel has been involved in five major wars since 1948. See Chapter 12). Ethics education for the military in the past was correspondingly, and understandably, geared to producing troops fit for fighting primarily old-fashioned wars, such as the Falklands War, which involved the recapture of what was regarded as British sovereign territory wrongfully invaded by Argentina. The role of the military was, in general terms, to undertake the Defence of the Realm. The moral justification for undertaking and engaging in that war was by way an appeal to just war theory and to a suitably modified (and modernized) version of the Augustinian list of justificatory conditions, primarily the self-defence condition. But times have changed. Whilst the self-defence condition could be reasonably stretched to encompass what we have come to describe as pre-emptive and preventive wars, it does not appear to stretch widely enough to take in humanitarian interventions and peacekeeping or peace enforcing engagements (putting the problem succinctly, in such situations, just who or what are 'we' supposed to be defending ourselves against?). Tor Arne Berntsen and Raag Rolfsen suggest that we are moving from a situation in which the armed forces are regarded as having but a single function not needing any moral justification other than an appeal to self defence to a situation in which the military is seen 'as an instrument available to the state in pursuance of its own interests' (see Chapter 8).

This captures something of the reasoning which lies behind Paul Gilbert's recent very useful suggestion that 'old wars' characteristically embody 'the politics of role' and 'new wars' embody 'the politics of identity'. He argues that what distinguished old wars was that they were typically 'contests between *states* in which various actors behave in ways regulated by the requirements of their roles' (Gilbert 2003, 11, my emphasis). By contrast, new wars are 'fought against or on behalf of *peoples*, over the manner in which their *collective identities* should be politically recognised' (ibid., 8, my emphasis). Thus, for Gilbert, the soldier is his role *qua* soldier has no need of feelings such as love of country and presumably no need for any motivation other than the desire to carry out his role-defined duties, to the best of his ability, as the aforementioned instrument of the state. If, as Gilbert asserts (ibid., 87), 'the norms of the jus in bello ... derive from the role of the soldier' and the soldier is indeed (no more than) an instrument of the state, then it would seem that the *politics* of role could mark the limits of any *moral* motivation, on the part of the individual soldier, to abide by the rules of war. If a soldier steps outside the role and, as Paul Robinson says is his perceptive critical review of Gilbert's book (see Robinson 2006), 'starts viewing himself as the representative of a collective identity', then he becomes prone to breaking the rules of war.

Yet involvement in new wars and operations other than war does require the soldier to engage with the politics of identity, either indirectly, as in Iraq where American and British troops are unavoidably embroiled in the Sunni-Shia conflict (a clear 'politics of identity' clash) or directly, as in humanitarian interventions. An invasion of the sovereign territory of another state on humanitarian grounds is *not* undertaken in Defence of the Realm and cannot therefore be easily justified by appeal to just war theory.

Furthermore, these changes in the nature of warfare and related operations have been marked by a parallel changes, qualitative as well as quantitative, in the duties and responsibilities of the soldiers involved. The soldier of the future is likely to be not only on occasion soldier, policeman, 'hearts and minds' ambassador or general diplomat, but sometimes all of them alternately on a single occasion, in quick and confusing succession. Also, the soldiers involved in the operations in question are as likely to be 'strategic corporals' (or even 'strategic privates') as officers (see General George Krulak's classic tale of Corporal Hernandez's adventures in a 'Three Block War': Krulak 1999).

The Problem of 'Officer Bias'

So are we currently educating the wrong people to engage in the wrong operations? There seems to be little doubt that current ethics education programmes in the military are still overwhelmingly biased towards the production of (good) *officers*. A major pedagogical obstacle has to be surmounted here, as far as deciding upon the target audience for such education and development is concerned. Ethics education in the military has, until relatively recently, been aimed almost exclusively at the officer classes, not at the enlisted men, notwithstanding that, in past wars, it has been the enlisted men who have done by far the greater part of the face-to-face killing and breaking. Perusal of the papers in this volume suggests that in most training establishments, adherence to this practice is still firmly embedded in the mindsets of those responsible for the training of the military. The majority of the training establishments on show appear to regard ethics education as being confined to, and only needed by, officer cadets, with a few extending it to non-commissioned officers (such as the Netherlands and

Australia), and one extending it to all ranks but with one ethics programme for senior officers and one for junior officers and enlisted men (Norway). Only in the German armed forces is there any indication that the same programme of ethics education encompasses, without distinction, enlisted men and commissioned and non-commissioned officers (see Chapter 9).

But if the (good) soldiers of the future are indeed going to be 'strategic corporals' or 'strategic privates' involved in fighting 'Three Block Wars' and partaking in operations other than war, with a consequent shift of tactical *and moral* responsibility for decision-making in the field from officers to non-commissioned officers and enlisted men, then should not they be receiving the lion's share of the ethics teaching? Part of the problem may be a reluctance to admit that the ordinary footslogger has the intellectual capacity to be ethically educated in the first place. The presumptions and prejudices of 50 years ago still seem to linger on here. Samuel P. Huntington, for example, drew a sharp line between officers and the rest: 'The enlisted men subordinate to the officer corps are a part of the organizational bureaucracy but not of the professional bureaucracy. The enlisted personnel have *neither the intellectual skills not the professional responsibility* of the officer. They are specialists in the application of violence not the management of violence. *Their vocation is a trade not a profession*' (Huntington 1957, 17–18, my emphasis).

The question therefore is this: if we accept for present purposes that the Huntington 'us and them' thesis is now unjustifiable in theory and unworkable in practice, are we best advised to jettison it altogether and pin our hopes on the creation of an army consisting mainly of strategic corporals/privates, with the officer class being relegated to performing a much more limited managerial role (so to speak)? My own intuition is that there is a danger of a self-defeating overreaction here. A perception that the present generation of soldiers does *too little* thinking about the 'big' ethical picture and takes *too little* responsibility for decision-making might lead us to plunging headlong into an ethics education and development programme that has an inherent a risk of producing soldiers from whom *too much* thinking and *too much* decision making was demanded. The practical effect could be that, in attempting to produce the proverbial Jacks of all trades *from the ethical point of view*, we end up with a military comprised of masters of none.

In order to confront this problem more constructively, I must now go off at another tangent, by way of exercise in comparative analysis and evaluation, via the notions of 'profession' and 'role morality', and of the ethics training of the military, legal and medical professions.

Professions and Role Morality

That the armed forces have been (and in most countries and cultures still are) regarded without question as a *profession* should not come as a surprise. The military are one of the three original professions (although the label 'profession' is of relatively recent origin); Law, Medicine, and the Military. The following criteria (or some variation of them) are often quoted as being individually necessary and jointly sufficient as to what a 'profession' comprises:

- professions provide an important public service;
- professional practitioners require a high degree of individual autonomy – independence of judgment – for effective practice;
- professions involve theoretically as well as practically guided expertise;
- they require organization and regulation for purposes of recruitment and discipline; and
- they have a distinct ethical dimension which calls for expression in a code of practice.

The last condition seems to have attracted the most emphasis amongst writers on professional ethics. Indeed, one writer virtually ignores the first four criteria and defines a profession as comprising 'a number of individuals in the same occupation voluntary organized to earn a living *by openly serving a certain moral ideal* in a morally-permissible way *beyond what law, market and morality would otherwise require*' (Davis 2002, 3, my emphasis. I have in fact criticized Davis's approach elsewhere and I quote his definition as illustrative, not by way of implying approval of it. See Carrick 2004). He goes on to say that 'the moral authority of professional codes seems to rest on an auxiliary rule. We might state it briefly as "obey your profession's code"' (ibid., 26). These ideals – the teleological targets, so to speak, of the three professions – are (traditionally again) assumed to be Justice, Health and (as previously stated) Defence of the Realm. But one problem with the 'old' military ideal now becomes even more obvious; if undertaking at least some of the varieties of new wars and, more especially, operations other than war such as peacekeeping and humanitarian intervention, cannot be justified on the grounds of self-defence, then how can the profession go on to claim that they are still aiming at their stated ideal? Of course, they could make a standard re-conceptualizing move and say that the ideal is better expressed as, say, 'Defence of the Innocent', although that smacks of making a virtue of necessity. But I do not want to dismiss the possibility entirely; I shall leave the question hanging for the moment and turn to the unpacking of the second notion, 'role morality'.

The concept of role morality first made its appearance in the field of sociology, where it was deployed primarily as a descriptive device, useful in describing the morality peculiar to performance of a particular role in a particular society or culture. Latterly, it has been adopted by philosophers and used in evaluative and normative contexts. Crucially, for my purposes, it has proved to be a very useful notion to which members of each of the three professions can appeal in order to justify the adoption of actions practices *within* the professional role in question which are putatively morally dubious or morally prohibited if undertaken *outside* the role. For example, the actions of cutting people open and removing their body parts are ordinarily (that is, by the standards of 'everyday' morality) regarded as (morally, and also legally) very wrong indeed, but if *surgeons* perform these actions on a *patient* in an *operating theatre*, the actions become not only morally permissibly but mandatory; acting in the role of surgeon carries with it the *duty* to perform such actions, in pursuance of the ideal of Health. One noteworthy result is that such actions become so embedded in the role that the role-language changes over time to accommodate and reflect the fact that the putatively wrong actions have metamorphosed, within their own closed moral sphere, into indubitably right actions.

Similarly with the legal profession. Outside the role of lawyer, we consider that ruthlessly hectoring and haranguing people and possibly causing them great distress is wrong; it constitutes bullying. But when a *lawyer* undertakes a *cross-examination* of a *witness* in a court of law, the action becomes permissible and the lawyer becomes duty-bound to perform the action in pursuance of the ideal of Justice.

Two common factors emerge at this point. Firstly, the ideals of both professions – the Goods being aimed at – are likely to remain unchanged indefinitely. Health and Justice will always be regarded as Goods. Secondly, in both cases, the *means* of attaining the desired ideal – respectively, performing surgery in order to cure the disease (or whatever) and restore Health, and undertaking cross-examination in order to establish the truth and bring about Justice are (or are assumed to be) the only means available to the surgeon or the lawyer, and thus immune from moral criticism.

Against this background, it becomes easier to appreciate why the education and training of would-be members of all three of our traditional professions has until very recently (recently in historical terms, that is) consisted mainly in drawing the attention of trainees to that profession's *code of conduct*; a set of law-like rules comprising mainly a list of dos and don'ts. In the case of the codes of conduct of lawyers, for example, one writer on professional ethics whom I have already quoted could say a mere five years ago that 'the moral authority of professional codes seems to rest on an auxiliary rule. We might state it briefly as "obey your profession's code"' (Davies 2002, 26). When deontology held sway in the military as well the same imperative could be addressed equally to soldiers ('Honor, Duty, Country' is as much an imperative as it is a motto or set of guidelines).

Yet in the case of ethics education in the medical profession, reliance on an underpinning law-like morality has all but disappeared and in the case of the legal profession it is, in some countries at least, it is being overlaid (although not replaced) by something like a virtue ethics approach. So it would seem that the military are the last in line to undergo this change. I believe that this is more than coincidental.

Ethics education for medical students is now based on what is, in all but name, a virtue ethics approach. It has been grounded for some time in the 'principlism' approach developed by Tom Beauchamp and James Childress and contained in what is now a standard text in the subject (Beauchamp and Childress 1979). Ethical behaviour is grounded in abiding by four *principles*, namely beneficence, non-maleficence, justice and autonomy. There are still rules to be followed, as set out in the relevant code of conduct (e.g. in the UK, that of the British Medical Association) and sanctions to be imposed after instances of breach of the code, but inculcation of the code, or of a supporting law-like morality in the students, is simply not thought necessary or desirable (although it is pertinent to note that the second principle, non-maleficence, is a direct descendant of the law-like opening to the original Hippocratic Oath: 'First, do no harm'). Would-be doctors and other healthcare professionals are assumed to be people of basically good character anyway, before they even enter upon their professional training. When they do come to undergo 'ethics education', what they get at the medical school where I teach the subject is a lecture or two on ethical theory followed by a series of seminar case studies on morally sensitive aspects of the doctor-patient relationship, such as patient confidentiality. But things were not always so. Fifty years ago, the law-like morality still pervaded the relationship and dictated the rules of conduct. The relationship was also decidedly paternalistic. The patient did what the doctor said she should do, and questioning the doctor's authority was, in most cases, unthinkable. Social attitudes then changed, and the balance of power shifted. Patient-centred medicine replaced the old paternalism, and the result is that the patient-doctor dialogue is now perceived as one between equals. However, this transition has been reasonably smooth for all concerned. More importantly, the methodology has changed in order to 'give the patient a voice' and shift the emphasis from the realm of duty to the realm of personal interaction, mutual trust and 'the ethics of care'. Doctors are still living in harmony with the moral requirements and imperatives of their role.

Would-be lawyers are also generally perceived to be basically 'good people', at least when they approach their careers in the law (when I attended many years ago, as a callow teenager, an initial interview with the Law Society of England and Wales to assess my fitness to join the legal profession, I was asked the stock question 'Why do you want to become a lawyer?' and gave the stock answer 'Because I want to help people'). That the general public perception of them can be, shall we say, somewhat negative, does nothing to deny the fact that, in the main, individual clients do trust their own lawyers and regard them as good people. Lawyers, in turn, regard themselves as in little or no need of ethics education (at least in the UK. In the USA, and consequent upon the perceived involvement of lawyers in the Watergate affair, ethics education for lawyers has been a compulsory course in their education syllabus since the 1970s; another classic example of a teaching programme being introduced as a response to a specific scandal, as noted by Martin Cook in respect of the USAFA programme (see Chapter 5)). Lawyers, too, seem comfortable in their role, although it is noteworthy that there is some evidence that not all trainee lawyers manage to adjust easily to the need to make the change from regarding aggressive haranguing as bullying (a bad thing) to accepting it as cross-examination (a good, or at least permissible, thing).

But what of soldiers? Why is so much made of the need to adhere to their honour codes and of loyalty to their mates, their company and their regiment? Part of the answer is that virtues and character traits such as honour, trust, loyalty and truthfulness are essential ingredients in the creation of a solid, cohesive unit; soldiering is the team game *par excellence*. But another part of the answer has to do with what might be called moral self-defence. The act of *intentional killing* is not just slightly wrong or very wrong. It is the ultimate wrong. That we regard the act as wrong is not just the result of a Kantian reasoning process. The reasons and causes go much deeper – *all the way down* (to paraphrase Bernard Williams in a different context) – we feel a revulsion about the act, not just squeamishness. At first sight, it would seem that those who perform the act of killing in legal and medical contexts (respectively, in cases of judicial execution and euthanasia) seem to be fully protected by their role-morality 'shields' against psychological disturbance and twinges of conscience. But even here, the protection is not absolute and universally accepted as such. Not all jurisdictions sanction judicial execution as a form of punishment and few sanction euthanasia (and amongst those, only passive euthanasia is condoned; active euthanasia is still considered 'beyond the (moral) pale' even though there are impeccable arguments available to show that the two are *logically* indistinguishable).

It is hardly surprising, therefore, that soldiers are in need of the strongest possible justification to 'reinforce' themselves and preserve their integrity and identity whilst engaged in the act of killing. The psychological barriers can all too easily break, as Albert Ball, one the leading British 'aces' of the Royal Flying Corps in the First World War, soon found; 'Oh, it was a good fight, and the Huns were fine sports. One tried to ram me after he was hit and only missed me by inches. Am indeed looked after by God, but Oh! I do get tired of living always to kill and am really beginning to feel like a murderer. I shall be so pleased when I have finished' (diary entry shortly before Ball's death in combat in May 1917, quoted in Gilbert 1988, 130). Furthermore, all soldiers involved in combat, particularly during prolonged wars, run the risk of becoming morally disillusioned. The simple certainties of 'Honor, Duty, Country' become increasingly distant and irrelevant. This has been commented on many times but is no less true for that; 'the strongest influence of war upon most of those who endure it is to blur their belief in absolute moral values, and to foster a sense of common experience with those who have shared it, even a barbarous enemy' (Hastings 1987, 18).

Summary

All that I have said so far might be taken as implying support for some form of moral relativism. This would be entirely wrong. My concerns can been encapsulated in a simple imperative; one fundamental objective of any ethics education programme must be to protect the soldier against the sort of moral schizophrenia that can affect anyone who is brought up on a diet of unqualified moral rules (Do not lie, Do not break other people's things, Do not harm, Do not *kill*) but who is then told that he is entirely justified in going out and doing the exact opposite, namely undertaking as much breaking, harming and killing as possible. I am suggesting that the only possible means of reconciling these two conflicting behavioural indoctrinations (so to speak) is to ring-fence them within the notion of professional role morality. By all means educate soldiers in the manner of Plato's Guardians and use Kantian philosophy and Kohlbergian psychology to underpin the pedagogy, but be very aware of the dangers of attempting to *replace* the underpinning with a neo-Aristotelean or virtue ethics approach. Basing the ethics education of the military on a perfectionist, idealist morality and psychology like Kant's and Kohlberg's is an unavoidable necessity. If the educators want to bring virtue ethics, care ethics and so on into the pedagogic equation, then they run a serious risk of taking the soldier outside his role and into situations where he does no longer have a reliable moral compass to guide him; he can find himself having to deal with people 'simply' on the basis of common humanity, fellow-feeling and a universal morality.

The Way Forward

There may be no single solution to the problems I have outlined, but some form of compromise may be workable. I have hinted at a possible reconceptualization of the professional role of the soldier. One possibility might be to regard the soldier-*policeman* as a permanent reality rather than as being a requirement of an occasional dual-role undertaking. This could involve a corresponding redefinition of the Good to be achieved by way of bringing in a reference to Justice (as is already alluded to in classical just war theory in any case in the condition that after victory in war, it is incumbent on the victor to secure a *just* peace). This conceptual widening might even allow the introduction of a common Good that I earlier criticized as being rather too wide, namely Defence of the Innocent.

This is still philosophers' talk to a great extent, of course, but perhaps not entirely unrealistic. From a practical point of view, and bearing in mind the emergence of the strategic corporal, such a project would entail setting up a common ethics education programme for all ranks. It is probably too much to hope for that a more radical proposal would find favour, namely a requirement that *all* military personnel must rise through the ranks and therefore take on the suggested two versions of ethics training (one self-regarding, one other-regarding, to put it crudely) right from the start. But this is what happens with most police training in any case, and such a system does already seem to operate well in the Israeli armed forces (see Chapter 12).

Whether or not this is yet another idealist bubble ready to burst remains to be seen, but there seems little doubt that change is inevitable. The papers collected here are proof positive that the challenges now facing the educators of the military have been taken up with great enthusiasm by those involved, and the collective wisdom on display does, in itself, give great hope for the future.

Acknowledgment

I am most grateful to the students of the Philosophy Society at the University of Hull for their helpful comments on an earlier version of this chapter.

Bibliography

Anscombe, E. (1958), 'Modern Moral Philosophy', *Philosophy*, 1–19. Reprinted in G. Wallace and A. Walker (eds) (1970), *The Definition of Morality* (London: Methuen and Co. Ltd).

Beauchamp, T and Childress, J. (1979), *Principles of Biomedical Ethics*, 5th edition 2001 (New York: Oxford University Press).

Carrick, D. (2004), Review of Davis (2002), *Journal of Applied Philosophy* 21, 101–5.

Chapman, J. (2002), 'Why Teach Legal Ethics to Undergraduates', *Legal Ethics* 5:1 and 2, Spring, 68–89.

Davis, M. (2002), *Profession Code and Ethics* (Aldershot: Ashgate).

Gilbert, P. (2003), *New Terror, New Wars* (Edinburgh: Edinburgh Univertsity Press).

Hastings, M. (1987), *The Korean War* (London: Michael Joseph).

Huntington, S.P. (1957), *The Soldier and the State: the Theory and Politics of Civil-Military Relations*, 12th edition 1995 (Cambridge, MA: Belknap Press of Harvard University Press).

Kahlenberg, R. (1992), *Broken Contract: A Memoir of Harvard Law School* (Amherst: University of Massachusetts Press).

Krulak, C. (1999), 'The Strategic Corporal: Leadership in the Three Block War', *Marines Magazine*, January, <www.au.af.mil/au/awc/awcgate/usmc/strategic_corporal.htm>.

MacIntyre, A. (1981), *After Virtue: a Study in Moral Theory* (London: Duckworth).

Nicholson, D. and Webb, J. (1999), *Professional Legal Ethics* (Oxford: Oxford University Press).

Robinson, P. (2006), 'Old Wars in New Battles' (review of Gilbert 2003), *Journal of Applied Philosophy* 23:3, 375–9.

Williams, B. (1985), *Ethics and the Limits of Philosophy* (London: Fontana Press at HarperCollins).

Chapter 17

Conclusion

Paul Robinson, Nigel de Lee and Don Carrick

Ethics training should not be a substitute for moral leadership. Even the best instruction, conducted according to the best thought out principles, will count for nothing if soldiers can see that their commanders do not in fact value what they say they value. Nor should ethics training allow commanders to close their eyes to the systemic failings of their institutions. One of the pitfalls of the military's favoured approach to ethics training – virtue ethics – is that because the emphasis is on character development, ethical failures may well be interpreted purely in terms of the character flaws of the individuals involved. As one presenter told the 2007 International Symposium on Military Ethics, thousands of people are subjected to stressful conditions, and work within systems which are dysfunctional, and the vast majority of them do not commit crimes. On the other hand, everybody is capable of immoral actions if placed in the right conditions. As Christopher Browning has pointed out, the perpetrators of Nazi war crimes were not for the most part especially 'evil' persons with noticeably deficient characters; they were thoroughly 'ordinary men' (Browning 2001). Leaders must accept responsibility for creating the circumstances in which virtue can flourish. They must continually assess the institutions which they lead, the missions which they undertake, and the tasks which they ask their subordinates to perform, to ascertain if these are well suited to encouraging ethical behaviour.

That said, as John Mark Mattox notes, 'Virtue *can* be taught; people *can* be transformed into something better than they are today' (Mattox 2002, 310). Anybody who has read all the chapters in this book cannot but admire the seriousness with which the military institutions under study have addressed this task. The effort is sincere; it is impressive. Whether it is successful is a different matter. Given the relative paucity of serious abuses of military power and authority, it appears so, but we have no clear evidence as to what extent this is the result of the ethics training that soldiers receive. We likewise have no solid data comparing the different techniques used in different systems to confirm which are the more effective. Inevitably, our conclusions are somewhat impressionistic and anecdotal. A more thorough analysis represents an obvious avenue for future research.

Moreover, even if ethics training and development appear on the surface to be relatively successful, there is considerable evidence in these pages that there is room for improvement. Several authors describe incoherent policies, confused objectives, and poor implementation. Some of the problems arise from fundamental disagreements about basic principles, most importantly concerning what the purpose of ethics training and development in the military should be. Is it to change character, as most authors suggest, or to build professional identity and change behaviour? Is it purely functional – designed to create soldiers who will possess the virtues required to function effectively as soldiers – or is it aspirational – designed to create people who are in some sense morally 'good'? There is no clear agreement, and often these aims are muddled up with one another and pursued simultaneously. Similarly, as in the case of the British Army's combination of virtue ethics and a utilitarian Service Test, contradictory philosophical systems are sometimes mixed together in a manner which can only cause confusion.

The problems reflect even deeper uncertainties about what the purposes of armed forces actually are. In a book on the *Future of Army Professionalism* published in the United States in 2002, we find within a few pages two entirely different views of the moral purpose of the US Army: first that 'the first absolute of any warrior ethic and of all genuine soldiers – is to *protect innocent life*' (Toner 2002, 326), and second, the position proposed by Don Snider, John Nagl and Tony Pfaff, that the army exists to serve the state and society, 'fighting the conflicts they approve, when they approve them' (Don Snider, John Nagl and Tony Pfaff, cited in Cook 2002, 341). These views inevitably lead to different conclusions as to the purpose of ethics education and development in the military. The former position would tend towards what Jessica Wolfendale calls the aspirational approach, and the latter towards the functional one. As J. Joseph Miller comments, 'one is left with the uncomfortable feeling that for Snider, Nagl and Pfaff, if acting virtuously were not necessary to successful soldiering, they would abandon all pretense of moral education' (Miller 2004, 202, footnote 3). The obvious conclusion is that before further progress can be made in the field of ethics education in the military, we may need to some extent to return to basics, and examine in more detail what we consider the moral purpose of armed forces to be, and what therefore the purpose of ethics training should be also.

These are, of course, not easy questions to answer, and perhaps it will never be possible to reach a consensus on them. In these circumstances, one can see the attraction of the British approach, of avoiding intellectualizing the problem, and instead sticking to what is tried and tested. It may be, however, that the pressures of an increasingly demanding public and a changing military environment will not allow commanders the luxury of such conservatism. The insistence of politicians and publics that institutions and systems be transparent, and that results be quantifiable, is likely to force further change. This volume does not pretend to provide all the solutions. It is but a first step in a process of analyzing more deeply what ethics training and development in the military should involve. There is much that people from different countries can learn from one another.

Bibliography

Browning, C.R. (2001), *Ordinary Men: Reserve Police Battalion 101 and the Final Solution in Poland* (London: Penguin).

Cook, M. (2002), 'Army Professionalism: Service to What End?', in L.J. Matthews (ed.), *The Future of the Army Profession*, pp. 337–56.

Matthews, L.J. (ed.) (2002), *The Future of the Army Profession* (Boston: McGraw-Hill).

Mattox, J.M. (2002), 'The Ties that Bind: the Army Officer's Moral Obligations', in L.J. Matthews (ed.), *The Future of the Army Profession*, pp. 293–312.

Miller, J.J. (2004), 'Squaring the Circle: Teaching Philosophical Ethics in the Military', *Journal of Military Ethics* 3:3, 199–215.

Toner, J.H. (2002), 'A Message to Garcia: Leading Soldiers in Moral Mayhem', in L.J. Matthews (ed.), *The Future of the Army Profession*, pp. 313–36.

Index